A Guide to Kodály

To the memory of Antal Doráti

János Breuer

A Guide to Kodály

Corvina

Translated by Maria Steiner
Consultant: Paul Merrick
Design by János Szalma

© János Breuer, 1990

Published by Corvina Books
Budapest V. Vörösmarty tér 1.
1051 Hungary

ISBN 963 13 2908 9

Contents

Preface	7
Summer Evening	9
First String Quartet (opus 2)	19
Sonata for Cello and Piano (opus 4)	28
Duo for Violin and Cello (opus 7)	37
Sonata for Solo Cello (opus 8)	46
Second String Quartet (opus 10)	57
Serenade for Two Violins and Viola (opus 12)	65
Psalmus Hungaricus (opus 13)	74
Háry János—comic opera (opus 15)	91
Háry János—orchestral suite	103
Ballet Music	109
Theatre Overture	110
Dances of Marosszék	111
The Spinning Room	120
Galánta Dances	131
Te Deum	139
The Peacock — Variations on a Hungarian Folksong	149
Concerto for Orchestra	161
Mass Versions	172
Symphony	183
Songs	195
Choral Works	204
Biographical Survey	217

Preface

In 1962, the year of Kodály's 80th birthday, Corvina Press, Budapest, together with MacMillan, London, published László Eősze's *Zoltán Kodály. His Life and Work*, and two years later, Ernest Benn Limited of London brought out *Zoltán Kodály, a Hungarian Musician* by Percy M. Young. In 1964 László Eősze's standard work also appeared in German (Corvina Press—Boosey & Hawkes, Bonn). Since then, no work discussing Kodály's lifework has been published in any of the widely spoken languages, the only volume to pay tribute to the composer being a Kodály iconography collected and prefaced by László Eősze (*Kodály—His Life in Pictures*, Corvina Press, 1971, 1982). "The rest is silence." Over the past twenty-odd years public opinion, both in Hungary and abroad, has undoubtedly kept to the fore mainly Kodály's work as a teacher. The work of Kodály the musicologist furthermore is available in English: Corvina Press published *The Selected Writings of Zoltán Kodály* in 1974, and his *Folk Music of Hungary* has seen several editions, the latest appearing in 1982. Yet the compositions of Kodály enjoy unvarying popularity in the great concert halls of the world.

Nonetheless, the fact that recently emphasis has shifted increasingly in the direction of Kodály the music teacher has upset somewhat the unity of the three strands within his lifework. There is in reality an organic relationship between the work of the composer, the ethnomusicologist and the great educator. The significance of the educationalist was increased by the fact that the furthering of music education was engaged in by a sovereign creator, while the path of the composer and the educator was influenced by folk-music research. No part of Kodály's tremendous œuvre could have been fully accomplished without the other two.

This book is in fact a *guide for concert-goers*, written with the aim of drawing attention to Kodály the composer. It gives an account of the origin of each work in relation to the main events of the composer's life, traces its subsequent career, and its popularity in Hungary and abroad, also providing analytical information.

At the time the book was written, research into Kodály's lifework was just gaining a new impulse in Hungary, and scholarly exploration of his œuvre had not yet reached the level it had, for example, in the case of Bartók. I was thus left basically to my own results obtained during my work collecting information and material over the previous 15 years. Of course I could not dispense with the existing literature on Kodály, above all the standard works by László Eősze and the research work and useful advice of Ferenc Bónis, Mihály Ittzés and István Kecskeméti. The Ministry of Culture made it possible for me to carry out research in libraries abroad, and by courtesy of Mrs. Zoltán Kodály, I was able to study the composer's legacy. I wish to express special thanks to my wife, for her assistance in the collection of the material.

The volume cannot cover all the works by Zoltán Kodály. It omits pieces with a strictly educational purpose, minor piano pieces, and folksong arrangements for voice and piano. Nor does it treat transcriptions which count as autonomous compositions, and the songs and choruses which play such an important role in Kodály's œuvre are summarized in separate chapters.

The volume ends with a biographical survey, which is intended to help orientate the reader through the many events of a long life.

No bibliographical references of footnotes have been included to support the author's statements, as, in compliance with my intention, this is not a scholarly work but one desiring to point out the value of Kodály's music. If I have succeeded in doing so, then the efforts of the 15 years taken to write it have not been in vain.

Budapest, August 1990 János Breuer

Summer Evening

COMPOSITION:	1906. Date of completion: September. Revision: 1929.
FIRST PERFORMANCE:	First version: Budapest, October 22, 1906, Hungarian Royal Opera House Orchestra, conducted by István Kerner. Revised version: New York, April 3, 1930, New York Philharmonic Orchestra, conducted by Arturo Toscanini.
INSTRUMENTATION:	flute, oboe, cor anglais, 2 clarinets, 2 bassoons, 2 horns, strings.
DURATION:	*c.* 20 minutes*.
PUBLISHER:	Universal Edition, Wiener Philharmonischer Verlag.

In the autumn of 1900, a young country lad by the name of Zoltán Kodály went to Budapest to continue his studies. After writing a great many compositions during his grammar school years, the young man enrolled in the Composition Department (under the direction of the Bavarian János Koessler) of the Royal Academy of Music (Conservatoire), and at Budapest University, where he studied Hungarian and German. Some 30 years later, Kodály related his impressions of those times: *At that time the Wagner cult was at its climax here. If it had not been for the fact that the programme was in Hungarian, the music played at concerts would have made one think one was in a small German town ... No wonder that in this great German world we were overcome by a terrific longing for the real Hungary, which was not to be found anywhere in Pest, for here German was vir-*

---

* Kodály only marked the duration of performance on a few scores. Durations given as *c.* are averages taken from recordings. *J. B.*

tually the official language of music. We were amazed at this, for Budapest had been (at least in the newspapers from which we had known it until then) the focal point of Hungarian life, reflected in the glory of the millennium. We were unable to reconcile ourselves to this great disappointment. (Confession, 1932.)

Kodály worked quietly, tenaciously, and very hard at both of his studies. Although from the first term onwards he was exempted from paying school fees at the Royal Academy of Music, his name was not yet linked with anything really outstanding. He carried off no scholarships and prizes. Perhaps he did not even strive for such distinctions. The acclaimed and recognized talent was not Kodály but Leó Weiner, who won four different awards. Imre Kálmán and Albert Szirmai also seemed to be more promising composers in those years.

During a conversation with Denijs Dille in 1963, Kodály recalled his years of study in Budapest. *It was not easy to reconcile the two kinds of study. I had to devote more time now to one and now to the other. With the approach of the examinations one field always had to be neglected, and so I could not work in either the way one would do if one studied only one thing ... Trying to balance between two such completely different studies, I was unable to write anything apart from* 'Summer Evening' *which was finished.*

The four years intended for music studies in fact proved to be insufficient, and in 1904–5 Kodály stayed for a further year in the fourth year, only writing *Summer Evening*, the composition for his final examination, in 1906.

It was around this time, in the summer of 1905 that Kodály set out on the first of his folksong collecting tours, which were to be of key importance in his lifework. He incorporated the results of his first tours straight away in his Ph. D. thesis, which appeared in 1906 under the title *The Verse Construction of Hungarian Folksong*. After a great many pseudo-scientific papers, this was the first work of truly scholarly value concerning the nature of Hungarian folksong. Kodály also made use in his conclusions of the collections of Hungarian folk poetry published (without music) in the 19th century. In fact at the time when he wrote his thesis, his knowledge of Hungarian folksongs was not based only on the pieces he had himself so far collected, since from 1903 he had been regularly studying folk music recordings preserved in the National Museum, melodies recorded on phonograph cylinders but not yet transcribed to paper.

After subsequent collecting tours, in the summer and autumn of 1906 he composed *Summer Evening* in Cirkvenica, on the Dalmatian coast. Nothing is known about exactly when Kodály began the composition, but the approximate date of its being finished may be inferred from the diary of the poet Béla Balázs, librettist of Bartók's two stage works (*Bluebeard's Castle* and *The Wooden Prince*), a close friend: *I've just received a postcard from Zoltán. Yesterday he finished his orchestral piece*, reads the diary for September 24.

This means that the score was completed scarcely a month before its first performance. It was first heard on the birthday of Ferenc Liszt at a concert featuring works by the graduating students of the Academy of Music.

Summer Evening had a most contradictory press reaction. *It lacks the beauties of Hungarian motifs. ...He has spun it out excessively. It is a slow, diffuse mixture of colours, which does not cohere into pregnant ideas. One encounters a few evocative details, yet as a whole it is broken up into so many little, uncharacteristic episodes.* Even Géza Csáth, the most sensitive critic of the time, who soon recognized real Hungarian music in Kodály's work, wrote: *Zoltán Kodály still has a headache from all his great learning. The many complicated counterpoints, which look fine only on paper, are unpleasant in his work.*

On the other hand: *Zoltán Kodály's symphonic picture entitled 'Summer Evening' is successful only in some details, yet it reveals the personality of a worthy, serious-minded, thinking person. One can sense from his work that this young artist had given much thought to how to liberate the Hungarian symphonic style from the shackles of stereotyped rhythmic cliché. He is one of those who want to bring about a Hungarian musical style that is freer, and broader in perspective than the present one. May he continue to deliberate and work: his melodies spring from the depth of the Hungarian soul, even if not all can derive pleasure from them.* The critic who recognized the significance of the young Kodály was none other than Imre Kálmán, the later world-famous composer of *The Gypsy Princess* and many more operettas.

After the première, this first version of *Summer Evening* was performed twice more in Budapest: January 8 and 22, 1911, both times at concerts by the National Symphony Orchestra conducted by László Kun, on one occasion for adults, and on the other for young audiences. Hereafter it presumably would have shared the fate of others of Kodály's youthful works by appearing no more before an audience, had Kodály not met the greatest conductor of the day, Arturo Toscanini, who conducted the *Psalmus Hungaricus* in the composer's presence in La Scala, Milan on October 10 and 12, 1928. On July 23, 1929 Toscanini sent a telegram to Kodály to ask, obviously in reference to a previous agreement, whether he could count on a new work by the composer for his American tour. Kodály suggested an orchestrated version of the *Dances of Marosszék* or *Summer Evening*. Toscanini opted for the latter, and on January 21, 1930 his secretary wrote to Kodály's wife: *The maestro was greatly interested in the 'Dances of Marosszék', yet he thinks it would be better for Kodály if he were to perform a completely new work of his, as this after all is rather a transcription. Do please send 'Summer Evening' immediately, so that he can look it through at once.* All this was brought to light by László Eősze, together with the fact that the revised version of *Summer Evening* was completed in November 1929.

Toscanini premièred the work with the New York Philharmonic Orchestra on April 3, 1930. Typical of the minute care with which Kodály was accustomed to work, was a letter of March 12, which in the postal conditions of the time must have arrived in New York at the very last minute, if not too late, and in which he wrote (in Italian):

My Dear Maestro,
While correcting the proofs of the score I have discovered a few faults and errors, which can presumably be found in the orchestral parts too, and which, however, I could not correct, as they had been sent out straight from Vienna. Should these corrections arrive too late, please forgive me for troubling you. Mea culpa.

The thought of seeing you soon almost seems a dream. We hope you will stand the great strain of the journey in the best health.
Yours sincerely,
Z. Kodály

One can sense from this letter that the première took place in great haste, altogether only two and a half months having passed between Toscanini's asking for *Summer Evening* and his conducting the work. This is why Kodály had no time to correct the material and prepare the proofs adequately. Even so it seems unusual for Kodály to have put the work to press before listening to its revised form. There are many documents to attest the great importance Kodály attached to a final test of listening to a work. In a letter of June 9, 1930 he warned his Viennese publisher with some measure of reproach: *Please caution those involved in preparing the orchestral material to use the utmost care. Toscanini has shown me a great many mistakes in the parts, which he himself had to correct.* This must have happened on or about May 21, at the first Budapest performance of *Summer Evening*, which was conducted by Toscanini. This performance was an act of courtesy towards Kodály and the Budapest audience on the part of Toscanini, who had set out on a European tour with the New York Philharmonic Orchestra.

To return to the New York première, Olin Downes reviewed the event thus in *The New York Times* (April 4, 1930):

There was a first performance of a delightful, poetic, but overdeveloped work of Kodály, his symphonic poem 'Summer Evening', composed years ago, refashioned very recently, dedicated to Mr. Toscanini and performed under his direction from manuscript for the first time anywhere. There is a serene and harmonically orthodox opening. A contrasting section, livelier and more modern, suggests folksongs and dances, and gay festivity. It is full of simple life and feeling, and it has a melodic quality presumably racial. But the piece is drawn out. Does Kodály succeed best in extended forms? His most engaging music known here is a suite from the comic opera 'Háry János'. His 'Psalmus Hungaricus' has powerful choral pages, but not sustained and enchained inspiration. But his music today seems to have far more juice and human feeling than the highly intellectualized product of his country-

man, Bartók. To contrast Bartók and Kodály, playing one off against the other, was a fairly common mode of appraisal of the day.

Summer Evening was not well received in its revised form either. Even the tremendous initial momentum of a première under the baton of Toscanini brought no lasting acclaim. Apart from the Budapest performance mentioned, Toscanini himself never conducted it again, and up until the 1960s, the great American orchestras performed the piece on just two occasions. In London it was first performed on September 16, 1930 at a Promenade Concert in Queen's Hall, with the BBC orchestra conducted by Sir Henry Wood, a dedicated exponent of Kodály's music. Yet by 1944 only two more performances of the piece are known of in Britain, a country with such a considerable Kodály cult. At the first Berlin performance (January 27, 1931) the Philharmonic Orchestra was conducted by Wilhelm Furtwängler. Still, even these great names did not suffice to ensure for the work a real popularity. Recording companies, always responsive to success, characteristically showed the utmost reserve; by 1974 just two recordings had been made of the work—both Hungarian—whereas at the same time, for instance, there were 26 different recordings of the *Háry János Suite* in circulation.

The miniature score of *Summer Evening*, published in May 1930, included an English translation of Kodály's preface:

If one surveys occasionally one's own creation from a critical point of view, one recognizes clearer than any stranger all the faults and imperfections of the work. This and that would succeed better today, if one only could do it again!

But the former self appears as a stranger in this work and it seldom occurs that we have the courage to demolish the statue in order to refound it. I wrote this work first in 1906 ... If I should succeed today in removing the old failures, I have to thank a great master, whose example and requests have roused again in me the feeling of responsibility and a constant dissatisfaction, which want to begin all again.

The title means only that the work was conceived on summer evenings by newly cut cornfields and the murmuring Adriatic waves. It may remain as a reminiscence.

The original tone-colour has remained unaltered: the instruments are the same, only the 3rd horn has been removed.

The musical material is in general the old one; only it succeeds perhaps better in this new form...

The score of the first version of the work, completed in 1906, has not survived, nor is the fate known of the orchestral parts used at the première. It is thus impossible to establish what exactly the "reworking" meant.

Summer Evening employs a reduced orchestra, with the wind mostly given solo treatment, the strings at points double, or even triple division. This signifies a turning away from the sound of the mammoth orchestra of the turn of the century, so forming an integral part of the whole range of new music at the beginning of the century. Schoenberg's *Chamber Symphony*, op. 9, for 15 instruments itself dates from 1906. Bartók's *Suite No. 2* for small orchestra also dates from about this time (1905–7), while, somewhat later, the orchestral version of Ravel's *Ma mère l'oye* (Mother Goose) also employs small forces. However, different these works may be, they exhibit the common feature of consciously turning away from the huge symphonic ensembles of Strauss, Reger and Mahler.

Listening to *Summer Evening*, and the series of nature pictures it suggests, a more direct parallel emerges: Debussy's *L'Après-midi d'un faune* (The Afternoon of a Faun), first performed in Budapest on January 10, 1906. Although Kodály repeatedly asserted both in speech and writing, that he got to know Debussy's works in 1907 in Paris, this referred possibly to a thorough study of his works, since the pastel colours in *Summer Evening* are almost inconceivable without Debussy.

The musical material of the piece includes pentatonic progressions, or more exactly progressions fundamentally pentatonic and modal, in origin deriving from Hungarian folk music, with all its melodic and harmonic implications. All the many forms appear of the structure termed heptatonia secunda by the musicologist Lajos Bárdos and which was highly characteristic of Kodály. Kodály's own collections of folk music hitherto are not themselves enough to explain all these folkloristic effects. What he had noted down by 1906 could not yet have become in way part of his flesh and blood. Still as mentioned before, Kodály had been studying Hungarian folk music from 1903.

Performing the work presents the orchestra, and especially the conductor, with an extremely difficult and by no means unrewarding task. Aside from a few fairly animated sections, the whole piece is in fact a single, lengthy, slow movement. The basic tempo is Andante assai, a sustained pulse which becomes rather slower than faster. This is Kodály's only orchestral slow movement in sonata form, and the changes and contrasts of character are to be measured against this pace. Another difficulty of performance arises from the continual floating quality of the material. Although the performance directions do not include many rubatos, the whole composition is in fact characterized by a parlandorubato formation after the performing style of old Hungarian folk music. Now the parlando of "speaking" melodies comes to the fore, now the rubato of ornamented peasant song. The outline of the closing theme, which resembles a dance and refers to the *verbunkos* (a popular dance music from the turn of the 18th–19th century), alone differs from this basic character, but, as it were by way of a curbing effect, Kodály incorporates the second subject, which is slower than the basic tempo. This particular "floating quality" is achieved by a written out rubato, by dividing the bar $3/2 + \frac{1}{4}$ (a kind of "syllable lengthening", as it were) in the first subject group, which characteristically is in pairs of bars, and by the metre changing from bar to bar in the second subject, in places the parts being virtually a crowded multitude of ornamentation, improvisatory in effect. The composition hardens, its dream world dispersing immediately, if the performance does not suggest an almost unbroken, ceaseless movement of the parts. On the other hand, if the composed rubato prevails excessively, the piece loses its firmness of outline and its effect is lost the same as when it is performed rigidly.

With its decreasing proportions, the plan of the form is put off the composition. The sonata exposition contains 165 bars, the development 143 bars, the recapitulation 91, and the coda 34 bars. It is true that, mainly due to the first subject being treated in variations, nearly two thirds of the exposition consist of development material, with a short second subject and an even shorter closing theme, itself echoing the first subject. In the recapitulation is it mostly the first subject in the opening section already presented from so many aspects that undergoes a radical abbreviation. It is as if the whole formal design were trying to suggest the waning light of sunset, the gilded rays of a darkening, peaceful, weary, brown evening.

A solo cor anglais states the three layers of the main theme, as infinitely gentle, melancholic, cantabile melody. Its division does not follow the classical model of 2+2, 4+4 bars, the inner division is asymmetric in a most delicate and variegated manner, every feature bearing a gesture of opening and continuation. This perfectly balanced, irregular yet regular, figuration is one of Kodály's real gems of melodic invention. The emotional and musical logic of it may be developed, and in fact is developed, in countless directions, right up to the huge melodic arch of passionate outcry. A horn solo—by way of a distant echo—leads to the second subject. For centuries, F major has been a pastoral key, and here too it first appears with a pastoral character. The oboe and flute solos seem to bring the sound of a faraway pipe—the performing instruction soave (sweetly) indicating the character. This too is a Janus-faced melody, dropping into dark keys far removed from the pastoral F major and releasing tremendous energies. It is supposed to be performed pesante (heavily), and fff, an instruction only occurring at this one point of the work. The cello, one of Kodály's favourite instruments, relieves the suddenly heightened tension in a kind of meditation, and the melody of the codetta soars in dance-mood, its tonality confusing and with more than one meaning, as if we were witnessing a refractive iridescence. The play of pictures near and far lends depth of focus to this section. In conclusion the second subject bids farewell on solo flute, oboe and horn.

The development section begins with a dance-like melody arranged as a *csárdás* (a 19th-century Hungarian folk dance). The main theme emerges only fragmentarily, as if looking for words in an ecstasy of exuberant emotion. A new, passionately fervent melody also surfaces. The elements of the musical material, which so far have been heard consecutively, now sound simultaneously, and an increasingly dense structure prepares for the recapitulation, the incandescent return of the first subject. It is a moment signifying the last sparkle of the evening light, the recapitulation, followed by a coda, suggests the calm and peaceful picture of a summer evening; the melody that opened the work is again stated by the cor anglais, even the dance scene flashing up once again, though more a memory than a reality. The music becomes more and more static, as the sound slowly dies away. The direction for the last bars is morendo, the musical landscape created by artistic imagination now being shrouded in darkness.

First String Quartet

opus 2

COMPOSITION: 1908–9.
FIRST PERFORMANCE: Budapest, March 17, 1910, Waldbauer String Quartet (Imre Waldbauer, János Temesváry, Antal Molnár, Jenő Kerpely). Private performance: Budapest Academy of Music, March 14, 1910.
DURATION: *c.* 35 minutes.
PUBLISHER: Rózsavölgyi, Universal Edition, Editio Musica.

Kodály became acquainted with string-quartet performance as a secondary-school student in the 1890s in a strange way. To play the cello in Haydn's quartets, he had to reconstruct the cello part from the other three parts, as the part was missing. *Later, when I could get hold of the original cello part*, recalled Kodály about this performance practice of his student years, *I was pleased to discover that there was relatively little difference between the genuine Haydn part and mine.* It was so that he could play in a string quartet that he had taught himself to play the cello. Later he again took up his violin studies, begun at the age of ten. *And so, on one day I was playing the cello, the other the violin. Even within the quartet we switched parts. I began with the cello, then handed it to another boy and continued with the viola. The playing was just good enough for use in a quartet.* (1964) One could hardly imagine a better school for a would-be composer of chamber music.

When Kodály went to Budapest, from the second term onwards chamber music featured in the curriculum of Hans Koessler's class: *We do more interesting things too, we write for quartet*, Kodály wrote on November 23, 1901 to Mikuláš Schneider-Trnavsky, a friend of his who was studying composition in Vienna. In 1963, when Kodály recalled his preparatory years, he said: *I composed ... parts of string quartets.* A string quartet third movement, possibly a scherzo, was performed on June 20, 1905 at an end-of-term concert given by composition students of the Academy of Music, together with Kodály's *Intermezzo* for string trio. This occasion almost certainly marked public début of the composer in Budapest.

This string-quartet movement was a type of workshop product and has not been performed since. In a letter of June 23, 1907 to his future wife, Kodály mentioned among his plans for the summer the writing of a quartet in C minor, but on July 23 he wrote he was not getting on with the work. As the key of his *First String Quartet* is C minor, perhaps in the summer of 1907 he was already occupied with plans for the work. Be that as it may, he completed the four-movement string quartet in the first half of 1909, as a young teacher at the Budapest Academy of Music. As in the case of so many of his works, Kodály dedicated the piece, which he marked op. 2, to "Emma", who had been his pupil since February 1905, and became his wife in 1910. According to the recollections of Antal Molnár, a founder member of the Waldbauer String Quartet that premièred the work, the quartet rehearsed the work for a year, with altogether 90 rehearsals, until finally the members knew the composition by heart.

Bartók set about organizing a performance of the work abroad even before it had had its première in Budapest. In 1910 the Allgemeiner Deutscher Musikverein held its annual festival, the most important festival of modern music of the time, at the end of May in Zurich. In a letter of December 12, 1909, Bartók brought the work to the notice of the composer and conductor Volkmar Andreae, who was the Swiss member of the jury: *As far as its poetic contents, ingenuity and accomplishment are concerned, I dare say it belongs among the best chamber works written today. Regarding poetic depth, I should mention in particular the second, slow movement, which is practically without compare. The work is fairly difficult but sounds very well and, although it adheres to the strictest chamber style throughout, it includes the most wonderful sound effects ever written for four stringed instruments.* Bartók's efforts were not in vain, for the jury accepted the piece and had it performed on May 29, 1910.

Bartók in fact spared no trouble in propagating Kodály's works, and during certain periods of his life, Kodály returned his efforts. No one knows to what extent the two students of composition attending different classes at the Academy were acquainted with each other at the beginning of the century. What brought the two musicians close together was the idea of collecting and categorizing folk music. By July 7, 1910 Bartók was already writing to a new friend of his, the composer Frederick Delius: *I am very much alone here apart from my one friend Kodály; I have nobody to talk to, and I have never before met anyone to whom from the very first I could feel so close.*

The *First String Quartet* had it first public performance on March 17, 1910, at Kodály's composer's evening, which had been organized by the most well-known Hungarian concert agency and music publishing firm. Two days later they put on a composer's evening for Bartók.

At the time Bartók was doubtless more widely known than Kodály both in Budapest and throughout Europe. Of the pieces coming from Kodály's workshop, practically nothing had reached Budapest audiences since his end-of-term examinations at the Academy of Music. The only exception were the concert performances of some pieces from the *Hungarian Folksongs* with piano accompaniment, which Kodály, together with Bartók, had published in 1906. Now, alongside the string quartet, the programme of the composer's evening included the world première of his op. 3 *Piano Music* (which, with the omission of "Valsette", became known later under the title *Nine Piano Pieces*), and the first Hungarian performance of the op. 4, *Sonata for Cello and Piano*, which had been premièred not long before in Paris.

The Hungarian press carried contradictory reviews of these works by a practically unknown composer. *At first his music seems strange, unfamiliar and novel, but after becoming immersed in it, we see the dawn of a new world.... Two qualities of the approximately 25-year-old poet should be mentioned: namely that he is a revolutionary and a Hungarian ... This was most clearly to be seen in the string quartet. ... Such sensationalism at any price, this manufacturing of tonal ideas with physical pain—this is either deliberate posing or pathology. Whichever it is, it has nothing to do with music.* Zealous reviews and rude contrary opinions clashed around Kodály's works. Yet after all, most twentieth-century composers have given issue to similar opinions with their early works.

The Waldbauer String Quartet performed op. 2 in several European cities in 1911—in Vienna, on November 1 in Amsterdam, on November 4 in Haarlem, and in the first days of December in Berlin. According to unsupported information, there was a performance in Paris too. Much later, on February 29, 1924, it was again the Waldbauer Quartet which gave the first local performance of the work in London (Aeolian Hall). In 1915 the Kneisel String Quartet took the work to five cities in the United States, presumably the very first performance of a Kodály work overseas. The first movement was performed on April 22, 1932 by the string section of the Budapest Concert Orchestra, conducted by Nándor Zsolt. (We do not know who had arranged the work.) Nonetheless, the *First String Quartet* has to a certain extent been dwarfed by Kodály's later, more mature chamber works. In later years too, it has featured mainly on the programmes of Hungarian ensembles; and quartets abroad, noted for the cultivation of contemporary music, have rarely included it in their repertoires.

Even Bartók's enthusiasm was not unambiguous when writing about Kodály's op. 2 for British readers: *The most important among the Hungarian composers ... is Zoltán Kodály ... Already his first published work, the String Quartet No. 1, reveals a complete picture of his personality. The first movement, it is true, still shows certain inequalities and a struggle with form, but the second is written with the greatest **surety** of technique, depth of emotion and—more important still—with complete originality of musical thought and means of expression. The influence of old Hungarian music reveals itself here in a highly personal way.* ("The Development of Art Music in Hungary", *The Chesterian London*, January 1922.)

The critic of the London performance, signing himself E.E. (Edwin Evans) was also not unequivocal in his review: *It is an early work (op.2) and antedates all the music we have hitherto heard of his in London. Whilst displaying certain attractive qualities of a somewhat Schubertian aspect (and even recalling that composer's longwindedness) it does not prove much more than that at this period Kodály had learned most of the requisites of his art—except perhaps how to 'carry on', for he comes now and then to a dead stop and starts afresh. That at least is how it strikes us at present, but casting the mind back a few years it is easy to realize that such a Quartet as this, with its personal vein of melody and its freshness of treatment, would have made quite a stir, besides prompting predictions—which, happily, have meanwhile been realized.* (*The Musical Times*, April 1924.)

The *First String Quartet* is the only work by Kodály of which the composer wrote a detailed analysis, adding music examples too. It appeared in the programme of the Zurich festival and in the festival numbers of German music periodicals, here and there with minor differences in the text.

First movement (Andante poco rubato–Allegro). The introduction (Andante poco rubato) is a Hungarian folksong theme, which opens the work by way of a motto, Kodály wrote. The folksong, or according to its origin rather a popular art song, represents with its domed structure the new style in Hungarian folk music.

In the course of all its many transformations, the folksong surfaces at countless points in the work virtually as a subterranean stream. Is it perhaps a grand form, a classical formal design built out of a folk melody? Kodály's analysis does not refer to this. In fact, he stated on countless occasions, and in many different ways that in its original form the folksong is unsuited for the creation of a sonata structure, an art-music grand form, with the exception of rondo and variations. His notion fully tallies with Arnold Schoenberg's oft-repeated view, which he set forth most pithily in 1947: *The discrepancy between the requirements of larger forms and the simple construction of folk tunes has never been solved and cannot be solved.* (Schoenberg: "Folkloristic Symphonies".)

Still, there is no contradiction between Kodály's theory and his practice. He solved the conundrum himself in 1963: . . . *The first movement of my first string quartet really feels as if I had wanted to write a string quartet out of a folksong. But the truth is just the opposite. The first half of the work was almost ready when I noticed that my first theme showed a certain connection with folksong, so much so that one might say it had developed out of it. Thus subsequently I placed the folksong, like a motto, at the head of the movement, but the work had not originated from it. I did not set about intending to elaborate the folksong as a sonata form, because I knew immediately that this was impossible.*

It cannot be considered fortuitous, however, that Kodály's own melodic invention led him to write notes so close to Hungarian folksong, as he had been studying folk melodies since 1903, and collecting them since 1905, thus by the time he wrote his *First String Quartet*, their tenor must have imbued his very being.

According to Imre Waldbauer, the first violinist of the quartet that bore his name, and who stood close to Kodály, the melodic material of only the first two movements of op.2 originates from folksong *(Cobbet's Cyclopaedic Survey of Chamber Music)*. Later, however, this melodiousness turns out to appear in all four movements of the work, the string quartet thus being of a monothematic structure. The model might have been the formal design of Debussy's string quartet. Kodály became acquainted with Debussy's works in Paris in the spring of 1907, and studied his quartet so thoroughly that on October 24, 1907 he wrote out the entire third movement of the work from memory. Also in 1907, Kodály wrote his piano piece entitled *Meditation* on one of the themes of the Debussy work. Even so, in different forms monothematic construction characterizes all of Kodály's chamber music.

Knowing that the folksong motto is a subsequent addition, it is easier to understand how a cyclic work in C minor opens in F sharp, a tonality regarded in 1910 as differing greatly from the main key, though by present day concepts it counts as its polar opposite. The broadly phrased, warm cello melody follows the aeolian scale, but the harmonies that accompany it, as in the slow introductions to the sonatas of the Viennese Classical composers, constantly call the tonality into question, lending the introductory pseudo-folk melody almost a floating effect.

The C minor quartet, lasting about 35 minutes, is Kodály's largest instrumental work. Later, the Waldbauer Quartet omitted the fugato from the last movement, obviously with the composer's assent, while subsequent performers of the work, with the composer's approval, shortened the slow movement, left out the middle section of the scherzo, and, naturally, the recapitulation of the main section. But all performers have adhered faithfully to the opening Allegro, the early sonata composition of Kodály which even Bartók had considered problematical. Listening to the work for the first time, several contemporaries heard in it the influence of Beethoven, although this may rather have reached the work via Brahms. It was perhaps the last time the direct influence of Brahms could be discerned in Kodály's technique. Listening to the convoluted melodies, a reference to *Sezession* also seems justified—not the Belgian and French *Art Nouveau*, nor the German *Jugendstil*, nor even the Viennese *Sezession*, but their Hungarian equivalent, which employs folk or supposedly folk ornaments. The dramatic Allegro first subject ascending in the cello, and the tremendous intensification that develops from it, immediately strike a note reminiscent of Brahms. The calm second melody recalls typical folksong features, its lyrical manner called into question by hard accents. In place of a closing theme, the conclusion of the formal unit is marked only by a flexible motif. The development is one of the lengthiest and most complicated of Kodály's similar constructions. The parts are piled up upon one another, the harmonies set out on wild adventures, and the floodgates open up before the message that comes from bursting, exorbitant emotions. Amidst these bold changes from fortissimo to pianissimo, the effect of the recapitulation is almost blurred. In a great unison the four instruments raise up the folksong motto as it were, in apotheosis, then after a muscular stretto where one of the motifs of the first subject is *transformed to resemble a funeral march, the movement suddenly closes.* (Kodály's analysis.)

The slow movement, Lento assai, tranquillo, is in Kodály's words, a *ternary form*. The typically cantabile first and third sections are determined by a variant of the *folksong theme* in swaying 6/8 and 9/8 barcarolle rhythm. The second theme, which forms the middle section, has a semplice opening, and, accompanied by sensitive rhythms which embrace the melody, arrives to a climax, and then continues downward again (fugato). The pizzicato double fugue before the recapitulation seems excessively polyphonic, and so, with the composer's consent, it has mostly been abandoned in performances of the work. The unison version of a cell from the folksong motif marks the arrival of the recapitulation. The emotional climax of the movement consists of a few unison bars accentuated by the performance direction of molto feroce (very wildly), followed by fortissimo espressivo. Both in texture and dynamics the recapitulation is an even more refined and differentiated version of the opening of the movement. Its sensitive, mysterious world fades away on harmonics. In his analysis, Kodály calls attention to the melodic relationship between the material of the first and second movements.

As a gesture to the monothematic concept, the scherzo, marked Presto, is also related to what went before, although with its firm rhythm it forms an extreme contrast with the resolved, variegated rhythm of the slow music. Above the "basses de musette" of the cello the rubato folksong theme turns into a taut dance melody, which justifies as hearing in it the robust rhythm of Hungarian folk dance. The melody of the middle section, in a somewhat more moderate tempo, is practically the inversion of the opening melody of the scherzo, and so the third movement itself too displays monothematism.

The finale with variations (Allegro–Allegretto semplice) displays an unusual construction. The C minor work ends in C major, as do Beethoven's Fifth and Brahms's First Symphonies. But the first moment of its "fast" introduction, like the slow introduction to the opening movement, suggests the polar F sharp tonality, so that there is a tonal symmetry between the outer movements. This unconcluded motif really suggests an opening up, recalling now an Aeolian, now a Dorian modality, and also taking part in the variations. Is it then *the over-torturing of the poor Greek scale*, as one of the critics of the time wrote disapprovingly? The rhythmic lilt of the motif mainly recalls those of Hungarian popular songs. It is an introduction to fantasia, its harmonies leading ever further away from the C major to come, with constantly wavering tempos, like a great rubato concealed within an allegro. The principal themes of the opening movement and the scherzo emerge timidly, almost questioningly, both to be virtually swept away by the motif that opened the finale, as if the gesture of the ode to joy from Beethoven's Ninth were here emerging: "nicht diese Töne". Out of the whirling parts the theme of the variations arises, but before it is heard in full, it suggests A flat minor with a key signature of seven flats, the most distant key from C major. This is followed by the principal melody, marked Allegretto semplice, of the variations, an extremely well balanced, self-contained melody with a four-line strophic structure, woven from Hungarian popular song elements which basically differ from folk music. The five variations treat the open motif that introduces the movement and the closed, four-line melody, in alternation. Kodály pointed out that *the variations preserve the outlines of the theme fairly well*. And this is true. Variation 4, in 5/8 time is by Emma Sándor, who later became Kodály's wife. The fugato structure woven from the opening motif is followed, after an episode in the minor, by another, faster fugato, adding a specific colour to the ceaseless alternation of opening and closing, animation and quietude. At this juncture the formal balance calls for a calm, broadly phrased, cantabile introduction of the melody with a song structure. And the coda, with its sudden stops, reveals the real meaning of this consistent double play, as if saving the surprise effect for the last minute—namely that the open and closed material of the variations, which so far had seemed to be different, in fact represent the dual features of one and the same melody.

Sonata for Cello and Piano

opus 4

COMPOSITION: 1909–10. Completed February 1910.
FIRST PERFORMANCE: Festival Hongrois, Paris, March 12, 1910, second and third movements only, János Mihálkovics (cello), Béla Bartók (piano). Budapest, March 17, 1910, all three movements, Jenő Kerpely (cello), Béla Bartók (piano).
DURATION: *c.* 18–19 minutes.
PUBLISHER: Universal Edition.

In 1964, recalling his student years after more than seven decades, Kodály said he had begun to study the violin and have piano lessons at the age of ten. To be able to play an instrument, he said, *was never the main thing for me. From the outset I spent much more time composing than performing. But I wanted to play string quartets with my school fellows and since we had no cellist, I simply decided to learn to play that instrument too. I ordered a cello method and learned all the exercises in succession—there was no cello teacher at Nagyszombat* (today Trnava, Czechoslovakia)— *and I very soon got to the stage where I could play Haydn quartets.* It was thus practical considerations that led Kodály to an intimate acquaintanceship with the cello, an instrument which played such a significant part in both his chamber music and orchestral music.

In a monograph published in 1936, Antal Molnár (1890–1983), Kodály's first biographer, mentioned a cello sonata in the style of Brahms, which Kodály later rejected as a juvenile work. The first music example in Molnár's work is the cantabile first subject of the Allegro in G minor of this sonata. On September 13, 1906 Kodály wrote to his future first wife: ... *then I'll get the sonata done right through*... On November 17, he wrote: *Cello-*

son. verrons, and on December 10 he said of the sonata that *... It has not grown at all... .*On June 23, 1907 he wrote hopefully from Paris: *If the summer is fine and sunny, I'll perhaps forge out ... the cello son., for which I have still no adagio, nor a good last allegro movement.* On July 23 he wrote that the cello sonata would not be completed during the summer. According to the dates Kodály wrote in the printed score of the work, he completed the slow, first movement on December 5, 1909, and the final movement in February 1910. In a letter of January 12, 1910 Bartók wrote of Kodály's *cello sonata now in progress.*

The score shows no signs of haste, though Kodály had good reason to be in a hurry, as scarcely was the work completed, when he immediately set out for Paris. In the French capital Sándor Kovács, the eminent pianist, teacher and aesthete, organized, with Bartók's help, a concert of Hungarian works, that is a "festival", as programmes devoted to a single theme are called in France to the present day. It was here that Kodály's sonata was first heard, on March 12, 1910. This date also marks, as far as we at present know, the first performance of a Kodály work abroad.

No sooner was the work completed than Kodály began to have second thoughts. *Kodály would prefer us to include only the second and third movements of his sonata,* Bartók wrote on February 18, 1910 to Sándor Kovács in Paris. As the programme shows, this request was fulfilled.

Before deciding finally on the form of the work, Kodály tried out the three-movement conception as well. The programme of his composer's evening on March 17, 1910 in Budapest described the work as 1. Allegro, 2. Fantasia Andante, 3. Allegro. (The programme included no opus number and the tempo markings for the second and third movements differ from those featuring in the printed score.) The press reviews of the composer's evening also speak of a three-movement version. In 1957, still in the composer's lifetime, Antal Molnár issued for scholarly purposes a previously unknown Kodály work under the title *Cello Sonata Movement, 1909.* As a practical edition it was prepared for the press in 1969 by the Soviet cello professor L. Ginzburg, under the title *Sonatina for Cello and Piano.* It is possible, though not certain, that this is the discarded opening movement of op. 4. Kodály's letter of June 23, 1907 quoted above, seems to suggest that the opening movement of the *Sonata* was completed in some form or other by that time. Certainly the *Sonatina* shows considerable difference in style from the op. 4, and it is understandable why the composer ultimately omitted it from the final version of the *Sonata for Cello and Piano*.

Before 1914, the two-movement version of the piece had been played in several cities abroad both by Hungarians and non-Hungarians. On May 3, 1913 it was heard for the second time in Paris, this time at a concert of the Société Musicale Indépendante, played by Diran Alexanian, the Armenian-born cello professor of the Conservatoire, and Alfredo Casella, who later made his name as a composer.

Michel D. Calvocoressi, the musical writer born in Marseille, who after the First World War settled in Britain, where he rendered much service to Kodály as a translator and as a musical staff-member of Oxford University Press, sent a review to London of both this concert and an earlier performance of Kodály's works in Paris (*The Monthly Musical Record*, June 2, 1913). To my knowledge this is the first thing to have been written about Kodály in the English-speaking world: *After a long interruption the Société Musicale Indépendante has resumed its concerts. The first evening ... began with a 'cello sonata by M. ZOLTÁN KODÁLY ... who is, with M. BÉLA BARTÓK at the head of the modern Hungarian School. M. Kodály, until now, was known to the Paris public solely by a set of pianoforte pieces ... which has been played at the same Society, three years ago, by M. Teodor Szanto—daring, bewildering little pieces, the purport of which seems at first most recondite, but which on closer acquaintance prove as delightful as they are original. They may be given as typical instances of what Hungarian music of today is. ... The 'cello sonata, though instinct with absolute originality, is less forbidding, and perhaps, the would-be students of modern Hungarian music will do well to begin with it ... A remarkable feature from the more technical point of view is the easy, simple way in which both instruments associate. In that respect M. Kodály has achieved a high feat of workmanship.*

The *Sonata* was the first work by Kodály to be performed in the English-speaking world. It was played by the cellist Livio

Boni and the pianist Franz Liebich in the Aeolian Hall in London on March 11, 1914. It remains to this day a mystery how the performers acquired the manuscript of the piece, and they themselves do not feature in any handbooks or encyclopaedias.

Hence the work already had a fine career in its manuscript form, its subsequent course being paved by Kodály's Viennese publishers, Universal Edition. Through Bartók's mediation, Kodály offered the *Sonata* for publication in a letter of May 22, 1920, returning to the subject on December 31, 1920. On November 17, 1922 he notified the Vienna AKM (the Austrian Copyright Society), which handled his royalties, to register the work as a composition in print. Soon afterwards, the *Sonata* was performed in Switzerland by Joachim Stutschewsky, who later became the cellist in Rudolf Kolisch's string quartet, and in Holland by Maurits Frank, the later cellist of the Amar-Hindemith quartet. As is shown by documents of the period between 1928 and 1932, the composition featured in the repertoires of six German cellists, and formed to my knowledge part of the programmes of six musicians in Britain also, during the years leading up to 1944.

In 1964 Kodály related the history of the origin of the work: *What happened in connection with my first cello sonata was... well, many composers have written down everything up to the first exposition in one breath, but it quite frequently causes a problem how to carry on from there... As I have said already, it is easier to arrive at the exposition, as the piece is either monothematic or has two themes; and if one has to search long for the second, then only in the rarest case will it fit the first, so that the two should occur to one simultaneously... indeed, what happened to me on one occasion was—the exposition having long been completed, but me somehow not wanting to, or not being able to, continue with the work, since I had always taken heard of Goethe's advice: if something does not go of itself, one should leave the whole thing and rather embark on something else, because if something has to be forced, then nothing good will come of it—that I suddenly hit upon sections way beyond the double bar. They virtually thrust themselves upon me, till the final point of the modulations, so that I did not have to think any further, as they rushed at me quite of themselves, up to the recapitulation. Of course, this happens most rarely*. Unfortunately we do not know which movement Kodály might have been referring to, the first which he later discarded, or one of the ones he retained.

The *Sonata for Cello and Piano*, in the form we know it today, is the first example in Kodály's instrumental music of that typical style in which all its melodic, rhythmic and harmonic elements, spring from Hungarian folk music, without, however, including any folk-music quotations or original folklore material. Equally evident is the influence of Debussy, particularly in the first movement. Of course it is not a question of servile imitation, or a derivative use of his style, rather a creative development of it. When Kodály paid his last tribute to Debussy in 1918, he summarized, as it were, what he had learnt from the French composer: *In his harmonies he often renounced the advantage of combining chords in a customary way, thereby increasing the expressive power of the chords he used. His melodies move in the new manner that avoids chromatics. At this point his music touches both ancient and folk music. But it is the culture of tone colours which owes most to him. He discovered previously unsuspected colour possibilities with the orchestra and piano alike. His works are conceived in terms of colours.*

The first movement of the *Sonata* is marked Fantasia. Adagio di molto. According to the programme of the first Budapest performance, the original tempo marking was Andante, but the reviewer of the day already noted that it was "very slow, almost in a largo tempo". While a composition exists in manuscript form alone, the composer may, to some extent, exercise control over its performance, and correct many details, including the tempo; the printed work, however, already takes on an independent life, and in the published score the tempo marking has been changed accordingly.

The Fantasia opens with twelve bars of dream music from the solo cello. It is marked molto espressivo—one of Kodály's most frequent performing instructions, calling for expressive intensity. Before the melody appears in a fully developed form, its framework of fourths and fifths is presented as a symmetrically arranged, four-note fragment of pentatonic music, typical of the old-style Hungarian folk music. This motto, however, refers not only to Hungarian folk-music sources, but also to

Brahms, whom Kodály held in such high esteem; here he virtually quotes the opening of the slow movement of the great predecessor's op.102, *Double Concerto for Violin and Cello*. The melody is of a closed structure, in a calm, 6/8 rhythm, the typical lilt of Kodály's later slow movements. As contrasting material, the piano brings an open-ended motif, first stirring and then restrained move restricted in movement, intended for continuation —also marked espressivo. The piano part seems to capture an instrumental improvisation, a broadly phrased rubato, accompanied, as it were, by the cello; the wavering metre changes practically bar by bar while leading to a great climax, developed from the piano motif with increasing passion, the tremendous emotion nourished by a fragmentation of the melody and a compression of the accompanying figures. The music switches to a quicker pulse, the ascending, arched line of the opening melody being followed, by way of response, by a sharply marked, descending motif first on the piano and then, in an intensified and animated setting, on the cello. The climax, bearing the dynamic character and tempo markings fortissimo, appassionato, and più agitato, is built from the piano motif from the beginning of the movement, and at this focal point all the melodic elements move along an upward soaring line. The recapitulation follows a favourite course of Bartók's later works: the building material is heard in reverse order, travelling along a bridge form. The order of instruments is also "reversed": the characteristic piano melody of the first section of the movement returns on the cello, completely different in mood, smoothed out into a molto espressivo. The cello melody engraved pentatonically in the first bars is now completed by the piano, while in the lowest register of the bowed instrument only the first two notes of the theme are heard, also in reverse order, a reference to the "bridge" form. By way of reminiscence, the first bar of the open-ended melody, assigned to the keyboard instrument, at the moment of farewell appears again on the piano, but now for the first time with an espressivo marking, and as an echo, is responded to for the last time by the ascending melodic motto on the cello, reinforcing the F sharp key of the movement.

The programme of the composer's evening in Budapest in

1910 still gave the title of the work as *Sonata in G major*, but later performances and the printed score no longer referred to the key. The anonymous reviewer of the second Paris performance of the *Sonata* (in *Le Courrier Musical* on June 1, 1913) described Kodály as a Cubist composer, while according to some critics of the 1920s, op. 4 is an atonal work. Contemporaries must have been confused by the two movements of the final version of the piece being in the keys of F sharp and G, although, according to the axis system of the musicologist Ernő Lendvai, in relation to G, F sharp is a subdominant tonality, and thus the scoring is in the customary key for a slow movement.

The tonal arrangement of the Fantasia movement, which remained typical of Kodály also in his later works, must have seemed surprisingly new for the time. As the composer András Mihály pointed out: *Kodály, as an organizer of melodies, explores a path which runs surprisingly parallel to Bartók's experiments ... As Bartók does so frequently, Kodály opposes or links two pentatonic structures which complement one another. This applies to both movements, but slightly differently. If, however, ... one confines oneself to the first movement, it may be said that this new manner of construction includes no modulation, nor do any functions in the old sense of the term play any role in it. The stability of the melodies and the form are ensured by the two pentatonic structures, and their diversity by the nimbly varied modes...* András Mihály has drawn attention to the polypentatonic-polymodal diatonicism of Kodály's style, a mode of construction whose starting point is identical with Bartók's scales, but differs in its final outcome, since the same basis led Bartók to chromaticism. One should not forget that Kodály emphasized on countless occasions that his musical mentality rested on a vocal base, which calls for an essentially diatonic world.

The final movement, marked Allegro con spirito (in 1910, Allegro), although having no title inscription, is also in effect a fantasia, a hard, fast-pace dance fantasia, virtually prising apart the frames of sonata form. The vision of a speeded up rural dance is suggested by the hard, 2/4 pulse that runs through the movement, whose even pace is broken only for fleeting moments by delicate accelerations and retardations. The large number of rhythmic effects taken from folk music for string instruments, plus the use of typical figures from bagpipe music all refer to the dance, certain melodic elements having almost the effect of a quotation, though their lilting dance-melody does not make an appearance as folksong. None of the motifs are rounded off in themselves, so that every moment of the piece is bursting with energy and dynamic development.

The pulsating pendulum of fourths and fifths from the opening four-bar cello motif, which in intervallic content parallels the beginning of the slow movement, contains in embryo the complete music of the finale. Is this the main theme? Or is it again a motto? From it unfolds the broader subject, as well as the second subject, and all the transitional, bridging material too As a result of the constant movement, these melodies and motifs move continually into tonal areas other than the ones they started from—different from what their characteristic features promised. In the grandiose development section it becomes obvious that the two instruments in fact represent *three* parts— (according to melody, rhythm and colour)—as complete equals. The composer creates an almost stereoscopic effect when he develops his material in three dimensions, increasing extraordinarily the depth of focus of the music. The recapitulation which is varied and augmented, also holds out the promise of further elaboration, but then comes a phrase heard previously with a closing function, rising from pianissimo to an intense dynamic intensification, and which is rhythmically "irregular", incorporating, through melodic division, 3/8 time into 2/4. The beginning of the cello phrase which opened the movement is now heard in the bass of the piano, with its ending superimposed above it in the high register. A downward run seems ready to prepare the final conclusion of this dance fantasia—but instead, a long pause, a deep breath is followed by the return of the slow movement, as a close, lending the sonata a monothematic framework. The beautiful arch of the cello melody is rised to an apotheosis, supported, like boldly constructed pillars, by dense piano chords rich in harmonic content. In 1910 the piano part was thinner and less richly ornamented, and only later did receive its final form. One can feel here the instrumental accompaniment to Kodály's songs dating from after the op.4. The blazing harmonies burn themselves out, and the cello melody slowly dies away. The resigned quotation of the end of the first movement erases from our memory; the ecstatic vortex of the dance scenes, these fleeting notes lead us toward the secret poetry of a solitary introvert, after the strong light, evoking at the close nocturnal colours and moods.

Duo for Violin and Cello

opus 7

COMPOSITION: Budapest, 1914.
FIRST PERFORMANCE: Budapest, May 7, 1918, Imre Waldbauer (violin), Jenő Kerpely (cello).
DURATION: *c*. 24 minutes.
PUBLISHER: Universal Edition.

Surprisingly, the favourable reception given to Kodály in Budapest at his début as a composer on his composer's evening of March 1910 brought no change in the fortunes of his works. True, on April 30 the Rózsavölgyi publishing house signed a contract with him for the publication of two of the works heard at the composer's evening (*First String Quartet* and *Piano Music*) as well as the *Adagio*, but the issuing of these three works seems to have exhausted the publisher's enthusiasm, and they were not followed by any more of Kodály's scores until 1921.

The initial effect of the composer's evening made itself felt for some time to come, but nevertheless, from March 1912 until 1917 none of Kodály's works were performed in Hungary, even though they were abroad. This meant that the works Kodály wrote after op.4. were for a long time confined to his workshop, his song cycles as well as new chamber works and piano pieces.

But even if for many years the new works did not reach the public, many documents attest to Kodály's activity during this period. As a teacher at the Academy of Music, from the autumn of 1912 onwards he was assigned the second year composition class as well as the first, which meant that whereas in the year 1911–12 he had eight students of composition, the next year this number had grown to twelve. By 1913 he felt the time was ripe to start to systematize and publish the Hungarian folk music he had collected with Béla Bartók and a few younger colleagues. He drew up a "Project for a New Complete Collection of Folksongs", jointly signed by Bartók and Kodály and which appeared the same year. Without financial support and public interest, however, only forty years later could the first volume appear of *Corpus Musicae Popularis Hungariae*. (A Complete Edition of Hungarian Folk Music.)

It was in the midst of such fervent activity that Kodály completed the next piece of his series of chamber music, the *Duo for Violin and Cello*. It took four years for the piece to be premièred, on May 7, 1918, at Kodály's second composer's evening in Budapest, together with the *Sonata for Solo Cello*, the *Second String Quartet* and the song cycle *Late Melodies* (minus two of the pieces).

In date of origin, the *Duo* is the earliest work of Kodály's to secure itself a permanent place in the twenties on the programmes of modern music societies.

The September-October 1922 issue of the Viennese periodical, *Musikblätter des Anbruch* carried the first news of the publication of the score of the work. The first performance abroad took place at a concert held on November 20, 1922 by the Prague Society for Private Performances of Music, which was affiliated to Arnold Schoenberg's Verein für mus. Privatauffürrungen in Vienna. The performers, Rudolf Kolisch (violin) and Wilhelm Winkler (cello), were among Schoenberg's most intimate colleagues. Early in 1923 the piece was performed in Zurich by the 'cellist Joachim Stutschewsky, the name of the violinist not being known. It was performed in London on February 13, 1924 by Jenő Léner and Imre Hartmann, and for a second time on March 2, 1926, when it was billed by the Contemporary Music Centre, performed by Kodály's former students of composition, Zoltán Székely and Paul Hermann, who both repeated the work in London on March 8, 1929, also taking it to a number of cities in Europe. In the 1920s the *Duo* was performed in several German cities by József Szigeti and Gregor Piatigorsky, and Licco Amar and Mauritz Frank (the latter members of the legendary Amar-Hindemith String Quartet).

Apart from the publication of the score, a major factor in the work's becoming known was its performance at the second ISCM festival (Salzburg, August 6, 1924), by Imre Waldbauer and Paul Hermann.

Violin and cello is a rare instrumental combination, perhaps an aftermath of the child Kodály's instrumental studies, and particularly counted as such in 1914, the year it was composed. In the Baroque violin sonata with figured bass accompaniment, the cello merely reinforced the bass of the keyboard instrument, and from the second half of the 18th century onwards, such duos were written mainly with an instructive purpose, for violin students. The parts for the two instruments in these pieces are not equal in rank. In 1909 the Russian Reinhold Glière wrote a duo for violin and cello, as did the Hungarian Emánuel Moór in 1910. We do not know whether Kodály was familiar in 1914 with these works. All the duos for these two string instruments known—or rather not much known—in 20th century music are of later date: Ravel's *Sonata* was written in 1922, Hans Eisler's in 1925, and works for violin and cello by Tibor Harsányi, Emil Schulhoff, Zoltán Székely and Boleslav Vomačka also all date from after Kodály's work. It would seem therefore that it must have been Kodály who discovered this instrumental combination for 20th century music.

The value of this discovery, even so, was not really appreciated by the contemporaries. Most performers of the *Duo* have been Hungarian, and the work has not found a famous patron abroad as did the *Sonata for Solo Cello* in the person of the British Beatrice Harrison. The *Sonata for Solo Cello* received its first English performance in London on February 5, 1924 in the Contemporary Music Centre, played by Harrison, and this was followed on February 13 by the performance of the *Duo* by Jenő Léner and Imre Hartmann, members of the Léner String Quartet. The two performances were received together in the March 1, 1924 number of *The Musical Times* in an article signed E. E. (Edwin Evans): *The Duo for Violin and 'Cello . . . is a much less arresting work . . . the opportunity for instrumental conversation tempts the composer to meander round subjects which are not always of sufficient interest to animate the dialogue. At other times the conversational character is dropped, and the 'cello is occupied with a pedal accompaniment, by which it ceases to be an equal partner, and the interest becomes lop-sided. This is not to say that the music is poor. A great deal of it is very good, but somehow it does not convince us, as the 'Cello Sonata does, that it has found its right vehicle of expression or its right form, which, when you come to think of it, is much the same thing.*

Imre Waldbauer's analysis in W. W. Cobbet's *Cyclopedic Survey of Chamber Music* (London, 1929) did not pave the way effectively for the spread of the work either: *With Kodály the inter-relation of the two instruments is based on perfect equality: each is the natural complement of the other, and everything is made to subserve a single principle, that of obtaining the ideal tone colour and form in an ensemble made up of two contrasting and yet parallel elements.* In September 1965 Kodály wrote with a measure of resignation to Eugene Ormandy, the eminent Hungarian-born American conductor of his orchestral works in Philadelphia: *Well, the poor Duo had to wait for 50 years to be heard by Ormándy.* So the work had no possibility to enjoy much popularity in the United States either.

Kodály was unusually very reticent about his own composition. Before the London performance of the *Duo*, the Léner ensemble asked him for a note on the work. The letter arrived fairly late in Budapest, and Kodály answered it on February 8, 1924, being aware of the fact that his reply would arrive in Britain too late for the concert: *In the summer of 1914 I spent a few weeks in Switzerland in an excellent mental and physical disposition. The day of the declaration of war found me, together with my wife in Zermatt. The whole resort became empty in a few days, and we too had to bid farewell to the most monumental mountain sights, as the hotels were closing down. We had to make the last stretch to the Swiss border in a truck, since Switzerland too was mobilizing. We had to stay put for several days in a village along the Tyrolean border (Feldkirch). It was there the vision of the Duo suddenly appeared to me. Never before had I thought of scoring for a combination such as this. I thought no one ever had done so before either. (Later I became acquainted with Haydn's and I also read that it had been fairly frequent in the 18th century.) No music-paper was to be had in Feldkirch, and so the first movement, which I put on paper there, is written in a school music exercise book, practically without any change throughout. Whether others will ever find anything either of the indescribable grandeur of the gigantic mountains or the dim presentiment of a precipitate war in it, remains a great question.*

Imre Waldbauer, who as a performer, was in perman[ent] contact with the composer, added in his analysis quoted abo[ve:] *In this work, more than perhaps in any other chamber [work] Kodály's heroic note is effectively sounded.*

The heroic tone of the opening movement of the *Duo* [(]serioso, non troppo) is familiar from the culminating n[umbers] of *Summer Evening* and also from some of the piano pi[eces] op. 3, yet it is completely new in Kodály as the principal me[ans] of a large-scale sonata structure. Another novelty is that [the] heroic tone bursts into the composition not at the forma[l] climax, as the outcome of the development, but immediately animates feverishly the first subject which opens the movement, played resolutely (risoluto) and broadly (un poco largamente) by the cello. This infinitely variegated and at the same time very massive melody gives the effect of an exclamation mark, and is further intensified by the accompanying chords from the violin. The key of the work as a whole is D, the first subject circumscribing this tonality, with extremely rich nuances. Tone and character change immediately when the violin takes over the melody from the cello. The transition assails the main key from two directions towards the dominant, and, with its pizzicato accompaniment, has a strict imitation structure. The piercing, active first subject, rich and eventful, is followed by a seemingly simple cantabile second subject, first on the violin and then on the cello. "Non espressivo", Kodály warns the performer and the listener, not intending it to be a moment of lulling intimacy. Indeed, before one can lose oneself in its simple beauty, this melody too blazes forth with volcanic power. The two instruments unite in the same melody, the first unison in the movement, and the growing tension arrives at a *fff* peak, with the instruction con fucco for the performer. After a long pause the codetta brings a sharp change in volume (pianissimo), unfolding against a background of carefully elaborated accompaniment. In fact all three melodies spring from the same source, since they all branch off from the opening bar, revealing the composer's monothematic thinking. The development gives way to fantastic instrumental adventures. In particular, the cello part abounds in elements each more virtuoso than the other. In fact Kodály withholds the original first subject from the develop-

section. Why? The first subject appears in full at the cli- and this also marks the recapitulation. But while at the g of the movement it was presented by the cello, now it in the high register of the violin, with a completely new animent, embedded in the undulating runs of the low strument. This elemental surge calms down gradually, e music becomes strongly expressive and wavering, as if olitary cello had turned it into a lament. The parlando e of old Hungarian folksong anticipates the emotional monothematic beginning of the slow movement, and leads, in the recapitulation, to a much more extended elaboration of the second subject and codetta than there was at their first appearance. The message of the movement dies away in ever softer fragments of the heroic principal idea.

The cello melody which opens the Adagio belongs among the most subjective and intimate moments of Kodály's dreamworld. Its melodic type is first encountered in *Summer Evening*, and one can trace countless later emotional variants of it in the composer's instrumental music. While the expressiveness of the opening movement avoided the instruction espressivo, now the sensitive melody in the first passage of the slow section calls for a molto espressivo performance. The new tempo, Andante, signifies the boundaries of its form: the apparently calm nocturnal picture of nature becomes full with visions, the smooth melodic surface shattered by the dramatic weight of expression. The sweeping melodies and melodic fragments accompanied by rustling effects, the increasingly condensed harmonic treatment, and the predominance of expressive elements, constitute a vision not to be found in Kodály's previous works. Following the rules of ternary form, the theme and mood of the beginning return, but the opening melody no longer resumes its original smoothness, and the eerie passages of harmonics on the cello bring no acquiescence, rather conjuring up a new vision. After this return of human inflection in a declamatory appassionata moment, the vision dies away.

The finale promises another slow movement: maestoso e largamente, ma non troppo lento. It is a free instrumental improvisation, a violin cadenza, providing the only point in the work absolutely dominated by the high-registered string instrument.

The thematic material recalls, by way of a monothematic construction, characteristic moments from the preceding movements, in this referring to the preparatory section of the finale of the *First String Quartet*. This introductory music is marked by a perfectly relaxed atmosphere, a rubato written out in full, indicated by bar division or formulated in tempo directions—this already foreshadowing the introduction to the finale of the *Second String Quartet*. The smooth flow of tiny motifs in it is most typical of Kodály's manner of composition. Chronologically the relative closest to this method features in the instrumental setting of the song *Winter Approaching*, to the poem by the Romantic Hungarian poet Dániel Berzsenyi. Prior to that it appeared in the second movement (Andante poco rubato) of the op. 3 piano pieces, and was to reappear, for instance, in the folksong arrangement "Tiszán innen, Dunán túl" (This Side of the Tisza, Beyond the Danube) in the comic opera *Háry János*.

Dramatically, this violin cadenza has a dual function. It serves partly to sum up what has gone before, and partly, owing to its improvisatory character, to prepare the fast principal section of the finale. Before it comes full circle, turning back to its own beginning, and thus providing a firm frame for the seemingly free fantasia which proceeds so tentatively, the actual Finale (Presto) bursts in, releasing irrepressible rhythmic energies. This is the first folk-dance rondo in Kodály's œuvre, even though it stems from imaginary, reconstructed folk material. The composer was to employ this form later in countless varieties. The presentation of the rondo theme immediately contradicts the rule of the violin in the slow introduction. Here the cello takes the initiative, and up till the middle section introduces all the new thematic material. The rondo melody seems to promise the structure of a four-line dance tune (A-A-B and, as expected—A). Yet the theme is by no means so regular. The promised symmetry is valid only for the first three phrases, in each of which the first bar gains its rhythm through note repetition, with the second bar being the vehicle of melodic energy. The symmetry is broken by the closing gesture, which in fact not only has a concluding function but an opening one as well. Listening to this melody, or any other analogous piece of music by Kodály, we might think that this form founded a school of Hungarian divertimento finales of many decades later. But in the *Duo* the rondo theme eschews any stereotyped form precisely by its "limping" closing formula, which, with an unexpected turn lends the piece a unique and individual character. Compared to its closed structure, the melody has a relatively open ending, and so it offers many varied possibilities for melodic and tonal continuation. The intervals too expand and diminish constantly, and the imaginary dance tune finally resounds over long sections, like some brief cry of the dance, and rhythmic pulse and the rotating motif of its melodic cell coming alternately to the fore. As a particular formal invention, another variant of the monothematic concept, the outline of the lyrical second theme parallels the codetta of the first movement, while its accompaniment unites both elements that made up the effect of the rondo theme.

After this extremely animated musical sequence, the trio (Poco meno mosso) brings an unexpected change. Another dance melody is heard from the violin, above the cello's long sustained bagpipe fifth—a four-phrase fifth repeating melody with a syllable count of eight to a line, yet neither the rhythm nor the metric division are typical of Hungarian folk music. Here again one encounters a characteristic structure, but in an individual variety.

As soon as the melody is taken over by the cello, its contrapuntal accompaniment is built out of one of its descending lines. The graceful melody carries in itself the possibility of countless forms of tonal tension, and Kodály makes ample use of them by augmented and diminished intervals and the transfer of melodic elements. The middle section is of a development type, and indeed, in some sense even the recapitulation may be considered such, since the rondo theme at this point has a completely new effect, as the two elements of its effectiveness are heard divided between the two instruments. Kodály also condenses the material and does not mechanically repeat what has been heard once already. In the strongly accentuated formal part that precedes the final conclusion, he practically gives space for an abbreviated recapitulation of the middle section too. Still, while at its first appearance the material was tense and playful, now it takes on a capriciously rubato character on the violin, above the even, sombre E flat minor chords of the cello. The rhythm crumbles away, the tempo slows down, and the ornamentation becomes richer and richer. These few retarding bars abound in variants that reflect the influences of instrumental folk music, only to allow the irresistible surge of the first presto, and presently a più presto stretto, to burst in all the more effectively.

Sonata for Solo Cello

opus 8

COMPOSITION: 1915.
FIRST PERFORMANCE: Budapest, May 7, 1918, Jenő Kerpely.
DURATION: *c.* 30 minutes.
PUBLISHER: Universal Edition.

At the outbreak of the First World War Kodály was declared unfit for military service, but he joined, in the first autumn of the war, the voluntary garrison set up to defend the chief monuments of Budapest. *Last year, instead of going for walks, I kept guard; this year, however, I cannot give any time to it,* Kodály wrote in November 1916 to János Rolla, the engineer, who was commanding officer of the garrison, asking to be released. The *last year* of 1915 marks the origin of the *Sonata for Solo Cello*. In an undated letter, probably from December 1916, Kodály explained in detail why he had undertaken the guard duty and why he could no longer do it. Listing his commissions as an ethnomusicologist, he continued: *These I could not avoid, I am obliged by the position I occupy ... Alongside all of this, I have to perform my official duties as before, indeed, the number of my students has again increased. And I am also by the way working continuously in the field of composition.*

This then was the balance of the first two war years: comprehensive scholarly work, stepped up educational activity, and, as a "by the way", composition. The fact that he mentioned his creative work last may easily be explained by the complete neglect in Hungary of Kodály the composer. His works were ousted from the concert hall, and after 1910 Hungarian publishers showed no interest in his new compositions. If he did still compose, it was for his desk drawer, with no hope of any encounter with the public.

It was in this situation, and under such conditions, that Kodály composed for his desk drawer the *Sonata for Solo Cello*, one of his monumentous works. In fact, it is so immensely difficult technically, presenting the performer with such novel demands, that there may have been little hope for a performance.

After Bach's solo suites it took nearly two centuries for the cello to be assigned any major role as a solo instrument. Indeed, practically no works were written for it at all, as even the fairly meagre sonata output relied inevitably upon the chordal support of the piano. In Kodály's sonata both the genre and certain features of the instrumental treatment refer to Bach, but the texture, abounding in three and four-part chords, alludes also to the cello technique of Brahms. According to the Hungarian composer Pál Kadosa, a former pupil of Kodály: *Kodály held Brahms in very high esteem and considered him extremely important*. Although there is no proof, I think it probable that Kodály studied the works of this Romantic composer, when writing for the cello, if indeed he had not already done so during his studies at the Academy under János Koessler, a Brahms disciple. But there is no prototype in musical literature for the veritable orchestral effects Kodály brought forth in his work on a single string instrument. Though Max Reger's suite for solo violin appeared in print in 1914 and the one for solo cello in 1915, it is highly improbable that their scores reached Kodály during the wartime years. Also, he did not much relish Reger's music. In 1907 he wrote of him to Bartók from Berlin: ... *I did not really feel tempted to read him*. Thus, he had no desire to study Reger's scores.

Disagreeing with views now forgotten, in 1920 Bartók emphasized: "... *This is a work which, unlike Reger's violin solo sonatas, is not an imitation of Bach's polyphonic style*. (*Musical Courier*, New York, August 19, 1920.) Possibly some of his contemporaries, in reviewing Kodály's work, referred to the influence of Reger.

One of the unusual ideas in the *Sonata* is that Kodály revives a practice of Baroque instrumental music, using scordatura; that is he has the cello strings tuned to notes other than the original. The two low strings (C and G) are tuned down a semitone (B and F sharp, respectively). He indicates the scordatura at the beginning of the work, rather than notating it in the score. This strange mistuning seems to overshadow and darken the timbre of the cello. The four open strings, if sounded in their natural tuning, add up to a natural seventh chord of B, which suggests the work's fundamental tonality of B, even though the chord does not appear at all during the whole of the work's approximately 30 minutes. A much more frequent effect on the other hand, is the use of three and even four-part chords in which two or three open strings are heard, with other notes formed by two, or one "stopped" positions, a finger pressed on the appropriate string. The composer makes maximum use of the possibilities inherent in scordatura.

1915 also saw the composition of another work for cello, *Capriccio*, which appeared in print in 1969. In this too Kodály used scordatura, but only tuned the lowest string a semitone lower. It remains a question whether he intended the piece as one of the movements of op.8 or merely as a sketch in which to elaborate the new technique. Its tonality (E) would fit into the sonata as a movement in the subdominant, but the material makes this less likely. For *Capriccio* is a fantasia on the Hungarian folksong "Hej, a mohi hegy borának" (Hey, the Wine of Mohi Hill), which Kodály later arranged for voice and piano in the cycle *Hungarian Folk Music*. Even the scale passage that opens the cello piece tallies note for note with the beginning of the piano accompaniment in the folksong arrangement (it also returns in the orchestral opening of Marci the coachman's song "Ó mely sok hal..." (O, How Many Fish) in *Háry János*, a melody related to the folksong "Hej, a mohi hegy borának". Kodály, however, held the view that folksong did not lend itself to higher musical art forms. Perhaps the choice of melody was prompted by conditions of the time, as one of the lines of the folksong serving as the basis for the fantasia reads: "igen sok pénz nem jó" (too much money is not good), perhaps a reference to wartime inflation. Whatever the case, *Capriccio* was in all probability a compositional warm-up for the *Sonata* rather than a piece intended as one of its movements but later rejected.

The *Sonata for Solo Cello* was first performed on May 7, 1918, on Kodály's second composer's evening. It was performed by Jenő Kerpely, to whom the work is dedicated. According, however, to the recollections of the rapidly dwindling number of eye and ear-witnesses, Kerpely, an extremely sensitive and refined musician, lacked the technique necessary for an accurate performance of the *Sonata*, and he was not really able to accomplish the enormous task. The première thus in all probability did not produce the intended effect.

The first time the *Sonata for Solo Cello* was heard in a way closely following the score, practically as the work's real première, came at a private performance, nearly two years later in Vienna, at Arnold Schoenberg's Verein für mus. Privataufführungen. This was the first performance of the piece abroad at the time still in manuscript, which took place on April 16, 1920. It was performed by the 18-year-old virtuoso cellist Paul Hermann, a pupil of Adolf Schiffer at the Budapest Academy of Music. Hermann studied composition privately with Kodály, who in 1919 had been deprived of his chair at the Academy.

The *Sonata for Solo Cello* was the first work of Kodály's to be printed in Vienna, and indeed the first piece of his to have been published since 1910. The July-August 1921 number of the *Musikblätter des Anbruch*, the Universal Edition periodical, advertised it under the headline "Just Out", but a review of the score had appeared already in the June issue. The first foreign performer of the work, the Dutch Maurits Frank, included it in his repertoire in the spring of 1922, and first played it in Rotterdam.

A few months before the *Sonata for Solo Cello* appeared in print, the première of another work by Kodály, *Two Songs* with orchestral accompaniment (op.5) produced attacks in most of the Budapest newspapers, describing the composer as an ungifted Bartók imitator. Bartók himself rejected the accusation in the progressive literary periodical *Nyugat* (The West). He wrote (February 1, 1921): *Fortunately the question of Kodály will be settled not here, but abroad. Through the good offices of a Vienna publishing firm, Kodály's hitherto buried works are to appear in swift succession, so that we shall soon hear foreign opinion of them.* (*Béla Bartók Essays*, Faber and Faber.)

Bartók himself played a great part in organizing this "foreign opinion". On November 24, 1920 he wrote to Philip Heseltine, who under the pseudonym Peter Warlock was to become famous as the composer of bold works novel in tone: *I would like to call your attention to an excellent Hungarian composer:*

Zoltán Kodály. That his efforts were not in vain is borne out by Heseltine's study, "Modern Hungarian Composers" in the March 1922 issue of *The Musical Times*, in which he analysed four works by Kodály, and pointed out: *The most remarkable is the 'Cello Sonata', a veritable* t o u r d e f o r c e *of immense technical difficulty but of compensating musical interest which is wonderfully well sustained throughout its three movements.*

Also through the mediation of Bartók the music critic Cecil Gray made the acquaintance not only of Kodály's works but of the composer himself. *Here you will be the guest of Mr. Kodály*, Bartók wrote on May 16, 1921 to Gray, who was about to come to Budapest. The following year Cecil Gray wrote a thorough study of Kodály, illustrating it with music examples ("Zoltán Kodály", *The Musical Times*, May 1922): *To write an unaccompanied 'Cello Sonata in three movements, as Kodály has done, demands considerable courage, but his musicianship is more than equal to the test. Our attention is held from first to last, as much by the abstract musical interest of each movement as by the wealth of resource and ingenuity of treatment which so eloquently testify to the intimate understanding of the nature and capabilities of the instrument for which the work is written.*

From London Michel D. Calvocoressi asked Béla Bartók for information on Kodály. On July 31, 1921 Bartók informed him about the works which had been published by Universal Edition and those that were to appear in the near future. He also gave Calvocoressi Kodály's address so that he could contact the composer directly. Calvocoressi translated the texts of many works by Kodály into English, and presumably as a result of Bartók's mediation, wrote a detailed study of Kodály in *The Monthly Musical Record* (April 1, 1922). This is how he evaluated the *Sonata: Kodály's 'Sonata for 'cello solo' (op.8) is a superb instance of broad, firm and beautiful form in which repetition of patterns occurs freely without ever resulting in monotony. From the architectural point of view, as well as from that of exploiting the instrument's resources to good artistic purpose, it is a wonderful* t o u r d e f o r c e. *The Finale, for instance, will test the performer's technique to the utmost, and display it in every possible light, but without ever exceeding the bounds of the possible, and never for mere purposes of effect. As a whole, the 'Sonata' affords as conclusive evidence of skill, imagination, and ingenuity as we may wish to find in the work of any composer.*

Béla Bartók was the first to inform the international public about Kodály's *Sonata*, in the issue of *The Musical Courier* quoted already: *This composition embodies an attempt to serve the demands of modern music with the simplest possible means—a single melodic instrument. I lay stress upon the word modern, for this is a work which ... presents a wholly new treatment of the instrument as well as new and original musical material. The sonata, in three movements, replete with astounding technical difficulties and incredible instrumental effects, is truly an enrichment of violincello literature...*

From the 1920s onwards, all this turned the attention of the international press towards Kodály's works. The progress of his works, however, including the *Sonata for Solo Cello*, was presumably more effectively assisted by positive performances, such for example as that of op.8 in Salzburg on August 7, 1923 at the first ISCM festival, arranged by a jury. The festival was attended by all the eminent, and less eminent, members of the community of composers the world over, and the critics from all the major dailies and periodicals. Kodály's *Sonata*, already known from the published score and reviews, was heard by the festival audience in the able interpretation of Paul Hermann. If one may believe the critics, the work scored a tremendous success.

The Salzburg performance seems to have prompted societies of contemporary music to include the work in their programmes. Paul Hermann and Maurits Frank performed it all over Europe. On February 5, 1924 Beatrice Harrison played the *Sonata* at a private concert of the Contemporary Music Centre in London, and she later performed it in several other cities in both Britain and on the continent. In Paris it was performed by Madeleine Monnier at one of the regular Tuesday programmes of *La Revue musicale*, on May 17, 1924.

Kodály employed a wide range of imaginative instrumental effects in his *Sonata for Solo Cello*. The technique of mistuning has already been mentioned and he also used four-part chords to be played with the bow or pizzicato, floating harmonics (including chords), the rustling sul ponticello effect, polyphonic voice-leading, melodies with pizzicato accompaniment, and melodies above sustained pedal points—all this not by way of some new, spicy stimulus, but as part of the structure, alongside the melodic world, the harmony and rhythm, and the many elements derived from folk music.

The opening movement (Allegro maestoso ma appassionato) is in sonata form, but differs from the model Kodály had employed previously. It contrasts "only" two thematic groups, instead of three—and even these grow from the same melodic root. The foreground theme, without yielding its unified character, reveals so many facets (being rounded out from four different elements) that it offers possibilities for monothematic development. Its maestoso character recalls the lilt of saraband movements in the suites of old. The movement begins right at the apex, with a blaze of passion, radiating heroic power. It is as though the sublime tone of the odes of Kodály's favourite Hungarian poet, Dániel Berzsenyi were put into music. This swelling melodic passage constantly breaks through its given metric frame; although the notation suggests 3/4 time, if one looks for the weighty, four-part chords or the accents marked sforzato, one finds them placed in a constantly changing, extending and diminishing metric arrangement, a sensitive, expressive pulse behind the saraband. At first hearing certain features of the first subject seem to act as bridging elements, devices for connecting or separating, which articulate the music. The development section, eventually, convinces us that each and every note of the theme forms an organic part of its structure. The kinetic energy of the beginning springs from a single stamping sweep, which loses its strength in the passages of downward rolling convolutions. After a world of wide intervals held together by organic ornamental elements, the second subject—for want of a better denomination—employs the contrast of small intervals, and resolves the taut rhythmic and metric organization into a composed rubato. Its mood is expressed by a doleful sospirato motif. The mysterious, rustling sound of sul ponticello bowing dimly outlines distant will-o'-the-wisps. After the chiselled melody of the first subject, suggestive of a steel engraving, this is sure to create a pastel effect, its tone anticipating the resignation of the work's great Adagio.

The sospirato motif is eventually heard in the lower register in a long extended form, preparing for the "Out of the depths I cry" gesture of the development section, with its wild melodic and harmonic excursions. After the minor typed B tonality of the opening of the movement, the outlines of E flat major and E flat minor now appear simultaneously at the beginning of the development—a minor melody above a major harmony. The ambiguous sound branches off into countless tonal directions. Every note in this middle section refers to the first subject group, making us suspect dramatic considerations, as the "second subject" is more directly linked to the tone of the Adagio. The idea seems to not have the first movement, the gate opening wide to the whole work, consume prematurely all the emotional reserves of the composition, exhausting the atmosphere of the slow section. But however multifaceted the melody has been at the head of the movement, it still contains enough new possibilities to bring surprises in the development section, such as the development of some of its elements, or the chain of screeching trills in the recapitulation. In the whole movement it is only here that Kodály employs trills, not as mere embellishment, but as a structural element. Rubato is the instruction for the compact, two-bar cadenza, which prepares directly for the recapitulation. From this point onwards the musical processes all become extremely condensed. The first subject group, which enjoyed full rights in the development section, here is only recapitulated in its beginning by way of reference this time in a rich, four-part harmonization marked *grave*. The second subject is also—out of dramatic consideration—given a more heroic colouring, as the beginning of the slow movement approaches. The opening section of the movement was full of downward pulling flat key signatures, but now the direction is towards upward tending sharps. The sospirato motif grows in expressive power before it dies away. The two opening chords, hard as granite, return at the closing moment of the movement like an exclamation mark.

The Adagio is one of Kodály's most intimate movements. The direction "con grand' espressione" seems to refer to Beethoven—the Largo of his *Piano Sonata in E flat major*, op.7, or one of the sections in the slow movement of the *Hammerklavier*

Sonata. After the heroic opening, again reminiscent of Beethoven, this slow movement is perhaps the finest expression of the profound resignation so typical of the young Kodály. This deeply poetic Adagio points far into the future: it is perhaps the first harbinger of that notturno vision which found its ultimate expression in Bartók's "Night Music" (the fourth part turned into a slow-type movement of the piano cycle "Out of Doors", written in 1926). At first sight the Adagio appears to be in ternary form, the middle section more animated than the basic tempo, but in fact its structure is considerably more complex. The first large formal section alone consists of five units. Its arched melody is interrupted twice by fragments which turn into musical notes the shadows and noises of the night, and—remembering that it was war time—at the same time outline increasingly, strongly the Austro-Hungarian army bugle retreat.

The middle section (con moto) is a fantasia on the augmented second phrases and other typical melodic features of the folksongs sung during the Hungarian War of Independence led by Prince Ferenc Rákóczi II at the turn of the 17th and 18th centuries. (The lessons of the *Capriccio* thus not being lost, as the Hungarian folksong arranged in it is of the same origin.) There may feasibly be an intellectual relationship between the bugle retreat call, and this musical reference to the overthrown struggle for freedom. The middle section of the slow movements is the first sign, documented in musical notes, of how deep was Kodály's interest in the period of Prince Rákóczi and the folk music of the time, an interest reflected in many of his later works.

The beginning of the recapitulation seems rather to be a continuation of the animated trio. Instead of a "regular" recapitulation, Kodály reverses the order and constructs a bridge form. The Tempo I pursues further the fantasia tone using the bugle call; its completely loose rhythm and metre give it the effect of a written out improvisation. The continuation has the same effect—an improvisatory development of one of the germ motives of the Adagio's principal melody. Kodály perhaps here transferred to the cello certain effects of his early *Piano Music*. The highly sensitive melodic arch of the beginning of the movement has here the effect of an elaboration rather than a note for note recapitulation or even an abbreviated one. It might have been this excessively subjective treatment of melodic material which had once been solidified, this meditation on his own theme, this kind of popular improvisation put into art music, that some critics of the day felt to be excessive. Nevertheless, this dissolving tone, which at some of the peaks is so highly expressive, itself forms an organic part of the dramatic plan, since it prepares for the vortex of the finale's rapturous dance rondo.

The heroic passion of the opening movement and the nocturnal vision of the slow movement (which equally could have been subtitled *In tempore belli*—In Time of War—as nearly 30 years later was the *Missa brevis*) are followed by another vision in the Allegro molto vivace closing movement. It is not the oblivious round dance it seems at a first hearing; it is harder, more bitter and mysterious than the folk-dance finales written by Kodály's Hungarian imitators. It is an extremely complex movement, which is also true of the seemingly simple, eight-bar opening melody. The repeated notes of the first, two-bar phrase, which is launched from the note B as a stepping stone by the fourth bar grow out of being rhythm into being a melodic germ, the former quavers fragmented into semiquavers (Bars 5–6); the close of the melody already marks out a new direction. Thus, instead of being dance-like and rounded off, the beginning includes possibilities of opening further, indeed opening into many directions. Further on, an even quaver pulse comes to the fore, in a chordal pizzicato, with a surprising guitar or cimbalom effect, and there are lengthy sections of passages permeated by tiny energetic figures in semiquavers. Although the cello is not used as a folk instrument, in the finale Kodály transfers elements of folk fiddling and bagpiping to the solo cello without quoting or copying any actual Hungarian folk-music material.

The bagpipe sound gradually fades away, turning into eerie tremolos. The beginning of the middle, development section is marked by a pizzicato "dűvő" effect ("dűvő" being a characteristic accompanying rhythm of Hungarian folk music and gypsy music, with the accent on the weak beats). Unlike in the *First String Quartet* and the *Duo*, here Kodály recalls the slow movement—naturally in a varied form—and the beginning of the work, not as an introduction to the finale, but in the middle section of the movement, thus pointing to another, characteristic possibility in his monothematic thinking. This is followed by a double cadenza: an arpeggio study, and a tremolo trill study, starting from a mysterious pianissimo and gradually becoming stronger and faster, its sound determined by special bowing methods (sul ponticello, sulla tastiera, i.e. on the bridge and on the fingerboard, respectively). This section also includes chromatic passage, rare in Kodály, and leads to the recapitulation of the opening theme; as in the recapitulation of the first movement, rhyming with it as it were, it is heard in a chordal, full version. The arpeggio cadenza and the bagpipe music return, together with a fragmented version of the main theme, and then the sound of the lowest string, tuned to B, marks the end of these wanderings of the solo cello, never before heard or imagined.

Second String Quartet

opus 10

COMPOSITION:	1916–March 1918.
FIRST PERFORMANCE:	Budapest, May 7, 1918, Waldbauer-Kerpely String Quartet.
DURATION:	*c.* 17–18 minutes.
PUBLISHER:	Universal Edition.

It is an interesting parallel in the life and work of the two composers that the first and second string quartets of Bartók, and the two quartets of Kodály, were written at the same time, or nearly so. In the case of the first quartets, the years of composition are identical, while in the case of the second quartets Bartók slightly preceded Kodály, the date of his *String Quartet No. 2* being 1915–1917. There is documentary evidence at least on Bartók's side, of a relationship having existed between the two production processes. Zoltán Kodály's wife preserved the lengthy draft of the third movement of Bartók's *String Quartet No. 2*, a present from the composer to his friend. In the manuscript copy of his 1921 article on Kodály, in which he repudiated Hungarian accusations that Kodály was a mere Bartók imitation, Béla Bartók stressed the importance he attached to Kodály's advice in connection with the composition of his quartets: *... In the second movement of my first string quartet and the second movement of my second it was on his (Kodály's) advice that I have corrected certain imperfections of form, which the manuscript draft has preserved to the present day.* (For some reason this reference has been omitted from the printed version.) At least the working relations between the two composers engaged on their string quartets were not to the detriment of their independence of tone and style.

The composition of his *Second String Quartet* coincided with Kodály's growing public activity. He held his first public lectures on May 4, 11, 18 and 25, 1917 at the Free School of Intellectual Sciences, whose lecturers came from the most eminent representatives of progressive Hungary. His subject was Hungarian folk music, which, apart from a few researchers, was known to practically no one. After a few minor articles on musical folklore, he published the same year his first comprehensive study on Hungarian folk music entitled "The Pentatonic Scale in Hungarian Folk Music". Using a great many examples, he illustrated a special feature of the old layer of Hungarian folk music—the pentatonic style without semitones. He added a sentence on the role of these scales in new Hungarian composition, including his own: *No doubt, with their primitive but virile energy, pentatonic melodies provided refreshing novelty after the overchromaticized melodies of the previous period.*

From the autumn of 1917 onwards, Kodály also wrote musical criticism. In his articles he supported Bartók, argued for music to become public property, and sought recognition for new French music. In the period of the First World War, this last counted not merely as a musical opinion, but also as a political statement, since the warring parties considered the music of the opposite side hostile too, French music thus counting as hostile in Hungary, with the German hegemony becoming stronger than ever before.

An artistic testimony to the growing social radicalism was Kodály's participation in a "historic concert" mounted by the Centre for Music History of the Royal Imperial Ministry of War in Vienna on January 12, 1918. Entitled "Soliders' Songs in the Austro-Hungarian Army", officially it was a benefit concert whose proceeds were for war orphans and widows, but it was also intended to represent the unity and military strength of the crumbling monarchy. Kodály, together with Bartók, had been commissioned by the Centre of Music History several years earlier to collect Hungarian soldiers' songs. It is not difficult to imagine what martial enthusiasm he encountered in the songs of the workers and peasants dragged into the war. Kodály's orchestral rondo entitled *Old Hungarian Soldiers' Songs* (the formal archetype of his *Dances of Marosszék* and *Galánta Dances*), wedged among the peremptory marches of this pompous display, must have sounded like a foreign body, something even more true for *Kádár István*, an arrangement for voice and piano, which was to become widely known from his later cycle of *Hungarian Folk Music*. "Pannonia is heading for great disaster..." this is not the expression of a firm belief in victory.

This then was the musical and social background to the *Second String Quartet*. The work was first performed at Kodály's composer's evening in May 1918, and it sparked off a far from unanimous critical reception.

The career of the second quartet abroad exactly tallied with that of Bartók's *Second String Quartet*, which had its première in Budapest merely a few months earlier. Both works were first heard abroad in Vienna, at an Anbruch concert, performed by the Waldbauer Quartet. Kodály's work was heard on November 27, 1919 in the central auditorium of the Konzerthaus, at a time when the White Terror in Hungary meant a critical period for both Kodály and the performers of the work. One can well imagine what this first performance abroad after the overthrow of the Hungarian Republic of Councils (on August 1, 1919) must have meant to the composer.

The spread of the *Second String Quartet* was not furthered by ISCM festivals, as had been the case with the other chamber works by Kodály. Even so, this work too was propagated throughout Europe by circles and societies with the aim of popularizing contemporary music. A late development in the career of the work was its inclusion in the programme of the International Society for Contemporary Music in the spring of 1941 in New York, during its 18th festival, mangled so painfully due to the world war. (The festival heard works from countries and by composers standing against fascism. The Hungarian delegate to the society's general assembly was Béla Bartók, and Hungarian music was represented by Kodály and three of his students: Pál Kadosa, Ödön Pártos and Mátyás Seiber.)

The score and parts of the *Second String Quartet* appeared in print in the summer of 1921. In London the work was first performed by the Waldbauer Quartet in November 1922, and the same Hungarian quartet played it again in Vienna, on October 25, 1923, during a large-scale Modern Music Week. In September the same year Universal Edition of Vienna, in collaboration with the Moscow Mezhdunarodnaya Kniga, mounted a Soviet exhibition of its scores. The works judged the most valuable were then heard at a series of concerts by Soviet performers, and these included Kodály's *Second String Quartet*. The production was repeated the same year at a concert series held in the Moscow Conservatoire. In the spring of 1925, the work was heard a third time in Moscow, as part of the programme of a Kodály chamber music evening, organized by the Assotsiatsiya Sovremennoy Muziki, the Soviet section of the ISCM.

In 1925, the Wiener Quartet, led by Rudolf Kolisch, and formed in 1923 on the initiative of Arnold Schoenberg, with its main aim of the popularizing of the works of Schoenberg's circle, advertised the most attractive modern works in its repertoire in the *Musikblätter des Anbruch*. The list included Kodály's *Second String Quartet*. In the 1925-6 season alone, the Wiener Quartet performed the work during their tours of France, Italy, Rumania, Spain and Switzerland. It was a repertoire piece of Hungarian chamber music groups travelling all over the world. It was played by the illustrious Dresden String Quartet, and in the 1930s the work featured in the repertoires of four British quartets. It was broadcast by the BBC in London on December 5, 1927, and by Berlin Radio on March 20, 1931.

After the appearance of the score, the March 1922 issue of *The Musical Times* carried an extremely cordial review signed P. H. for Philip Heseltine (the same number of the periodical carried Heseltine's article on "Modern Hungarian Composers" in which he had some appreciative things to say about Kodály): *Zoltán Kodály's Second String Quartet (UE)—op.10, composed in his thirty-sixth year—is particularly interesting, not only for its intrinsic merit, but also for the enormous advance it shows upon the first Quartet, written eight or nine years earlier—an advance not towards conformity with the current musical jargon which is summed in the vague word 'modernity', but, on the contrary, towards a more direct and personal style of expression. This music is of a deceptive simplicity which will yield more to prolonged study than much that is of far greater apparent complexity—for simplicity and complexity in music are not, as some seem still to think, a mere matter of texture, harmony or form, but depend upon the internal significance of the work. A single line of melody may be more intensely charged with meaning than many pages* of the most elaborately fashionable 'aural phenomena' with which it is surrounded.

British musical circles seem to have attached major significance to the work, as in its November issue the same year, *The Musical Times* carried a review by Michel D. Calvocoressi in the column "Music in the Foreign Press", in which he returns to op.10 apropos a German review: *A Point of Form in a Kodály Quartet. In the Neue Musik-Zeitung (August)* Dr. Hermann Erpf writes: *In Kodály's String Quartet Op.10, the form is the outcome of a technique which was introduced by Schoenberg. We encounter no 'theme' out of which 'motives' crop up and are 'worked-out', but a group of motives which is the original unit. Several brief motives by their combination constitute a first section ... which we can discuss as such only by marking the way in which the motives cooperate within it. For instance, in the first movement of this quartet, Kodály has seven sections, in the sequence a-b-c-d-c-b-a. These sections, however, are not so sharply differentiated as we find them in the sonata form.* Kodály's music has rarely been mentioned together with Schoenberg's.

A clear indication of the work's success was that the first edition sold out in five years. In connection with the new edition Kodály made a most important comment in a letter of February 2, 1926 to his Vienna publisher: *The new instructions regarding the performance have been made urgently necessary by the lessons drawn from the performances so far. Actually I ought to rewrite the whole of the first movement in 3/8 time, as with the present notation most performers give an utterly false interpretation to the rhythm. This, however, would call for much too extensive changes, and so I have dispensed with it. I have endeavoured to help by giving a few performing directions, I hope they will suffice.* To avoid the necessity of engraving the music anew, an important note was added to the beginning of the score. *The performance of the first movement is to flow very naturally, without any particular stress given to the accented points of the bars.*

The reviewers of the day were justified in pointing out the individual character of the work. A specific feature appears right away in its large form, consisting of two movements, or more exactly, the outlines of a middle movement can be felt in the slow introductory music to the finale, were it not constructed in such a completely improvisatory manner.

The first movement (Allegro) differs completely in tone and character from the resolute, firmly outlined opening Allegros of Kodály's earlier cyclic chamber works. The basic, 6/8 pulse, which occasionally expands briefly into 9/8, and the whole melodic development, really plants the dreamworld of Kodály's slow movements into an opening sonata Allegro. The rhythm and melody outline the gentle swaying of the barcarolle. (Although much slower, the same lulling rhythm marks the opening movement of Bartók's *String Quartet No. 2*.) As Erpf has correctly noted, the material is woven out of motifs rather than sharply profiled themes, and this has an integrating rather than a differentiating effect, which would use contrast in keeping with the sonata principle. Due to a melodic or rhythmic relationship, or sometimes the similarity of both, these motifs spring virtually from the same root, and so the opening movement can justifiably be considered as a monothematic structure outlining a sonata form, a single large-scale development with a series of variations.

Although on the surface homogeneous, the material is in constant movement, undergoing changes and development. As far as the performing directions are concerned, it offers one of Kodály's richest scores, abounding in nuances. The basic tempo is in an almost continuous motion, while the great many dynamic shadings call the attention of the performers to the great number of contrasts within the basic character. The instrumental idiom is much airier, more transparent and relaxed than in the *First String Quartet*, projecting gleaming, sombre colours, or specific, flickering shadows.

The pastel shades, however, do not conceal the formal contours of this dream in sound. The opening ascending melodic line indicates the moment of recapitulation with a reversed, descending gesture. The group of motifs of the first subject, with an espressivo sospirato gesture in its axis, and the field of the suddenly curbed, calm second subject are linked by an agitato transition. The espressivo of the codetta is virtually a mere reference, but the imagery of the visionary fantasia of the development presents it from all the more aspects. After the middle section, abounding in events and inner action, the recapitulation is reduced practically to references.

Following the analogy of the *First String Quartet* and the *Duo*, the finale opens with slow introductory music. But in the second quartet the Andante is not a formal continuation of the procedure applied in the first quartet and the *Duo*, as this introduction brings no retrospection, summarizing what has been heard already. The "Quasi recit."(ativo) opening serves as a free, improvisatory filling of an interval of a fifth—as if one heard a violin and then a cello version of distant piping. This sound of a shepherd's pipe becomes almost ethereal and fleeting, as the harmony to go with it is formed, typically, of the notes that are missing from the "melody". The continuation both on the violin and the cello resembles speech melody, it almost asks for expressive words; it shows a kinship with the Hebraic-Gregorian funeral melody of Kodály's *Epitaph for piano* (op.11). In the profound silence the notes of a distant dance melody anticipate the actual, dance-like finale (Allegretto). This version of a pseudo-folk dance *csárdás* tune from the end of the last century, lent an almost unreal effect by its pizzicato accompaniment (heard only on the unaccented beats). This is followed by the return of the speech-like melody, and then climax woven from fragments of the flute intonation at the beginning of the movement leads on to the irresistible sweep of the dancing vortex of the Allegro giocoso. The resigned, reticent self-assertive poetry of the opening movement, and the distant, free improvisations of the slow introduction are followed by a series of dance scenes, in variety like a revolving stage, a virtual consummation of *esprit de corps*. Embedded in a "bagpipe" accompaniment, the first dance is heard on the viola and the violin. Next a less animated, cantabile dance melody (a possible second theme) is stated first by the viola, then taken over by the violin. This is followed by the *csárdás* from the introduction, now in a realistic rhythmic setting. The climax is developed from one of the motivic phrases of the *csárdás*, borrowed from folk dance, and then, with a sudden dynamic shift and a curb of the tempo, with only a distant suggestion of the dance-like pulse, the *csárdás* is developed in a unison of three instruments. The middle section opens with another dance melody—an imaginary bagpipe air with bagpipe accompaniment. It is a composed melody (not a folksong quotation), as are most of the sections in a popular tone in practically all of Kodály's early instrumental pieces. The dance melodies are interwoven, as are their individual elements, and the impulsive movement prizes apart the "regular" formal frame. After further headlong dashes and recoils, the tempestuous stretto only states motifs as the symbols of complete melodies, the composition closing with one of its characteristic augmented fourth gestures—a single heavy dance step—by way of a motto.

Serenade for Two Violins and Viola

opus 12

COMPOSITION:	1919–March 1920.
FIRST PERFORMANCE:	Budapest, April 8, 1920, Imre Waldbauer (first violin), János Temesváry (second violin), Egon Kornstein (Kenton) (viola).
DURATION:	*c.* 22–23 minutes.
PUBLISHER:	Universal Edition.

Two years elapsed between the completion of the *Second String Quartet* and the *Serenade*—two years of revolutions in Hungary. It was not a calm period, ideal for operation. As far as we have knowledge, Kodály wrote five, fairly short pieces in 1918—Nos. 2, 4 and 5 of the *Seven Piano Pieces*, a song to the poem "Adam Where Art Thou?" by Endre Ady, one of the greatest 20th century Hungarian poets, and the middle piece of what later became the cycle *Three Songs* ("Behold, My Heart is Open")—and completed no new work at all in 1919.

The autumn of 1918 saw the victory of a bourgeois democratic revolution in Hungary. Kodály became a member of many new cultural organizations. On February 17, 1919 the new government appointed him, back-dated to December 31, 1918, deputy director of the Ferenc Liszt Academy of Music (with Ernst von Dohnányi the director). On March 21 the proletarian revolution seized power and declared the Republic of Councils, whose cultural leadership appointed the three most prominent Hungarian musicians, Bartók, Dohnányi and Kodály, members of the Musical Directory.

There were no signs whatever of Kodály being a communist either in his ideology or his political attitude. He did his work—and this must have been far from little—to pave the way towards realizing, at long last, the musical reforms long awaited by all honest musicians, and which in part could still be considered bourgeois and democratic. However, since he did have a role in public life during the revolution, and as at the time he was the least widely known internationally of the members of the great Hungarian triad of musicians, the White Terror that followed the overthrow of the Republic of Councils wanted out of the three members of the Musical Directory to make a strict example of Kodály, although Bartók and Dohnányi were also uncompromising in their attitude.

On September 23, Kodály was suspended from his post as deputy director of the Academy of Music. On November 16, Miklós Horthy marched into Budapest, five days later Jenő Hubay, an outstanding violinist but a lesser composer, was appointed director of the Academy, and the following day Gyula Pekár, under-secretary of state at the Ministry of Culture, ordered a disciplinary action to be taken against Zoltán Kodály. The direct political aim was to declare him a Bolshevist, with the professional aim being to prove that as a musical functionary Kodály had brought ruin and demoralization to the Academy. The ultimate aim was to vilify in the court room the whole democratic music policy of the Republic of Councils. But the charges proved to be invalid, and it was the prosecutors of the ignominious trial who themselves came to the dock. Nonetheless it was a full year before Kodály could again teach at the Academy of Music.

The bitter experience of these two years of defamation found expression, two years later, in the *Psalmus Hungaricus*. I have here sketched out the events of the revolutions and counter-revolution only to try and give an idea of the social background of the origin of the *Serenade*.

At the end of the printed score is the indication that Kodály completed the three-movement work in March 1920. At that time the disciplinary proceedings were still in progress.

The *Serenade* is the concluding piece of Kodály's chamber music. The forces required themselves make it an unusual work. Kodály had in fact already written a trio for the same instrumentation while still a grammar-school student, and he himself played the viola part in it, in February 1899. *The piece, of course, was completely built on the fundamentals of Haydn and Mozart,* he said of it in 1964. In the past the combination of two violins and viola was principally used for educational purposes, mainly in the form of trios with a viola part that could be substituted by the cello. Apart from compositions and transcriptions for instructive purposes, altogether three trios for this combination of instruments are known before Kodály's *Serenade*: one by the Hungarian Károly Thern (1882), Dvořák's *Terzetto*, op. 74, also known as *Bagatelles* (1887) and a trio by the Russian Taneyev (1910). It is not known whether Kodály knew any of these.

The ink was hardly dry on the score when, on April 8, 1920, the *Serenade* was premièred in Budapest, performed by members of the Waldbauer Quartet, who played it again on May 12, 1921. The piece started its international career during the legendary festival of modern chamber music organized by Austrian musicians in Salzburg in August 1922. This was when the International Society for Contemporary Music was formed, with Kodály among the founding members, and this too was the period Kodály formed a friendship with the eminent British musicologist Edward J. Dent, who for several decades was the active president of the ISCM; the words of the *Psalmus Hungaricus* and *Jesus and the Traders* have ever since been sung in English in Dent's translation. In Salzburg Kodály's work was played by members of the Amar-Hindemith String Quartet, recently formed by Licco Amar, the Budapest-born child of a Turkish father and a Moravian mother (first violin), Walter Caspers (second violin) and Paul Hindemith (viola). They performed the work again two years later in Donaueschingen, though not at the "big" festival, but in a cycle of contemporary music held before it.

Apart from the best Hungarian performers, most of Kodály's works have attracted also at least one truly eminent ensemble or soloist from abroad. In the case of the *Serenade* this role was played by the Amars, who performed the piece at countless societies of modern music throughout Germany, and took it with them on their foreign tours as well (to Italy in 1925 and 1926, and the Soviet Union in the 1927–8 season). The Léner Quartet and the Budapest Quartet kept the *Serenade* permanently on their repertoire.

The Léner String Quartet were in charge of the first performance of the *Serenade* in London (November 11, 1922), and the Hungarian quartet gave the performance broadcast by the BBC's International Concert (Grotrian Hall, October 5, 1926).

After the Budapest première, Béla Bartók had much praise for the work: *A single musical event stands out in the last few months in Budapest, one, therefore, all the more important, namely; the first performance of Zoltán Kodály's string trio ... One may unhesitatingly call it the sole sensation of a season especially poor in novelties. Written for two violins and viola, and only recently completed, the composition represents the ripest and deepest work of Kodály ... The mere externals of the work—the choice of instruments and the overwhelming richness in instrumental effects achieved in spite of these spare means—are a sensation in themselves. The spiritual content is commensurate with the frame. It reveals a personality with a message truly new and capable of transmitting it to us in masterly, concentrated form. An effervescent wealth of melodies betraying in their exotic tendencies the powerful influence of the old sustained rubato airs of Magyar peasant-music flows through the entire work. It must be regarded as a genuine modern cultural product of the Magyar race. It exhibits, moreover, certain traits common to other modern Hungarian composers. The second movement of the string trio is the most remarkable of all: sustained double-thread of mysterious, drawn-out sevenths and ninths; tremolo passages of the second violin—pianissimo and con sordino—as harmonic framework; and a kind of dialogue between the first violin and the viola. Singularly swaying, passionate melodies of the viola alternate with spectre-like flickering motives of the first violin. We are transported to a tonal fairy-land, never heard nor dreamed of before.* (*Musical Courier*, New York, August 19, 1920.)

Interestingly, the reviewer of the concert broadcast by the BBC in 1926, signing himself as E.E. (Edwin Evans, *The Musical Times*, November 1926) set the least store by the slow movement. He also raised an important question concerning modern Hungarian music—whether it is justified to link the names of Bartók and Kodály: *Why Kodály is constantly bracketed with Bartók is a mystery. The latter is a daring spirit, scrupulous as to himself, but without compunction toward others. Kodály is a gentle, romantic soul, a kind of Magyar Schubert, even to that composer's not always heavenly length. His Serenade is a fine work, and the more rapid sections were not unsuited to the broadcast. But the peculiarly intimated meditation which forms its middle movement was wont to be enjoyed by three players and their nearest and dearest associates.*

The airy, floating sound of the *Serenade* derives from the unusual combination of instruments. Here Kodály eschews his favourite instrument, the cello, to which he entrusted significant ideas in his earlier chamber-music and orchestral works. The "bass" is provided by the viola, whose lowest note is an octave higher than that of the cello. Both the choice of instruments and the texture warrant the radiance and serenity of the fast movement, and the timbre, which plays such an important part in Kodály's music, becomes lighter. On the viola the bass does not lose its function of supporting and bearing the sound, only it moves into "tenor position", extending to the whole cyclic work an impression used as a special effect in Baroque music in the three-part passages above the tenor.

Where did the joyous tone of the outer, fast sections of the work spring from, when the indicated date of completion would seem to give no reason, or possibility for rejoicing? Still, a musical composition is not an exact mirror of the chronicle of historical events. It is perhaps not an arbitrary interpretation, nor an over-simplification, to hear an echo of the Hungarian revolutions in this "ode to joy" of Kodály's.

The character of the first subject group in the opening movement (Allegramente), and indeed a considerable portion of the whole section, is determined by a constant, tense anapaest rhythm (two short beats followed by one long). In European music this rhythm has served to express joy, at least as early as Bach's *Brandenburg Concerto No. 3* (first movement). One of its versions with larger rhythmic values dominates the middle section of both Liszt's and Berlioz's revolutionary *Rákóczi March*. But whereas the anapaest, in conformity with the iambic stress of the Indo-Germanic languages, typically follows unaccented beats by accented, Kodály modifies the classical Greek metrical foot into Hungarian, placing the accent on the two short beats, thus lending the melody a particular poise and ease. Kodály noted down the pattern of this rhythm from folk music.

The first subject, of course, is not a folksong quotation, nor has it any roots in folklore. It is a melody suited to sonata treatment, formed from one rhythmic and two melodic elements, which can be further developed. It is a march, but in three four time! Its layers are fused into a single, firm block, differing utterly in tone from Kodály's earlier sonata allegros. If one recalls the emphatic beginning of the *Duo*, the deep-rooted pathos of the *Sonata for Solo Cello*, or the floating dreamworld of the first section of the *Second String Quartet*, one feels how new and different the golden serenity is at the opening of the *Serenade*. In the most distant possible contrast to the taut giusto of the opening, the expressive, dreamy second subject dissolves into a rubato and develops in wide intervals. It is introduced by the viola, and taken over, with growing passion, by the violins. It is as if the images of *Summer Evening* were to return. The codetta is marked by an ascending melodic line on the viola and, by way of a symmetrical response, a descending line on the first violin.

Three pizzicato chords announce the beginning of the development. But in fact no development really follows. Just as in the Allegros of most of Mozart's serenades and divertimenti, in the first movement of his trio Kodály fights no pitched, dramatic battle. Instead, the second violin stubbornly persists with the anapaest rhythm over 21 bars, with a version of the codetta first below (on the viola), and then above (on the first violin). And is the way Kodály slips the first subject back into the musical texture practically motif by motif a development, or rather a recapitulation? This section is in any case dominated by the dream-like second and third melodies, stated in full before a high F, representing the tonality, peters out above pizzicato chords, and the serenade music dies away.

No one has given a finer characterization of the slow middle movement, Lento, ma non troppo, than Bartók in the excerpt quoted above. It is truly a unique masterpiece. In its typical 6/8 barcarolle rhythm it is related to the tone of the slow movements of Kodály's earlier chamber music. It is a nocturnal vision, a nature picture full of the noises of a stifling summer's night. Both its atmosphere and tonal structure are in several layers. Instead of the basic key of F, it is in the dominant C, but the two notes on the second violin which accompany the first melodic material (A flat–G flat) straight away alienate the basic key of the movement. Also, the concluding C major chord is given a completely different hue from the distant A flat minor (or A flat pentatonic?) segment. In his article quoted above, Bartók noted in connection with the *Trio*, but with a wider reference: *It must, however, be stated that this, as well as Kodály's other works, despite their unusual combination of chords and their striking originality, are wholly based on the principles of tonality (although not in the established sense of a rigid major and minor system). It will be seen that despite the 'atonality' tendencies of modern music, the possibilities of rearing new erections on the basis of 'key' architecture have not been exhausted by a very long way.*

Man also figures in this nocturnal nature picture. Though never authenticated, in the dialogue of the viola and violin contemporaries thought they recognized a dialogue between man and woman. The infinitely serious, speech-like, and truly virile melody of the viola is to be played espressivo, molto espressivo, dolce, molto dolce, and inquieto. The violin melody, entwined in coquettish appoggiaturas and a great many ornaments (or perhaps frippery) is to be played idendo, indifferente, and then disperato. In no other Kodály work are the performance directions so closely linked to a psychological picture of human attitudes. The serious viola melody heard at the beginning changes not only its position but also in character, when the first violin takes it over in the recapitulation, at this juncture the violin ornaments also take on a more gloomy sound when heard on the viola.

The opening melody is replete with sighs and entreaties. An increasingly fragmented melody and a high violin part woven from folk-music embellishments form an inflammatory combination. The middle section has an unexpected moment when the most important ideas from the first movement appear—the first and second subjects. Various monothematic procedures of construction had occupied Kodály constantly in practically all his early chamber works. The *Serenade* brings a new one: the first subject of the opening movement, firmly impressed on the listener's memory, is brought to a climax by the slow movement, and then the tension resolved by a violin cadenza fashioned from the second subject. A long-breathed rest is followed by an abbreviated recapitulation heard on the instruments in reverse (the viola's material taken over by the first violin and *vice versa*). This exchange of roles is more than a simple formal invention; it intensifies, by "pure" instrumental means, the dialectical relationship between nature and man.

Kodály also adheres to the principle of monothematic construction in the monumental dance scene of the finale (Vivo), even if not by such an obvious means as the quotations in the slow movement. The second subject of the first movement here becomes the second subject in a dance rhythm, deprived of its speech-like, meditative elements. Indeed, the familiar melody appears again, as the inversion of the original second subject from the first movement, in the Andante poco rubato that precedes the coda, strongly checking at this point the sweep of the finale.

A completely dissonant passage of major and minor ninths opens wide the portals to this dance-like vortex. The movement is spurred on by the great variety and changeableness of Kodály's favourite rhythmic turns from folk music: stamping syncopation and bagpipe effects. Here and there fleeting, capricious moments break the sweep of the dance. As far as the motivic fabric and development technique are concerned, the movement is more mature than any of Kodály's previous works. The initially gracious second subject gathers tremendous energy in the course of its motivic treatment. The basic 2/4 pulse narrows down to 3/8, then expands into 5/8, 6/8 and 3/4, anticipating the process of supple rhythmic diminution and expansion in many of Bartók's later works. Pizzicato chords accompany the sturdy, highly variegated melody of the codetta. The middle section is both a development and a trio. A new melody in a more moderate tempo is slotted into the material, suggesting the new excitement and stimulus of the whole-tone scale. The portals wide open at the beginning of the movement return, and after a completely rearranged recapitulation, the flux of ceaseless motion finds rest in a quasi-folksong Andante poco rubato. Events follow now in an irresistible sweep. The unrestrained coda leads to a thematic unison of the three instruments; practically up to the last moment the material passes through fantastic harmonic and tonal adventures before arriving with a syncopated stamping rhythm at the work's main key of F.

The *Serenade* is a splendid farewell to the genre of instrumental chamber music which until 1920 played a central part in Kodály's œuvre. It ends the series of great works which, from the early 1920s onwards, marked out for Kodály a firm place in contemporary music throughout the world. It marks the end of a cycle in which instrumental idiom and expression at a high artistic level coalesced with Kodály's inherently vocal musicality.

Psalmus Hungaricus

opus 13
for tenor solo, choir and orchestra

COMPOSITION:	Budapest, 1923.
FIRST PERFORMANCE:	Extraordinary Philharmonic gala concert in the Vigadó, Budapest, November 19, 1923, on the occasion of the 50th anniversary of the unification of Pest, Buda and Óbuda into present-day Budapest: Dr Ferenc Székelyhidy, the Palestrina Choir, the Budapest Philharmonic Society Orchestra, conducted by Ernst von Dohnányi.
INSTRUMENTATION:	3 flutes, 2 oboes, 2 clarinets, 2 bassoons, 4 horns, 3 trumpets, 3 trombones, timpani, cymbals, harp, organ (ad lib.), strings, solo tenor, mixed choir, children's choir (ad. lib.).
DURATION:	*c.* 23–24 minutes.
PUBLISHER:	Universal Edition, Wiener Philharmonischer Verlag, Editio Musica Budapest.

In January 1923 a Budapest journalist asked a number of Hungarian composers what pieces they were working on. The answers appeared on January 21 in the daily newspaper *Újság*, and included among them was a surprisingly resigned reply from Zoltán Kodály: *I am not writing anything. Quite simply because nothing comes into my mind. For, when all is said and done, if you cannot think of something, then it is better not to write anything. Even the greatest had their dry, barren, sterile periods.*

After the *Serenade*, complete and premièred in 1920, no new works by Kodály were heard for several years. But the composer's answer was not entirely accurate, since he showed evidence of activity as a composer. On April, 1 1922 Kodály wrote to his

Viennese publishers, Universal Edition, that he was working on a cycle of arrangements for voice and piano of pieces from his own collection of Hungarian folk music, a plan he returned to in a letter of May 5. The cycle entitled *Hungarian Folk Music* was to appear from 1925 onwards, in ten volumes.

This was also the time when Kodály, together with Bartók, published 150 Transylvanian folksongs, the finest pieces of their collection. They compiled the volume in 1921 and it appeared in print in 1923, with an English preface written by Kodály, signed jointly by him and Bartók. Kodály was also working on the edition of his own collection of folk laments, but this valuable Hungarian folklore material did not reach the press in the early 1920s, only being published in 1966, supplemented by pieces from the collections of other ethnomusicologists. In the autumn of 1921 Kodály was reinstated to his post at the Academy of Music, his students including eminent musicians like Antal Doráti, Mátyás Seiber, who later settled in England, and Tibor Serly, who worked in the USA.

The year 1923 saw the 50th anniversary of the unification of the three towns of Pest, Buda and Óbuda into the modern Hungarian capital city of Budapest. To celebrate the event in a worthy manner, a gala concert was to be held including the premières of new Hungarian works. Three composers were commissioned to write new works; Bartók composed the *Dance Suite*, Ernst von Dohnányi a festive overture, and Kodály his *Psalmus Hungaricus*. We do not know the date of Kodály's commission, but it presumably coincided with Bartók's, April 11, 1923. The date at the end of the printed piano score of the *Psalmus* reads "Budapest, August 1923", marking the conclusion of the work. Knowing Kodály's circumspect working methods, he relatively had little time for the work if his plans for the *Psalmus Hungaricus* had reached back not prior to the commission; however, this cannot be ascertained for sure, as Kodály never dated his sketches.

The première met with tremendous acclaim in Budapest. The score appeared in print in 1924, with Hungarian and German texts, but it took three years before the work was first heard abroad. It was first performed beyond the country's borders on June 18, 1926 at the fourth ISCM festival in Zurich, in the same programme as Honegger's *Le Roi David*, and during the same festival which heard Schoenberg's *Wind Quintet* and Anton Webern's *Six Orchestral Pieces*. *Psalmus Hungaricus* scored a huge and unanimous success. Enthusiasts of modern music found it sufficiently modern, those of conservative tastes considered it sufficiently traditional and all the critics recognized its great dramatic and poetic power. In an article entitled "The Zurich Festival", Basil Maine, the eminent music critic wrote in *The Musical Times* (August 1, 1926): *Kodály's 'Hungarian Psalm' for tenor voice, chorus and orchestra opened the Festival, and to the end its deep impression remained. The fervour of this single-minded music served to show up the shallow artifice of much that was to follow.*

This emphatic festival appearance was followed by a whole range of performances from the early spring of 1927 onwards: we know of more than 200 performances abroad by 1944. It was taken up by the greatest conductors of the time, including Mengelberg in New York, Toscanini in Milan and Anton Webern at one of the Worker's Symphony Concerts in Vienna. *Psalmus Hungaricus* lifted Kodály's music of the significant yet restricted medium of special concerts devoted strictly to contemporary music, and put it on the programmes of subscription concerts of orchestral music with a much wider mass audience.

Plans for a performance in Britain were also taking shape. In an undated letter, bearing the postmark August 30, 1925, Michel D. Calvocoressi wrote to Kodály about the English translation of the *Psalmus*. Edward Dent, who had attended the Zurich performance as the ISCM chairman, wrote to Kodály on March 9, 1927 that the Cambridge University Musical Society was considering performing the work. ... *Our conductor, my colleague Dr Roortham, would be pleased to perform the work. The choir is very good and intelligent and will display great understanding for the composition. My first question is whether there exists an English translation; if there is none, I would be ready to translate it myself...* (original in German). The first performance in Britain was scheduled for November 30, 1927, in Cambridge, with Kodály invited as the conductor. This was the first occasion he conducted in England. In a letter of November 14, 1927, Professor Dent expressed his delight over Kodály's trip to Britain (which in fact was the composer's first visit to that country), adding: *The soloist is the opera singer Frank Mullings, who has often sung Tristan and Othello; he is a highly intelligent man. . . . Our committee was not really satisfied with Calvocoressi's translation, and I have made a new one . . . in the style of the old English Bible, which is also better suited to the Hungarian rhythms.* He went on to inform Kodály that the London Symphony Orchestra was to perform at the concert. The excellent translation by Dent, which has been in use ever since, was added to the printed score in 1928, and went a long way to contribute to the great success the work has enjoyed in the English-speaking world. The BBC broadcast it on December 4, 1927 performed by the Wireless Chorus and Orchestra, conducted by Stanford Robinson, with Parry Jones as the soloist. (As one can see from the letters Kodály wrote in 1927 to Edward Clark, the principal programme maker of the BBC Music Department, there was originally talk of Kodály conducting the work himself.) Ten days later, on December 14, the piece was performed in the Queen's Hall by the Philharmonic Choir conducted by Kennedy Scott, the soloist being Stuart Wilson. This meant three performances in a matter of hardly more than two weeks, with three different soloists, conductors and choirs! Stuart Wilson also translated some of Kodály's folksong arrangements into English, and Kodály soon formed a close friendship with him.

In addition to the great success *Psalmus Hungaricus* brought for Kodály in England, it was through this work that he came into contact with the Three Choirs Festival, founded in the 18th century and held ever since in rotation in Gloucester, Hereford and Worcester, and through it, with the English choral scene he later held in such high esteem; he also met the eminent organizers of the Three Choirs Festival (the festival secretary A. G. Jones, Herbert Sumsion and the conductor Sir Ivor Atkins). Kodály conducted the *Psalmus* on September 6, 1928 in Gloucester, where he made the acquaintance of Edward Elgar and Ralph Vaughan Williams. From that time onwards, works by Kodály have been regularly included on the programmes of the Three Choirs Festival.

But to return to the first performance of the work in Britain, the Cambridge event was reviewed by Ferruccio Bonavia: *The performance of Kodály's 'Psalmus Hungaricus' (the first in England) proved an event of surprising interest. Interest indeed is not a rare ingredient of musical performance; but it is seldom a wholly musical interest, as was the case in Cambridge. In the 'Psalmus Hungaricus' one sees Kodály completely free from the obsession of those moderns who write music as if they hated it, and anxious only to go as far as they possibly can from musical traditions. He shows his modernity clearly enough in his treatment of harmony, but there is not a chord in the whole 'Psalm' that should cause annoyance to grammarians. The music is robust, and even violent, but so is the theme, which represents King David calling upon Heaven to avenge his wrongs and smite the offenders. Such sentiments cannot be adequately expressed in the methods of the 'bread-and-butter-Miss'. Dissonance here is not only justified, it is necessary, since it stands for a world that is out of time: for a mind distressed.* (*The Musical Times*, January 1928.) The same issue carried Michel D. Calvocoressi's review signed C. on the London performances: *The BBC Choir's performance of Kodály's 'Psalmus Hungaricus', which was the first in London, came in for severe criticism, but that of the Philharmonic Choir under Mr. Kennedy Scott, at Queen's Hall, on December 14—the first concert performance here—was of a festival standard. The work makes an immediate impression by its picturesqueness and passion. It is a cry from the heart, painful and angry. Although Kodály is admired by Mr. Cecil Gray, his Psalm will affright no one.*

The following performances (with occasional missing data) mark the triumphant career of the *Psalmus* in Britain: 28 December 1928, The Bach Choir London, conductor Adrian Boult, solo Dr Parry Jones; February 1929, The Glasgow Choral and Orchestral Union, conductor Wilfried Senior; April 1929, Glasgow, St. Matthew's U. F. Church, conductor Erik Chrisholm; April 1929, Cardiff, The National Orchestra of Wales, The Choir of the Cardiff Music Society and the Lyrian Singers; 21 November 1929, Manchester, the Hallé Orchestra; Autumn 1930, Leeds, Philharmonic Concert, director Dr. Bairstrow; 10 March 1931, Liverpool, Philharmonic Society, conductor Henry Wood; 17 March 1931, Sheffield, The Amateur Music Society, conductor Dr J. F. Staten, tenor solo Stuart Wilson; 4 November 1931, Birmingham, The City of Birmingham Choir, conductor G. D. Cunningham, tenor solo Frank Titteron; 28 March 1936, Birmingham, The City of Birmingham Choir, conductor G. D. Cunnungham, tenor solo Dr. Parry Jones; 29 November 1938, Newcastle-upon-Tyne, The Bach Choir, conductor S. M. T. Newmann (Kodály's *Te Deum* was solo in the programme); Spring 1940, Erewhon Philharmonic Concerts.

In 1963, speaking of the origin of the work, Kodály said: *Apart from philologists, no one was familiar with the poem of the Psalmus. So it turned out that the threads which one follows, even if unconsciously, in life, do in the end converge. If I had not studied old Hungarian literature, I would have never written the Psalmus, because I would not have found the text for it.*

The real meaning of this statement is solved by another. On the day of the world première of the *Psalmus Hungaricus*, Kodály wrote of his new composition in the programme sheet *Magyar Színpad* (Hungarian Stage): *As the text for my work for tenor voice, choir and orchestra, written fot the anniversary of the capital, I have chosen an old Hungarian psalm: the poem, by Mihály Kecskeméti Vég, dates from 1535, and I found it in György Gönczi's songbook published in 1620.* Thus the facsimile text variant "from a manuscript (Town Library Wrocław)" at the beginning of the printed piano score serves decorative purposes only. The copy in all probability was known to Kodály, but he used the seventeenth-century edition instead. A whole series of legends were later attached to the facsimile decoration about Kodály the researcher of literature and philology, these, however, have not been reinforced by the composer himself.

The versified transcription by Mihály Kecskeméti Vég of Psalm 55, in which King David complains of his troubles but comforts himself in God, is one of the finest Hungarian literary relics of the 16th century. It was written at the time when Protestantism was spreading in Hungary, and when the medieval Hungarian state, having reached a climax of Renaissance culture and power, went into decline. It was after a great historical disturbance too, that Kodály set the poem, and in the Hungarian psalm verse he found a poetic archetype of the tragic personal and communal experiences of the overthrown Hungarian revolutions of 1918–19 and the counter-revolution that followed.

Little is known of the translator. In 1521 a Hungarian student called Michael de Keckemety studied at Cracow University, and in the 1560s, the chief justice of Kecskemét (which was to become Kodály's native town) was called Mihály Vég. The two names may imply the same person: the translator of the psalm, who worked his name Michael Ueg Kecskeméti into the verses of Psalm 55. Whoever he was, Mihály Vég must have been a learned person, as he wrote smooth flowing verse, and made confident use of the Volta rhythm, widespread all over Europe, mainly in the dance music of the period, with its leaping triple time rhythms (a close relative of the equally popular Galliard). The rhythm was also known in Hungarian folk music, and in the sung versions of Hungarian poems of the 16th century, particularly those that mix lines with the syllable count of 5+5 and 5+6, found consistently throughout the poem of *Psalmus Hungaricus*. The dramatic force of the style of the poem based on the loosely structured psalm, its rich idiom, the graphic expression —preserved in Edward J. Dent's translation—and its richness of language raise beyond all doubt the prayer set to music by Kodály above the average poetic quality of 16th century Hungarian Protestant song.

Any answer to the question whether the idea of a musical setting of Psalm 55 sprang from Kodály's creative imagination while he was preparing for the commissioned work for the gala concert commemorating the anniversary of the Hungarian capital, or whether he made use of the occasion to elaborate an already existing plan, would be pure conjecture. If we reflect that between 1906, when his *Summer Evening* was heard as an end-of-term piece at the Academy of Music, and 1923, only three orchestral works by Kodály had been performed (on four occasions, including *Summer Evening*), it seems feasible that the attractive possibility of large forces acted as a stimulus. Who can know? Even so, for the previous 15 years or thereabouts, Kodály's works had included some in which elements virtually anticipate the music of the *Psalmus*, as if being "sketches" for it, but sketches elaborated in compositions. In his instrumental works, the chamber and piano pieces, and even the accompaniments of his songs, the form consists of two intonations supplementing one another. One is resolved, improvisatory in tone, soaring from resignation and a timid melancholy to dramatic outbursts of passion, and indeed pathos, always personal in its poetry. The other tone is firmly, stubbornly rhythmicized, with a dance character, resolving into a finished form and communal in character. The two intonations, though contrasted, are not rigidly divided; there are many passages indicating that in a higher artistic sense this duality forms a unity.

Of these two types of intonations the instrumental setting of the *Psalmus Hungaricus* is determined by the improvisatory, loose sound. The emphatic and explanatory violin melody in the orchestral introduction is already familiar from the piano part of *Énekszó* (Sixteen songs) op.1, some of the piano pieces of op.3 and op.11, and even from the opening of the *Sonata for Solo Cello*.

The other large group of "sketches" for the *Psalmus*, in the form of actual compositions, seem as it were to pave the way for the part of the psalmodist. In a broad sense, this group includes all of Kodály's songs, and his subjective, artistic empathy, based on scholarly experience, of the unity of poem and melody. More exactly, in practically each song there emerge melodic or rhythmic features later to characterize the imaginary character of the psalmist.

And even if not dance-like in quality, nevertheless the stiffening and hardening of the parlando elements can be observed in the *Psalmus* too.

By 1923 therefore, a great many of the means the composer employed in the *Psalmus Hungaricus* had matured and crystallized in Kodály's music. In a certain sense the work became a summarizing masterpiece. Yet it was at the same time also a pioneering work. At that time Kodály had had relatively little experience in choral setting and orchestration. Of the few choruses he had written before then, only the *Two Folksongs from the Area of Zobor* had been performed, and that only on a single occasion. Nor was he treated very generously by orchestras, although it is true that symphony orchestras were not treated generously by him either. Of his few orchestral works it is the *Two Songs* (op.5, 1913–6) which is illuminating in this context, as the orchestral rubato of "Approaching Winter" and the broad gesture of lament in "Cry, Cry, Cry" both lead up to the *Psalmus*. This slight orchestral experience seems to have been sufficient for Kodály to mix the orchestral colours of the *Psalmus Hungaricus* in virtually their final form even during the work of composition. It can be seen from the sketches that the sound of some sections suggested the final orchestral procedure at the very moment of their conception. The material was written straight away for strings, clarinet, or horn. As far as instrumental colour was concerned, Kodály had doubts only in one place about the correctness of his ideas. At the glimmering flute solo depicting the tenor's line "I would fly away far into the wilderness", he wrote: *Only low? fl.+bassoon?*, meaning whether the lowpitched flute melody should not be supported by the bassoon. It turned out, however, that this was not necessary.

If the surviving 32 pages represent the whole sketch material and Kodály made no more sketches for the psalm, it is virtually certain that he wrote practically the whole work in one single sweep, as if writing out a completed work from memory. He sketched out the whole rondo form with three themes on a single music sheet (the recurring elements being an orchestral introduction, "When as King David..." and "O hear the voice of my complaining"). It is true that the first formulation of the orchestral ritornello was lengthier than its present form, with the rhythm of the melody of "When as King David..." greatly differing from the final form, and it became increasingly taut and reticent during the course of the final elaboration. But the choral sections and solos were put to paper virtually in their final form.

The sketches, which throw light on his compositional activity, reveal which sections were those that called for additional work to support the moments of inspiration with the process of conscious construction. Like any other composer, Kodály worked out on paper the orchestral imitations and strettos to accompany the words "Nightly and daily go they about me" and "They take their evil counsel in secret", casting aside one possibility and retaining another. In many places the sketch only experiments with particular possibilities. A sheet of 20-stave manuscript is full of imitations and their different inversions, the composer's judgements added in the margin: *no, good, excellent*. This procedure recalls a remark made by Kodály several decades later: *For me a score by Bach is a work elaborated just as scientifically as a dissertation.* It was natural that he should construct the rapid imitations, fitting them to the tenor solo, then to the solo with the women's chorus without words especially since Kodály had not had much experience in previous works of such polyphonic and strictly contrapuntal structures extending over a wide area.

Kodály made most of the corrections, with minute care, in the choral sections. His search has already been mentioned for a suitable rhythm to go with the melody "When as King David ...". This melody appears in the sketch already in the form in which it is known today. From the outset the melody, with its communal voice, was unshakeable. But what about the rhythm? The sketches show Kodály's search for the final version. In one of the pencil sketches of "They take their evil counsel in secret", the "complaining" chords appear under the tenor solo, and Kodály remarks *Chorus?! without words.* On another sketch he writes *Death Chorus.* After the great outburst of "Smite them with destruction" he searches for the form of entry for the chorus. *The whole introd. + chorus unis. Included?* and elsewhere: *Chorus without text for either short or long introd.* The second suggestion became the final one, since "When as King David ..." had already been sung twice in unison by the choir, and was to be sung again at the end of the work. The question next was whether the tenor solo beginning "I give Thee honour, Lord" should be joined by the chorus's imitation: *it interrupts the solo pp, then takes it over,* noted Kodály. What should the vocal composition of the chorus be here? The sketch indicates a mixed chorus, but Kodály's question and answer may be read in the margin: *Women's choir? only.* The continuation was not yet decided upon either. *Chorus after 'I give Thee honour, Lord', until ff, a new strophe? Repeat of 'O hear the voice of my complaining'?* The latter idea was the one finalized in the score.

Having clarified the problematic sections, Kodály wrote a vocal score in ink. Though it includes many signs resembling shorthand symbols and pencilled references to the orchestration, it is practically a final version, up to the conclusion of the strophe "Thou are our One God". But after the choral march, in duple time, of the melody "When as King David...", the vocal score reverts to being an uncompleted sketch. New thematic material and structures appear, which Kodály later rejected. One suggestion has the strophe beginning "As for the righteous, Thou dost preserve" ascending from A minor into A major. Kodály handles the text using strict Palestrina four-part counterpoint with an incipit of a fourth (the early 1920s saw Kodály's discovery of Palestrina), and into this development he brings the tenor solo too. The melodic formula (recalling Bach's word-painting technique) of "Those that are mighty scatter'st and destroyest" already existed, as did the tenor counterpoint of the last strophe, "These words King David wrote in his Psalter", but the coda as a whole, in its present-day form had not yet emerged.

The composition process cannot be unambiguously reconstructed as the sketches were only meant for the composer's own use, and are not dated. But certainly in making use of a chorus, Kodály had to find answers to artistic questions he had not encountered before, or at least not in the same form. It is in this sense that the *Psalmus Hungaricus* opened a new path in Kodály's career as a composer. The unique master of choral writing found there and then the technique and expression that were to determine his activity for several decades.

Kodály did not consider his work to be ready even after the première; between the 1924 first and 1928 second editions of the score we find several hundred differences (in bowing, dynamic marking, accents and other notes for the performer). The second more elaborated score contains the practical experiences of Kodály who conducted the *Psalmus* from 1927 on. As there was no organ available at the second, 1924 December 1 performance, Kodály used children's choir to reinforce women's voices. This was the first time he worked with children's choir, which later played a most important part in his œuvre. In the notes to the score of *Psalmus* we read the following: *It is strongly recommended to employ a children's chorus (boys' voices)... especially if the female voices are not sufficiently strong in the middle register to balance the men's voices. When a very efficient children's chorus is available, it may be employed to reinforce the sopranos and altos from 33 to 35 and from 36 to 40.*

The secret of the overwhelming effect of the "Hungarian Psalm" lies in its magical unity of means and expression, its classic structural proportions, and the profoundly poetic conception. Moderation and proportion mark the overall form and the individual sections alike. The melody of "When as King David...", a vocal rondo theme, expanding the folk pentatonic into hexatonic music, as well as, in compliance with old Hungarian folkstyle, suggesting two tonalities in a double layer, belongs among the finest melodies in music; the means it employs—the rhythms just as much as the range of its intervals—bear the marks of the most perfect proportions. A wonderful instance of sense of artistic proportion is when this melody, inseparable from the human voice, reveals an instrumental face as well, in the orchestral opening, which proves to be an improvisatory unfolding and development of "When as King David...". The proportionate structure of the overall form is indicated by the fact that in this cantata, the first in music with a rondo form, the rondo theme, exhibiting duality in unity, with its identity of contrasting character—the introductory instrumental ritornello, and "When as King David..."—is heard in each form five times. Whilst carrying the burden of the structure like a supporting pillar, the rondo theme virtually determines the great parlandos and ariosos of the psalmist as well.

This world of music is essentially diatonic, but—which belongs also to the question of proportion—Kodály adds the chromatically meandering material of "O hear the voice of my complaining", suggesting doubt and despair, to the intonation that grows out of folk music. Bence Szabolcsi the outstanding Hungarian musicologist wrote: ...*Since the melodiousness of Kodály's music is basically of a vocal bent and attitude, narrow, chromatic melodiousness in fact only appears as a guest, in a section or a transition (like the great complaint music in the 'Psalmus')*. But in the *Psalmus*, this material has a function perhaps surpassing that of being confined to a section or a transition. It determines the character of the first tenor solo over a fairly lengthy section, and also changes the tone of "When as King David..." in its two reprises. And in the "Death Chorus" ("They take their evil counsel in secret") Kodály expands the musical portrayal of weeping into dodecaphonic chromaticism minus one note in harmony shifting further every two bars. At dramatically justified moments the melody and harmony of the "complaining" return almost as a new rondo theme.

Thus diatonic music and chromaticism serve to enrich the expression not only consecutively, by way of contrast, but also simultaneously. A particularly fine example of the unity and variety of means is shown in the most personal and most subjective section of the work, the tenor aria "So in Jehovah I will put my trust". From small units, the melodic lines develop using typically pentatonic intervals, but viewed over a longer context, they have a chromatically floating effect. This almost ethereal hovering is strengthened by the harmonic basis, the chords sometimes sliding over as many as nine semitones. It is furthermore inbuilt into the structure of the chords, the root typically not being in the lowest part. The section is marked by a complex interrelationship of colours, harmonies and melodic lines, while the sound is for the first time in the work characterized by the harp. In 1907 Kodály still spoke about the harp with strong contempt to his friend the poet Béla Balázs: *I don't like it. For me it is a much too soft instrument*. But in the glittering and harsh score of the *Psalmus*, he needed this previously rejected instrument for the iridescent music expressing the hope of the psalmist. The tone of "So in Jehovah I will put my trust" differs sharply from the style of the rest of the work, foreshadowing the late works of Kodály—the *Concerto* and the *Organ Mass*.

Kodály was a reticent composer, expressing his message always in a terse form, and also extremely sparing in his means. But by a few means he created a shatteringly authentic historical atmosphere, expressing social truths both past and present. The *Psalmus Hungaricus* breathes a historical atmosphere in a triple sense, compressing into one the biblical age, the Hungary of the 16th century, and the period of the failed revolutions of 1918-9.

The work opens with a fervently passionate cry, invoking history, at times seething towards a climax. At the same time, however, it strikes Kodály's note of resignation, and before dying out, gives way to the narrative chorus, the common multitudes of the people, at first, after the extreme animation, still hardly moving: "When as King David...". The historical invocation of the orchestra rises up again, in preparation for the first great tenor solo of the psalmist, whose motif of entreaty, bewailing and flight are followed again by the rondo melody in the chorus. As at its first appearance, it is heard in monophony, the register now shifted a fifth higher, and intoned only by the high choral voices, framed by the motif of the orchestral complaint. This region of heightened emotional tension is continued by the second episode of the tenor solo: "Nightly and daily go they about me." The orchestral accompaniment, with its many rustling, sliding counterpoints to a motif rotating about its axis, is a gem of late Bachian imagery. The time signature here switches from the 6/8 triple time, the "perfect time" of the Middle Ages *(tempus perfectum)* to the "imperfect" duple time *(tempus imperfectum)*. The psalmist's complaint hardens into accusation: "Violence and strife rage fierce in the city". For a moment the music conjures up another freedom struggle also overthrown, that fought by Prince Rákóczi II. The line "Ne'er in all the world saw I such deceivers!" blends in with the notes of a typical folksong from the freedom struggle. The bewailing, wordless female chorus, the "Death Chorus" as Kodály called it (modelled perhaps on "Sirens" in Debussy's Nocturnes, or the similar choral treatment of Delius) is the emotional low-point of the work. Consolation in this hopelessness rises from the community. The song "When as King David..." is heard for the third time during the work, set amid harmony, and transposed from the basic key of A minor to F minor. Into the first line the soprano weaves the weeping melody, indicating, as it were, that the uplift is still far away. Here the score refers to another layer of history: the world of suffering in Bach's Passions. The line "In his great anger bitterly grieving" is joined by the rising bass counterpoint from the opening chorus of the *St Matthew Passion* by J. S. Bach.

The burning passion of the chorus dies slowly away. The closing choral phrase is echoed on the horn and clarinet, leading on to the third solo episode, expressive of solitude, resignation and disappointment. The pathos of the orchestral introduction flares up for a second in a solo clarinet run, a musical memory amid the meditations of the psalmist. The expression mark for the soloist is *Con dolore* (with sadness). The almost stationary sound of the orchestra paints a sense of solitude and desolation, and the biblical curse which follows, a sweeping outburst of elementary passion, sounds all the more powerful: "Smite them with destruction". Words are not adequate to answer such a volcanic eruption. The refrain now is not "When as King David...", instead the choir intones the natural notes of the orchestral ritornello, without words. The chorus here reaches the highest regions, the long sustained B of the sopranos lingering in the listener's ear.

While so far private grief and that of the community have formed two layers of the work, now the two intermerge. The melody of the first episode of the tenor solo—"I give Thee honour, Lord, and worship Thee"—is followed by a canon from the women's choir, and then the soloist's melody is stated in a taut rhythm by the full chorus. Not only the rondo theme, but the interlude also returns in this huge structure. However, the recapitulation, though it faithfully follows in melodic outline the melody as it was first heard, in fact differs from it greatly. The free parlando of the psalmist's opening song is formed into a taut giusto, and the rhythm, instead of being a mere indication, now suggests with a realistic pulse the proximity of a solution. Here Kodály employs a masterful technique of retardation; the affirmative response from the mixed chorus is framed by the complaining motif, thus showing that the long-awaited liberation is not so easily attained.

The tenor aria which follows the creed of the community "So in Jehovah I will put my trust", a most profound, and subjective example of lyrical expression, also serves to slow down the emotional drama. Listening to it we can imagine how arias of a personal tone might have sounded in operas by Kodály built out of his own material—had he composed them. This aria differs completely from everything so far heard in the solos of the psalmist. It has almost the effect of a self-contained insertion; its melodic line and orchestration show no relationship with any other section of the work. Amid the orchestra's iridescent reflections the instrumental setting seems to recall Kodály's chamber music past. He casts the Adagio into a single large arch, opening it with harp runs, and with the dying away passages from the harp preparing for the sound of the last trumpet ("Thou art our One God"). This is a recapitulation, turned into a march, of the melody of "When as King David...", the work's multi-layered coda. The music personifies the God of justice, the Lord of the poor.

How utterly picturesque are the ascending, constantly enriched musical portraits of the "righteous", the "holy", and the "humble", together with following a centuries-old tradition, the falling melodic line of "Those that are mighty scatter'st and destroyest". The picturesque trills of "tried in the furnace" on the strings and woodwinds indicate the flicker of distant flames. A different depiction, but also of long-standing tradition, characterizes the shaping of the words "Forth from the fire thou suddenly taketh him, once more in honour Thou will raise him on high!" This is the only point in the work where Kodály employs alternating time signatures, when on two occasions he expands the 3/4 lilt into 4/8, lengthening the word "forth" to match the dimensions of "suddenly" and "honour".

In this section the music employs more word-painting than anywhere else in the whole work, not that the text here alone offers such possible solutions. The easily recognized sounds of musical realism are condensed into this part because now the work switches from the realistic realm of bitterness, complaint, curse, supplication and confidence to an unreal world—from reality to a dream. A minor is followed by A major! This is a tremendous uplift; the music is suffused in golden light, the notes of the orchestral introduction becoming lighter, and the rocking, dancing lilt of the choral parts expressing joy: "They will raise him on high". The last appearance of this line is answered by triumphant martial music, drumbeats, and flourishes on trumpet and trombone. All this, however, is only a dream, the dream of the people and the composer. For when we already believe in the triumph of the justice of the people, the music suddenly darkens—the only point in the work marked by a treble forte, making it dynamically the most extreme point—and relapses into the hopeless A minor of the beginning. Regarding its notes, this collapse is essentially identical with the orchestral section heard at the beginning of the the work, before the first appearance of "When as King David...". Even so, they are not fully identical. The orchestration is different, and perhaps still more important, there is a difference of expression: now, with the conclusion approaching, the instruction "espressivo" does not recur. (The performance indications most often used in the score are "espressivo" and "appassionato".) Now "it is finished", the tragedy has come to an end, darkness has again fallen on the world and the extinguishing fire of the orchestra can no longer be "espressivo" but must lead back to historic reality. The Epilogue presents the melody of "When as King David..." once more. It is not so objective as at its first appearance, the unison being replaced by fifths, referring to the organum of early medieval polyphony, as if the melody itself were shaken, living through the drama which has taken place on the inner stage. A few notes rise above the community: a flash of light from a tenor counterpoint—this actually marked espressivo— underlines the main message of the whole psalm: "And for the faithful, bitterly grieving, As consolation I from it made this song."

The Adventures of Háry János from Nagyabony to the Burg Castle

*comic opera in four (originally five) adventures
with prologue and epilogue
opus 15
together with excerpts performed independently
text by Béla Paulini and Zsolt Harsányi*

COMPOSITION: 1926 (1937–8, 1948–52).

FIRST PERFORMANCE: Budapest, October 16, 1926, Hungarian Royal Opera House, conductor: Nándor Rékai, producer: László Márkus, sets: Gusztáv Oláh, choirmaster: Vilmos Roubal

CAST: Háry János: Imre Palló, Örzse, his betrothed: Izabella Nagy; Emperor Franz: Sándor Pusztai; Empress: Sári Sebeők; Emperor's mother-in-law: Teréz Fazekas; Napoleon: Dr Viktor Dalnoki; Marie-Louise, Napoleon's wife: Rózsi Marschalko; Uncle Marci, imperial coachman: János Körmendy; Knight Ebelasztin: Gyula Toronyi (plus 14 spoken parts), Generals, Hungarian and French soldiers, Ruthenian girls, bands of soldiers, people on the borders and at court, dragons.

SET: The prologue and epilogue are set in the Nagyabony inn; I. Adventure, along the Muscovite (today Prussian) border; II. Adventure, in the garden of Emperor Franz II; III. Adventure, below Milan; IV. Adventure, at the end of the world (later omitted); V. Adventure, in Háry's room at the Vienna Burg

INSTRUMENTATION:	3 female soloists (voices undefined), 2 tenors, 2 baritones, children's choir, female and male choir, ballet. Performers: 3 flutes (changing to 3 piccolos), 2 oboes, 2 clarinets, saxophone, 2 bassoons, 4 horns, 3 trumpets, 3 cornets, 3 trombones, tuba, cimbaloongarese (if not available, may be substituted by harpsichord or piano), piano, celesta, timpani, cymbals, bass drum, side drum, triangle, military drum, strings. Military band (on stage).
DURATION:	full evening.
PUBLISHERS:	Universal Edition, Isdatelstvo Muzika, Moscow (vocal score)

HÁRY JÁNOS SUITE

COMPOSITION (compiled):	1926–7.
MOVEMENTS:	I. Prelude. The Fairy Tale Begins; II. Viennese Musical Clock; III. Song; IV. The Battle and Defeat of Napoleon; V. Intermezzo; VI. Entrance of the Emperor and His Court.
FIRST PERFORMANCE:	Barcelona, March 24, 1927, Gran Teatro del Liceo, Pau Casals Orchestra, conducted by Antal Fleischer.
INSTRUMENTATION:	as in the comic opera.
DURATION:	30 minutes.
PUBLISHERS:	Universal Edition, Wiener Philharmonischer Verlag, Boosey and Hawkes, Editio Musica Budapest.

BALLET MUSIC
("Dance of the Dragons" from the omitted IV. Adventure)

FIRST CONCERT PERFORMANCE:	Frankfurt am Main, August 22. 1927, Saxophon Hall, Budapest Philhar-

monic Society Orchestra, conducted by Ernst von Dohnányi (under the title "Dance of the Dragons").

INSTRUMENTATION: as in the comic opera.
DURATION: 5 minutes.
PUBLISHER: Universal Edition.

THEATRE OVERTURE

COMPOSITION: 1927, concert ending 1929–32 (?).
FIRST CONCERT PERFORMANCE: Vienna, between April 25, 1928 and end of June, Gesellschaft der Musikfreunde, conducted by Robert Heger (no documentary evidence of the name of the orchestra, but presumably the Vienna Symphony).
INSTRUMENTATION: as in the comic opera.
DURATION: 12 minutes (?).
PUBLISHER: Universal Edition.

The poet Béla Balázs, a friend of Kodály in his youth, reported in his diary a debate he had had with the composer: *Then we talked about Hungarian art and Hungarian drama. About our great task. Life of the people in Hungary is not rich and colourful enough for a play, Kodály said. I told him off.* (March 16, 1905)

This dialogue preceded by a few months Kodály's first folksong collecting tour in the summer of 1905. As we know from his letters and notes, his opinion changed diametrically after becoming personally acquainted with the life of the poverty-stricken Hungarian peasants. Plans and librettos for a number of stage works had come into Kodály's hands before *Háry János*, all of which he had found unsuited for a musical setting. They are part of the story not just of the stage works Kodály never composed, but also of the background to *Háry János*.

In 1924 the Hungarian press announced that the country's first prose theatre, the National, was to stage a *népszínmű* (a play about Hungarian village life with popular art-music interludes) entitled *Háry János*, adapted by the popular journalist and cabaret writer Béla Paulini and Zsolt Harsányi, a writer of light plays and novels from the epic poem "Az obsitos" (The Veteran) by the 19th century Hungarian poet János Garay. The incidental music was, according to the press, by Dezső Lavotta. (It should be noted here that János Háry is not a fictional character, but a real person who lived in the 19th century.)

In late February, 1925, Zsolt Harsányi wrote to Kodály: *...The little one-act piece of which we were speaking at the time* (it is not known when this was), *has grown into a full evening's Hungarian military and peasant Singspiel.* On March 7 the two authors read to Kodály the libretto of *Háry János*. The librettists had divided the work between themselves, Paulini developing the scenes and the conception of the plot, and Harsányi being responsible for the versification of the dialogues and the lyrics of the songs. The latter, since Kodály drew upon the valuable material of folk and art poetry, eventually proved unnecessary.

It was soon decided that *Háry János* would be staged not by the National Theatre but by the Opera House. In a letter of July 2, 1925 Paulini asked Kodály to go to the National the next day, as Sándor Hevesi, the director of the theatre, and the composer Miklós Radnai, the newly appointed director of the Opera House, wished to confer with the authors. In all probability this was Radnai's first undertaking in his capacity as director. It was most likely this consultation that sparked off work on the composition of the opera.

The first news report mentioning Kodály as the composer of *Háry János* and the Opera House as the site of the coming première appeared on July 14, 1925, followed by the first of several false reports on October 15: *The music of Háry János has been completed.* The next unfounded rumour to reach the press was on February 4, 1926, saying, *Z. Kodály has presented the score of* Háry János *to the Opera House.* In a polite but impatient letter of April 12, 1926, Radnai urged the composer: *this is to ask you to be so kind as to forward the full and the piano score of* Háry János *at your earliest convenience, so that the work of copying and the writing out of the parts can be completed.*

The work did not progress at the rate desired by the opera. On September 13, practically a month before the première, Radnai wrote to Kodály: *...The situation evolved during the* *rehearsals calls overwhelmingly for an intermezzo to fill the change of scene between the first and second parts ... This is a matter of some 3–4 minutes, so it would not involve too much work, whereas the play really needs this music enormously, a linking entr'acte to set the mood. I write these lines because you are working on the rest anyway. (We keenly await that too, principally for the writing out of the parts and the rehearsing of the choral part, lest there should be any delay).* And again on September 22: *...I respectfully ask you to let us have all the pieces on time, by which I mean October 1 at the latest...*

As these documents show, the *Intermezzo* (originally called Palotás—the name of a stately Hungarian dance), the most popular section of the opera did not feature in Kodály's composition plans at all, and only owes its origin to the advice of the Opera House spurred on by dramatic considerations. The director's imploring, even pleading also throw light on the tortuously slow process of the music's preparation.

In the autumn preparations were in full swing, even though the music was still very incomplete. By September 28, rehearsals with sets were already being held in the Budapest Opera House.

No one knows today which sections of the music, apart from the *Intermezzo*, were completed at the last minute, and which sections were even then not complete. Certainly after the première, Kodály turned and said to Miklós Radnai: *You are mistaken if you think Háry János is finished.* Radnai did not think it was either, and continued bombarding Kodály: *...Time passes and we are still waiting for the promised songs and the overture...* (letter of December 17, 1927). *We are very anxious that Háry János should feature on our programme for the following season rounded off with the new pieces...* (letter of May 21, 1927). On June 29, 1927 reports appeared in the press about the completion of the new overture and the vocal pieces.

For the time being, however, the piece became still shorter on the basis of three performances, from October 22, 1926 onwards, Kodály abandoned the scene set at the end of the world (including the "Dance of the Dragons" which later became an independent piece entitled *Ballet Music*). On January 10, 1928 the Opera House for the first time staged *Háry János* complete, with the *Theatre Overture* and three new vocal pieces.

This still, however, did not mean that the piece was finished. Indeed, it could be said never to have been completed in Kodály's lifetime. New abbreviations and additions to the opera continued to appear up until 1963.

It therefore is not easy to piece together the authentic musical fabric of *Háry János* from the legion of cuts and additions. Up to a point Kodály was presumably ready to adhere to the concepts of the direction, since he was amenable enough. But all his life there was one thing he never consented to, and that was a revision of the libretto. In vain did Gusztáv Oláh, the chief producer of the State Opera House in the 1950s, ask him to do so, even though the libretto could well have done with the beneficial improvements of a dramaturg.

But wherever the composer's personal control was absent—as at the first performance abroad (in Cologne, September 26, 1931), which won enormous acclaim, two months later in Aachen, and, after Kodály's death, at a Felsenstein production in the Komische Oper in Berlin—producers made drastic alterations in the plot to make the references which only mean something to Hungarian audiences, understandable to those abroad. A fate similar to that of Offenbach's operettas has overtaken the various stage adaptations of *Háry János*—as many variants of the libretto as there are stages.

The English language version of the whole work was staged by Juilliard Opera, the ensemble of the pupils of the famous New York Juilliard School of Music, on March 18, 19 and 20, 1960. The success was rather moderate, the daily papers also brought out unfriendly reviews. The British première was staged by amateurs, the 50-member orchestra and 150 singers, actors and choir members of Culham College, Abingdon, between March 14 and 17, 1972.

The first British performance by professionals was held in 1982, on the occasion of the Buxton Festival between July 24 and August 6. It was staged by Malcolm Fraser, conducted by Anthony Hose, with Alan Opie as Háry. Further contributors were Cynthia Buchan and Linda Ormiston, according to an account by Anthony Cross in *The Musisal Times* (November 1982, p. 709). The acceptance of neither of the two British performances did promote the further path of Háry János. Edward

J. Dent, chairman of the ISCM and a close friend of Kodály's, had already once tried to organize a performance in London. In the summer of 1938 he visited Hungary expressly to attend the open-air performance of *Háry János* on August 13, and he also planned to translate the play into English. But on January 15, 1939 he told Kodály of the failure of a London performance: *The Sadler's Wells is too much an opera house, and the Old Vic too much a theatre*, he wrote in his letter in German. However paradoxical it may sound, English-speaking listeners may obtain the best impression of this stage work from a recording. A double album was released in London in 1969 (Decca SET 399/400), on which the London Symphony Orchestra, assisted on this occasion by the English cimbalom player John Leach, the Edinburgh Festival Chorus and the Wandsworth School Boys' Choir are conducted by István Kertész, the solo vocalists being members of the Hungarian State Opera House. Kodály's folksong arrangements are sung by the English choirs in Hungarian. The prose scenes and all the dialogues linking the music are spoken by Peter Ustinov, in English, and the plot can thus be followed without the stage spectacle.

In Budapest *Háry János* scored great success. (The fact that the successful performances in Cologne and Aachen were not followed by productions in other German cities was doubtless due to the ban Hitler ordered on performances of works from abroad.) Soon after the première, on February 18, 1927, Kodály was able to write to his publisher: *Despite all kinds of obstacles, we have reached the 11th performance. The play is to remain on the bill*. In December 1930, the 25th performance was celebrated. To estimate the significance of this it is necessary to know that between the two world wars 20th century operas usually obtained five or six performances at the Budapest Opera House.

It would be difficult today to analyse the reasons for the effect the opera had in Hungary, but it seems probable that the audiences of the day forgave the peasant songs which sounded so out of place in the Opera House for the sake of the naivety intended by the libretto and the colourful spectacle. (Today on the other hand allowances are made for the problematic parts of the text for the sake of the music.)

Before the première, Kodály described his aims briefly:

As soon as Háry starts speaking, 'the tale begins'. This is the key to the Háry of the play, who contains Garay's undying veteran, but is also something more than that. He is much more than a jovial genre character, a Hungarian miles gloriosus *(swashbuckling soldier): he is the incarnation of the Hungarian story-telling imagination. He does not lie, he creates a tale; he is a poet. What he relates has never happened, but he has lived it through, and so it is truer than reality.*

In the music too something similar was needed for the play; I do not know how far I have succeeded. But I know that the songs of the actors are good. Each and every one of them comes from folk traditions, and at the cost of an hour or two's travel they can still be heard in the village. They are more suitable than any personal lyricism for giving the effect of 'lyrical authenticity' on the lips of the actors.

They are pearls, whose setting alone comes from me. I have tried to be worthy of them.

To my knowledge songs of the Hungarian people are here heard for the first time from the stage of the Opera House. I would like to think that in their wake might spring a little affection for the most forsaken children of a forsaken country.

Háry János is flanked by a prologue and an epilogue: in the Nagyabony inn the old man Háry relates his wonderful adventures during the Napoleonic wars. *I. Adventure*: Háry stands on guard at the Prussian (Muscovite) border. The Prussian sentry allows nobody cross the border, not even Marie-Louise, the daughter of Emperor Franz of Austria, whose retinue includes Knight Ebelastin, nor old Marci, the coachman of the imperial coach. Háry pushes the sentry-box, together with the lofty guests in it, over to Austrian ground. As a reward they take him, together with Örzse, his betrothed, to Vienna.

II. Adventure: In the courtyard of the Vienna Burg Háry tames Lucifer, the most unmanageable horse of the imperial stud, and as a reward is given a gilly-flower (stock) by Marie-Louise. Driven by jealousy, Knight Ebelastin uses Napoleon's authorization to present the French emperor's declaration of war against Austria.

III. Adventure: Hussars are camping below the castle of Milan. Napoleon launches an attack, but upon a wave of Háry's arm his army fall over, and he himself is taken prisoner. Marie-

Louise arrives, and requests János Háry instead of Napoleon for her husband. Örzse appears, she does not release her betrothed. Grand finale (Recruiting).

IV. Adventure: Preparations for the wedding of Marie-Louise and Háry are taking place at the Viennese court. The little princes recite to Háry what they have learned at school. The court enters. Háry does not desire Marie-Louise's hand, nor the princely title. He returns with Örzse to their native village of Nagyabony.

Although at a first hearing Kodály's music sounds like a loosely woven fabric of folksongs and composed instrumental movements, it is in fact much more firmly constructed than would seem. The folksong "Nagyabonyban csak két torony látszik" (In Nagyabony only two towers can be seen) stated at the beginning of the opera, in the third adventure, and as the conclusion, serves as a triple supporting pillar, with the message of the work expressed in the last lines of the song: "Inkább nézem az abonyi kettőt / mint Majlandban azt a harminckettőt" (I would rather look at the two in Abony / than the thirty-two in Milan). The increasingly tense counterpoint of the orchestral movement entitled "The Tale Begins" is smoothed out harmonically and melodiously by the end of the play, expressing, as it were, the resignation and lethargy of the return from fabulous adventures to drab reality, and thus providing a musical frame to the play. The *Intermezzo*, the most popular orchestral section, portrays first the first and second adventures, the voyage from the Prussian border to Vienna, as a solid dance movement with its principal section taken from a piano method published in 1802 and the trio from a score written between 1818 and 1820, naturally thoroughly reshaped. After the fourth adventure, the road back from Vienna to Háry's native village of Nagyabony is depicted by superimposing the trio onto the principal section, as if slowly tiring out the musical material. Another supporting pillar is the melody of "Tiszán innen, Dunán túl" (This side of the Tisza, beyond the Danube) from Bartók's collection, which in the first adventure appears first as an improvisatory fading instrumental piece with the title "The Piping Hussar", and then as a vocal duet, while at the end of the fourth adventure it is heard as a choral apotheosis "Szegény, derék magyar nép"

(Poor, honest Hungarian people) to a few lines of text by Zsolt Harsányi—this being the only instance where Kodály set the text suggested by the librettist. So that this should be fully understood, the apotheosis parallels the climax of "As for the righteous..." in *Psalmus Hungaricus*.

At the beginning of the second adventure (in the courtyard of the Vienna Burg) the precious, Rococo minuet sung by Marie-Louise, "Ku-ku-kukuskám, / Szállj le hozzám madárkám" (My little cock-cock-cock, / Fly down to me, my birdie) and the full-blooded folksong "Hej két tikom" (Hey, my two hens) sung by Örzse as she feeds the Austrian double-eagle, signify an inner symmetry. A similar subtle symmetry shows up between the Rococo minuet melody just mentioned and the minuet-like folksong, "Gyújtottam gyertyát" (I lighted a candle), which opens the fourth adventure, although in this folksong the volta rhythm of the older, 16th century Western European dance form also plays a part "Elment a két jány virágot szedni" (The two girls went to pick flowers). The music with a *verbunkos* swing which links the first and second adventures reappears as an instrumental insert entitled "Gypsy Music" in the third adventure, set near Milan. Retaining its *verbunkos* character, but with new material, it figures in the accompaniment of an 18th century college student song beginning "Hagyj békén viaskodó, oh!" (Leave off wrestling, oh!), and then in the form quoted by János Bihari, one of the greatest figures of 19th century Hungarian *verbunkos* dance music, in the middle section of "A jó lovas katonának" (The good horse-soldier). (The song, printed with the title "Verbunk" in Volume VI of the series *Hungarian Folk Music*, copyright 1925, does not include this Bihari quotation.)

It was around the period of the composition of *Háry János* that old Hungarian instrumental dance music, including the *verbunkos*, first began to attract Kodály as a scholarly matter, and the artistic lesson of these studies was first turned to account in *Háry* primarily in the *Intermezzo*, whose martial dance-like lilt could only have developed from the original vocal melody by a creative imagination.

The use of the cimbalom brings a new tone and sound effect. It lends colour to several instrumental combinations in the play (being heard, naturally, only at the folk layer), and it may have been these latticed chamber-music textures using the cimbalom that aroused Bartók's interest in exploiting the possibilities of the instrument. The cimbalom in fact first appears in Bartók's work in the orchestral version of his *Rhapsodies No. 1* and *No. 2* for violin and piano (1929).

The "Viennese Musical Clock" also draws attention to a particular relationship between folk music and composed art music. On the one hand it is a Couperin rondo of classical purity in a brilliant wind-percussion orchestration, but on the other hand the source of the rondo theme with its broken triad is a signal played on the swineherd's horn and folk trumpet from Kodály's collection. Another unique combination of art music with folk music appears in the stuttering song of the defeated Napoleon. Napoleon sings a Hungarian folksong to the accompaniment of a grotesque funeral march with a saxophone solo composed by Kodály. A variant of the folksong text is also known by Lajos Pósa, the popular writer of poetry for children in the late 19th century. This naive children's verse was described at the time by critics as *Chinese-Hungarian nonsense*. In his study entitled "Music in the Kindergarten" (1941), Kodály wrote that the critic *evidently did not know that the words originated from a traditional song well-known in Gömör County and that Pósa had certainly taken it from there*.

Although the attribute "Chinese-Hungarian" dates from the end of the last century, it could well characterize the scene of the "Entrance of the Emperor and His Court" to a grotesque brass orchestra, with its ceremonious "Chinese" consecutive intervals and pentatonic phrases. (Its influence survived in the orchestral *Peacock Variations* and the *Concerto*.) Kodály rarely placed side by side the "ideal" and the "grotesque" as did Liszt and Bartók, but here his other splendid "grotesque" is the battle "shrunk" into a deployment of tin soldiers, the condensed sequence of "The Battle and Defeat of Napoleon" in the orchestral suite (also only for wind and percussion).

The body of the play, however, still consists of folksongs lifted out of the life of the people onto the stage. In an unaccompanied song Örzse calls down curses on the lot of the peasant who has been dragged away for military service: "Sej! Verd meg Isten, aki eztet csinálta" (Hey, may God damn the one who did this). "Piros alma" (Red apple) is a love song with glowing harmonies, "Tiszán innen, Dunán túl" (This side of the Tisza, beyond the Danube) brings a delicate and sensuous duet, while old Marci's folksong grotesque, "Ó, mely sok hal" (Oh, how many fish) parallels the melody of *Capriccio* for solo cello.

These are not meek, harmless melodies. Old Marci's drinking song, or Örzse's playfully teasing song, "Hej két tikom tavali" (Hey, my two hens of last year) are overshadowed by the heart-rending harmonies, timbres and orchestral sospirato motifs of "Hogyan tudtál rózsám idejönni" (How could you, my rose, come here) of Örzse in the second adventure at the Vienna Burg, and "Szegény vagyok" (I'm poor) of Örzse in the fourth adventure.

The jaunty *Recruiting Song* "A jó lovas katonának" (The good horse-soldier) also features in the series *Hungarian Folk Music*, with the marking "Tempo di Verbunk". There it includes a strophe which is omitted in the opera "Nem parancsol sem vicispány, / Sem a szolgabíró, / Robotára senkit nem hajt / Ispány vagy tiszttartó" (I'm not ordered about by either the deputy-lieutenant / nor by the sheriff, / No one forces me to drudgery / neither the bailiff nor the steward); but the shining harmonies and trumpet flourishes of this song in *Háry János* express the desire for freedom even without the words. This is especially so, when the music in the camp that opens the third adventure (which ends with the *Recruiting Song*) voices the bitterness of the oppressed peasant in a direct continuation of Mussorgsky's popular realism, with an awesome, seething accompaniment on the low-pitched orchestral instruments to the folksong beginning "Sej besoroztak" (Hey, they've enlisted me). Mussorgsky's popular realism is further reflected in Háry's creed in the song in the fourth adventure: "Felszántom a császár udvarát" (I plough up the emperor's courtyard), a melody which conjures up earlier, overthrown Hungarian freedom struggles, and whose instrumental setting with its concentric movement and weeping phrases expresses the millennial grief of the Hungarian peasant. Its petition bursts from the depths of the soul: "Áldd meg Isten császár fölségét, / Ne sanyargassa magyar népét!" (Bless, o God, His Majest' the Emperor / So that he shouldn't scourge his Hungarian people!). At this sublime moment the instrumental setting reminds us that the melody is a close relation of old Marci's merry drinking song, as well as being akin to No. 15 in Volume III of the series *Hungarian Folk Music* "Akkor szép az erdő" (Fine is the forest).

This is perhaps the emotional climax of the piece, followed logically by the choral apotheosis of "Tiszán innen, Dunán túl", whose preceding statements also form a sharp contrast to the song of the people praying for a better fortune. For the fourth adventure, set in a room at the Vienna Burg, creates a serene Hungarian peasant Baroque atmosphere, through the presence of the little princes—their entry and exit marches, and the ABCD children's chorus—and the minuet-like suite of marrying off songs ("Gyújtottam gyertyát"... "Elment két jány"—Empress, Marie-Louise and women's choir).

Kodály replaced the sham peasants of the traditional *népszínmű* with the genuine, oppressed, suffering peasant. The play ends irrationally in an apotheosis, but justifiably so, as in the Hungary of the 1920s there seemed no other way of expressing the people's desire for freedom.

HÁRY JÁNOS
orchestral suite

The story goes, and may be believed, that the idea of the *Háry János Suite* came from Béla Bartók, who was enthusiastic about the comic opera. He discussed the idea with the Hungarian conductor Antal Fleischer, not long after the première of the stage work, on October 28, 1926, at a concert at the Berlin Singakademie, having in mind a première in Barcelona.

In an undated letter to Antal Fleischer, Kodály wrote:
I enclose the missing portions of the score. As far as the parts are concerned, M. Chomout brought a pile of them yesterday, and—if I understood his message to the maid correctly—he will bring the rest in ten days. You may perhaps find out if this is the case, and urge it upon him to be ready in time,

Yours truly,
Z. Kodály

I have just seen that No. 8 (Recruiting) is missing. I see no other solution but to send you the opera copy, which just happens to be with me, and ask you urgently to write it out yourself and send it back to me. The other pieces: 1. Duet, 2. French battle, 3. Entry, exist in two copies and so you can take them.

The final title of the "Palotás" was *Intermezzo*. We learn from this letter that at a certain phase during work on the suite, the first movement was still missing—"The Fairy Tale Begins" and the "Viennese Musical Clock".

The *Háry János Suite* was first performed in Barcelona on March 24, 1927, during a Hungarian evening of the Pau Casals Orchestra, conducted by Antal Fleischer. Doubtless as a result of the machinations of Kodály's Vienna publisher, the fact that this was the première was suppressed. The event was not considered distinguished enough to serve as publicity, and the performance by the New York Philharmonic Orchestra conducted by Willem Mengelberg, on December 15, 1927 was propagated as the world première of the *Háry János Suite*.

I do not know where the information in the programme notes of the first performance in Barcelona was obtained from, but certainly the order of movements, and even some of the titles, differ from how they are known today: I. The Tale Begins; II. Love Duet with a Russian Bride (today: third movement: Song "This Side of the Tisza, beyond the Danube"); III. Dance of the Hussars (presumably today's fifth movement: Intermezzo); IV. Viennese Musical Clock (today the second movement); V. Grotesque March (today the fourth movement: The Battle and Defeat of Napoleon); VI. Table Music—march during banqueting (today Entrance of the Emperor and His Court). This must mean that apart from the two outer movements, nothing at the first performance was yet in its final place, while the titles may have been the result of an arbitrary translation. As in most later instances too, the cimbalom part was substituted by a piano. In a letter to his publisher (September 15, 1927) this possibility was mentioned by Kodály. The score, however, in the first place suggests the harpsichord as supplementary to the cimbalom, but at the time most orchestras had no harpsichord and there thus only remained the piano. Occasionally music-reading cimbalom players from Hungarian gypsy bands may be found abroad.

If the world première of the suite in Barcelona under the baton of Antal Fleischer was a quiet event, the second performance, labelled as the première, and conducted by Willem Mengelberg, took place under conditions all the more effective. Typical of its acclaim, by the spring of 1931 the *Háry János Suite* had been performed in 100 cities throughout the world. Before 1944, it was heard in Germany alone on 82 occasions. Great Hungarian orchestras billed the work on 30 occasions, and there were 12 performances in Britain, conducted by the most eminent conductors of the time. Performed by the Chicago Symphony in 1928, 1929, 1930, 1934, 1938, 1939 and 1942; by the Philadelphia Symphony in 1928, 1931, 1933, 1937, and 1942. In the history of performing contemporary music I think it is unprecedented that the same orchestra should play the same new piece ever so often as a popular Classical or Romantic symphony. The suite was Kodály's first work of which a recording was made abroad; in 1931 Jenő Ormándy conducted the Minneapolis Symphony Orchestra for His Master's Voice, and in 1936 he recorded it with the Philadelphia Symphony, for the series *Columbia Masterpieces*.

Four years after its release by His Master's Voice, William McNaught wrote the following about the recording (DB 2456–58): "The 'Háry János' Suite by Kodály is humorous, melodious, picturesque, and startling music, but too much out of joint to make a good concert piece. I remember listening to a Queen's Hall performance of 'Petrouchka', with the stage action taking shape in my mind's eye at every point of the music. After a while people began to file out, in an evident state of boredom and disappointment. They lacked the clue of visual memory, and to them the music was a series of disconnected episodes and ejaculations. Possibly we who listen to the 'Háry János' music without any knowledge of what happens on the stage are as little able to understand what the composer is about. Moreover, a good deal of the scoring is of a kind which does not come off well on the gramophone. The possessor of these records may therefore find some difficulty in getting in touch with the music, though aware of its character and originality. The Suite is played by the Minneapolis Symphony Orchestra under Eugene Ormandy." (*The Musisal Times*, September 1935, p. 808.) The concert hall success of the suite was of course not influenced by this far not appreciative review. Surprisingly, there is no mention of the quality of the recording.

After the first performance abroad of the *Psalmus Hungaricus* in 1926, Kodály scored his second resounding world-wide success with the *Háry János Suite*. This piece took his work away from the world of select concerts billing exclusively contemporary composers to the utterly different environment of subscription concerts.

At the first performance of the *Háry János Suite* in England on August 23, 1928 at a Promenade Concert in Queen's Hall, Sir Henry Wood's orchestra was conducted by the composer. The Promenade Concerts were usually conducted by Wood, who yielded the baton only to eminent contemporary composers wishing to conduct their own work. Kodály would willingly have conducted the suite, together with the new overture and "Ballet Music" movement from the comic opera for the BBC on December 4, 1927, together with the studio performance of *Psalmus Hungaricus*. He had a long correspondence with Edward Clark, the chief programme organizer of the BBC Music Department, who did a great deal for new Hungarian music, but the plan eventually fell through and the *Psalmus* was conducted by Stanford Robinson.

In October 1928 *The Musical Times* carried an unsigned review entitled *Promenade Concert Novelties*, which wrote of Kodály's work: *August 23 gave us the first performance of a work that will probably be heard again, and frequently—Zoltán Kodály's Suite 'Háry János'. It consists of half a dozen movements arranged from a comic opera produced at Budapest in 1926. Háry János is not a mineral water, but a national character apparently compounded of Till Eulenspiegel and Baron Munchausen. The Suite is a very attractive affair, with scoring that can be described as fresh and original even in these days of brilliant orchestration. There is a real beauty in the two quiet movements. The composer conducted and was recalled many times.*

Kodály seemingly had the orchestral suite copied from the score of the opera practically without any change. Only the third movement ("Song"), the only section of the suite taken from a vocal piece (the duet "This Side of the Tisza, beyond the

Danube), has been expanded by a tiny orchestrational effect, a viola solo at the beginning intoning the folksong, while the original vocal lines are assigned to the wind parts. And the writing into one piece of the three short sections in the movement "The Battle and Defeat of Napoleon" was simply a job for a copist.

A symmetrical concept is achieved in the suite by the odd-numbered movements constituting the "ideal" layer, offering a vehicle for profound expression, while the even-numbered movements open out into the world of scherzo moods, the "grotesque" and caricature.

The sneezing effect as an ironic grimace at the opening of "The Fairy Tale Begins" (Con moto, tranquillo, molto moderato)—in the opera, the Student sneezes on Háry's tales founded within the piece to express that they are "true"—was both appreciated and criticized by its contemporaries. Although not featuring in the earliest plans of the work, the effect of striking a humorous-serious keynote expresses, balanced on a razor's edge, the tone of the whole work. With its constantly enriched canon structure, the great melody of the tale, rising from the depths, brings closer and closer its ancient atmosphere, and raises it from a gentle world of cantabile-espressivo to the heroic pathos of the four horns heard in unison (appassionato). This tremendous climax is followed by a long rest, then a final pole reflection of the heroic tone is projected, like a question mark, onto the progress of the tale. After the mists and warring heroism of the "once upon a time" opening, the "Viennese Musical" (Allegretto) is all light and sparkle. No dark bassoon, grave trombone and bass tuba feature in the wind section, whose scintillation is enhanced by a large number of percussion instruments. The form is the miniature rondo associated with Couperin, and even the sound seems to recall the French composer's harpsichord pieces and his favourite carillons. The major rondo melody with broken triads is shaped from instrumental folk music. Of course only the beginning of the melody stems from folklore, the continuation being the composer's own. The accompanying piano part, however, with its seconds and fourths, pleasantly estranges the major character of the theme. Kodály does not copy or adapt his formal model, at every return the gracile rondo theme is assigned new harmonies, new orchestral timbres, all of which contribute to the music being more playful, delicate and airy.

After this first interlude, the "Song" (Andante poco rubato) leads into the most profound conceptual layer of both the opera and the suite. It is less striking listening to the stage work than here in the suite that "Tiszán innen, Dunán túl" (This Side of the Tisza, beyond the Danube) gives rise to a miniature variation form. The theme is presented in the darker string colour of a solo cello, followed by three variations; the character of "theme and variations" is suggested by varying the instrumental effects which surround the folksong, which remains unchanged.

There follow an espressivo variation, one resembling a march, and a third one virtually unworldly, rapt and dreamy, while the melody, or rather its segments, are linked by improvisatory passages. These variated, improvisatory bridges fully resemble chamber music, as does the orchestration of the whole movement, with the solos in the strings, the cimbalom cadenzas and improvisations in the wind. There are no bassoons, trumpet or trombones, whether as colour elements or as a pedal to thicken the sound, and there is no place either in the ceaseless floating rubato or the realistic, metric pulsation of the percussion.

After the dream images of the "Song", the grotesque atmosphere of "The Battle and Defeat of Napoleon" (Alla marcia, Poco meno mosso, Tempo di Marcia Funebre) brings a radical change. The orchestration itself warns the listener not to take the battle scene too seriously. Of the woodwind Kodály only employs three piccolos and alto saxophone, while the array of piccolos and percussion suggests an ironic reference to "alla turca" music, played with "drums and pipes". The march heard at the beginning, with its caricaturing stressed tritones, appears altogether three times, in an increasingly sumptuous orchestration (1: trombones, 2: trombones and trumpets, 3: full brass), then at a wave from Háry's hand the armies of the French emperor fall like tin soldiers in this splendid musical battle scene sequence. Napoleon is represented by a supercilious, ridiculous portrait drawn with the bass trombone and tuba, and ridiculous also is the miniature funeral march with its choking saxophone solo. The "Intermezzo"—originally entitled "Palotás"—(Andante maestro, ma con fuoco), is a particularly fine example of what a creative imagination can see in a melody *simply taken over* from someone else. The simple, uniformly rhythmic melody of the main section is found as a vocal piece in István Gáti's piano method published in 1802. The snappy, dotted *verbunkos* rhythm, together with the dynamic contrasts and melodic configurations entrusted to the cimbalom, were added by Kodály. Stylistically the melody thus transformed forms a perfect unity with the thematic material of the trio. The heroism which in "The Fairy Tale Begins" becomes lost in the past, and in "The Battle and Defeat of Napoleon" is turned into the grotesque, in the "Intermezzo" becomes real and present. Like the second and fourth movements, the beginning of the "Entrance of the Emperor and His Court" (Alla marcia) promises to be musical grotesque in its combination of wind and percussion. Its two march melodies are heard simultaneously in splendid counterpoint. The string section joins the process only later with a significant new musical idea portraying, after the conceited march music, the bustle of the imperial court. After the great fanfare signalling the arrival of the emperor, the movement, and the suite, end with an increasingly animated chain of musical images to accompany the entry of the Viennese court. An ingenious idea of Kodály's tale-telling imagination, is that the movement does not refer to Vienna at all, apart from the reconstructions of a few sparkling Rococo moments. Taken all in all, the parallel fifths, glaring colours and pentatonic phrases seem rather to portray a procession of mandarins at the Chinese imperial court—the court of the Viennese Burg being as far away from Háry and his people as the Peking court. The last movement of the suite abounds to such an extent in orchestral invention that Kodály later incorporated certain of its ideas into his orchestral works, the *Peacock Variations* and the *Concerto*.

BALLET MUSIC

Kodály composed an orchestral "Dance of the Dragons" for the "end of the world" scene of *Háry János*, which, due to staging problems, was abandoned after the third Budapest performance. Kodály later published the movement lasting about 5 minutes under the title "Ballet Music". This lively little piece, which is rarely given, was first performed in London at a Henry Wood Promenade Concert, on August 24, 1937.

THEATRE OVERTURE

Kodály wrote a "Theatre Overture" for the Budapest revival of the opera in 1928. In its first form the large-scale sonata movement was left open-ended, leading straight into the stage action. Kodály later wrote a new conclusion for concert performance. This version was first performed in London, on December 5, 1932 by Malcolm Sargent (Queen's Hall, Courtauld-Sargent Concert).

Dances of Marosszék

a) for piano
b) for orchestra

COMPOSITION:	1923(?)–1927, orchestration concluded October 8, 1929.
FIRST PERFORMANCE:	Hungarian Radio, March 14, 1927. Concert performance: Budapest, March 17, 1927, Louis Kentner (piano version) Dresden Opera House, November 28, 1930, Sachsische Staatskapelle, conducted by Fritz Busch (orchestral version) Ballet: Hagen, between January and March, 1931, City Theatre, choreography: Günter Hess.
INSTRUMENTS:	2 flutes (second doubling piccolo), 2 oboes, 2 clarinets, bassoon, double-bassoon, 4 horns, 2 trumpets, kettledrum, side drum, bass drum, cymbals, strings.
DURATION:	*c.* 12 minutes.
PUBLICATION:	a) piano version: Universal Edition, Editio Musica Budapest,
	b) instrumental version: Universal Edition, Wiener Philharmonischer Verlag, Boosey and Hawkes, Editio Musica Budapest.

The *Dances of Marosszék* is one of the works by Kodály whose exact date of origin and the various phases of whose composition are virtually impossible to establish. In an interview with Denijs Dille, the Belgian music historian, in 1963, Kodály spoke of his relationship with Bartók: ... *I always avoided being his rival, and tried to do something different from him. When we received the commission for the anniversary of the unification of Pest and Buda, I asked him what he intended to do. He said he would do a dance suite, and wrote the* 'Dance Suite'. *I also had dances in mind, the dances of Marosszék and Galánta, but since that was what he was writing, I chose another theme, the* 'Psalmus'. The idea of the *Dances of Marosszék* accordingly stemmed from 1923, but it is not known when any of the music was committed to paper, since Kodály, as mentioned, never dated his sketches. However, the plan of the *Galánta Dances*, which he also mentioned in the interview, cannot date from 1923, as there is documentary evidence that Kodály became acquainted with the musical material used in the piece in 1927.

At least, the idea of a rondo built from folk and pseudo-popular material can be traced back prior to 1923, as the rondo for small orchestra entitled *Old Hungarian Soldiers' Songs* was first performed on January 12, 1918 in Vienna. Kodály, it is true, considered the piece a failure; he did not have it performed again and did not deem it worthy of print (the score was published in 1976, with the title *Hungarian Rondo*).

The piano version of the *Dances of Marosszék* had its first concert-hall performance on March 17, 1927 in Budapest, during one of Kodály's composer's evenings, held regularly in Budapest in the 1920s. At that time the Hungarian Radio had no adequate facilities for on-the-spot recording, and so the full programme of the evening was broadcast in the form of a studio concert three days previously. It was performed by the eminent pianist Lajos (Louis) Kentner, one of Kodály's former pupils, in the 1920s a regular contributor to his teacher's composer's evenings; he settled in England in the 1930s.

According to Kentner's recollections, on the morning of the day of the première, Kodály called him to his home and gave him the music of the *Dances of Marosszék*, which he was to perform in the evening, sheet by sheet, to practise. That the piece really was completed at the very last minute is borne out, if indirectly, by a letter of February 18, 1927, in which Kodály ordered the concert programme from the printers, and which does not mention the name of Kentner among the performers, the name of the pianist therefore being necessarily added at the last minute.

According to the programme, even the title was still unsettled, as it spoke of *Village Dances*:

1. *Of Kászon (Mrs Zoltán Kodály's transcription)*
2. *Of Marosszék.*

The final title was arrived on July 1, 1928, when Kodály informed his Viennese copyright office on completion of the work: *Marosszék—Hungarian folk dances from Marosszék*, written by him in German in the register; then, as this seemed too cumbersome, he modified it, finding the appropriate solution of *Dances of Marosszék*. At the time the work had not appeared in print. Kodály did not usually contact his copyright office in connection with unpublished works, but the *Dances of Marosszék* had been played abroad too, from the manuscript, by several Hungarian pianists, which made it necessary to settle the question of royalties. Even later, the piece was very rarely played by foreign pianists as the score is technically extremely demanding and does not offer a rewarding task.

In any case something induced the composer not to publish the piano version of the *Dances of Marosszék* for more than three years. Perhaps he had the orchestral version, envisaged as early as 1923, before his eyes. Eventually he published the two versions simultaneously, so much so that two additions in the orchestral score also feature in the piano score, as alternatives (or perhaps Kodály originally planned the piano piece so that at two points it would contain expanded orchestral versions as well). The possibility cannot be excluded either of the two versions having been written simultaneously, or indeed of the orchestral form having preceded the piano version. The comment of the London reviewer of the printed score, signing himself T. A. (for Thomas Armstrong) was perhaps not entirely without foundation: ...*This pianoforte version is only an arrangement from the orchestral*... (*The Musical Times*, November 1930.) Oscar Thompson, one of the critics of the first performance in the United States, wrote just the opposite, however; ...*Some orchestrated piano music by Zoltán Kodály, styled 'Dances of Marosszék'*. (*The New York Post*, December 12, 1930.)

It can scarcely be regarded as fortuitous that Béla Bartók, the main champion of Kodály's piano music, who, as can be proved, did have a copy of the piece by 1927 or 1928, only included the *Dances of Marosszék* in his repertoire in 1930, the year it appeared in print. He first performed it on November 24,

1930 in a radio concert broadcast by the Daventry transmitter in London, and by 1931 had played it on 11 further occasions.

Kodály received from Toscanini the main stimulus to orchestrate the *Dances of Marosszék*, that is, according to present knowledge, to realize his original concept. He formed a friendship with the conductor in October 1928, at the outstandingly successful performance of the *Psalmus Hungaricus* in Milan. László Eősze has reconstructed the sequence of events behind the origin of the score. On July 23, 1929 Toscanini sent a telegram to Kodály: *Making up my programme I'd like to know for sure if I can count on a new work from you which I could première in my next American concerts.* This means the subject of a new work had already cropped up between them. According to Eősze's research, Kodály completed the orchestration of the *Dances of Marosszék* on October 8, 1929, and he quickly sent the score to Toscanini (by the second half of the 1970s, the manuscript score was no longer to be found among the conductor's legacy). On January 21, 1930 Toscanini's secretary informed Mrs Kodály: *The maestro was keenly interested in the* 'Dances of Marosszék', *but he still thinks it would be better for Kodály if he were to perform a completely new work of his, this after all being rather a transcription.*

For nearly fifty years it was believed that the orchestral version of the *Dances of Marosszék* was premièred by the New York Philharmonic Orchestra, conducted by Toscanini. In fact, however, it was first performed by the Sachsische Staatskapelle under the baton of Fritz Busch, in the Dresden Opera House on November 28, 1930. The next performance took place in Budapest on December 1, at a concert of the Budapest Philharmonic Orchestra conducted by Ernst von Dohnányi, and Toscanini was the conductor of the third performance, heard on December 11, the same year, in New York. The Dresden press gave Kodály's work a fairly cool reception. In the article mentioned above, Oscar Thompson wrote much more warmly about the New York performance: *Inevitably these dances smacked more of the soil than the sort of Hungarian music that in the last century became all too popular in the restaurants of two continents. The full, dark scoring, rather strikingly relieved by lightly accom-*

panied woodwind solos, retained a rural savour that set off ruddily the folk rhythms and folk phraseology of the tunes.

The linking of the world première with the name of Toscanini must have been prompted mainly by publishing interests, as the news—even if unfounded—of the première having been undertaken by the greatest conductor of the day meant a great deal in paving the way for a rapid international success for the composition.

Certainly, the expectations of the publishers were fulfilled. In two years, until the end of 1932, according to the present, far from full information at my disposal, the work had 42 performances abroad, both in Europe and overseas. In Germany alone 22 performances are known of. Conductors of the *Dances of Marosszék* included—after Busch, Dohnányi and Toscanini—Eugene Ormándy, Fritz Reiner, Frederick Stock (USA), Busch (Rome), Vittorio Gui (Florence), Sir Henry Wood (BBC, March 29, 1931), Robert Heger (Halle Orchestra, Liverpool, November 2, 1931) and Carl Bamberger (Moscow, Leningrad, 1931).

After the *Anschluss*, the German occupation of Austria in 1938, Kodály was able to dispense with his Viennese publisher and have his works published by Boosey and Hawkes in London. The *Dances of Marosszék* was the first among Kodály's major works to have been published in London: the miniature score appeared in 1942, and was well received by E. H. M. (the émigré German composer Ernst Hermann Meyer) in *The Music Review* (November 1942): *The score is as transparent as glass. There is not a single superfluous or doubtful note in the spare but masterly writing.*

In form, material and harmony the piano version is essentially identical with the orchestral version (the orchestral piece being 28 bars longer). There is, however, a striking difference in the tonalities of the two: the piano piece is in C sharp, while the key of the orchestral piece is D. A possible reason for this may be that due to the use of open strings, the sound of string instruments in D is much fuller and more lustrous than in C sharp (it is no pure joy for pianists either to play in C sharp major, the key of the coda, but for violinists it is even more troublesome). The orchestration also includes tonal effects, ornaments and voice leading which could not be executed on the piano. There are about 50 differences in the two versions regarding performance directions, character, tempo and dynamics, which make the orchestral score much richer than the piano score. Perhaps it is only a consequence of the "nature" of the orchestra that the full score includes so many more instructions, but it is possible also that one is here faced with two pieces which in nuance and accent are not identical. For instance, the fact that the orchestral score very often includes the instructions espressivo, while it only occurs once in the piano score, seems to suggest that the piano piece is harder, steelier and more sparkling than the orchestral version.

In form, the *Dances of Marosszék* is a taut miniature rondo with three episodes and a coda, the rondo melody returning three times, always in varied form. It is as if, inspired by the folk-music material, Kodály were to return here to the roots, the original meaning of the rondo—the round dance. Several decades after completing the work, he formulated his artistic intentions in connection with it, though with no particular reference. *A popular theme, the melody of a folksong is completely unsuited for any higher form. As long as one applies the melodies in their original fashion, one must be content with forms which are not counter to these. Variation is the only form which leaves the folksong and its kernel untouched, which does not develop it any further, but rather reinforces it through all its variations ... or even more suited for this is a rondo with short episodes.* The *Dances of Marosszék* then was created from a combination of just these two principles—rondo and variation.

Kodály's preface to the score appeared in several languages, including English, in the edition published by Universal in October 1930:

'*My nurse, a Hungarian from Marosszék, was a good singer, a good Heyduc dancer*', writes John Kemény, prince of Transylvania *(1607–1662)*, in his autobiography.

It is perhaps no accident that most of the old folk-dance music has been preserved unto our days in the district of Marosszék and that some pieces are called 'Marosszéki' even in other regions.

It is probable that these pieces, known to us as instrumental, were originaliy sung. Of some of them the worded vocal form has even been found.

Until the war, one could hear such pieces in every village, played either on the violin or on a shepherd's flute; old people used to sing them.

Kodály collected the music he employed as the rondo theme in the *Dances of Marosszék* in 1910, and the melody that appears in the third episode of the work, in 1912. The first and second episodes, and the coda, include folk-music material from the collection of Béla Vikár (1859–1945), who was the first to use Edison's phonograph cylinders for recording folk music in the late 19th century. Kodály transcribed these three melodies from the phonograph recordings. None of the melodies come from the geographic region of Marosszék, and so the "Marosszék" of the title indicates a folk-music type, pointed out by Kodály in his preface. The melodies employed in the work, particularly the rondo theme, have an extremely large area of relatives in Eastern Europe, Rumanian and Ruthenian variants also being known. Hence it is perhaps not too arbitrary to attribute to the *Dances of Marosszék* a spirit showing kinship with Bartók's *Dance Suite*, uniting the peoples of Eastern Europe in a community of common dances.

Kodály was reproached more than once for getting an emphasis on simplified forms, types and models in Hungarian folk music. The rondo melody in the *Dances of Marosszék*, by contrast, is as far from any folk-music type as possible: the melody makes use of the full stock of all 12 notes, which is extremely rare in Hungarian folk music. This, of course, does not make it either atonal dodecaphonic, but still it may become the point of departure for a harmonic interpretation with several meanings. And everything in the discoloured, passing semitones of the original folk melody which seems rather to be ornamentation, in the composition is given emphasis. But even in structure it is an individual and unique melody, uniting the descending line of the old style folk-music structure with the arched, recapitulatory form of the new style.

At its first appearance (Maestoso, poco rubato), the multifaceted rondo melody unfolds with a dashing, slow *verbunkos* folk dance lilt and an increasingly full sound, like a long song showing extremely broad perspectives. The rhythms, the brilliant major harmonies, and the instrumental colours all underline the hard character of the melody. Every repeated element, the melodic lines heard repeatedly, is given a new garb, in the orchestral version a delicately woven counterpoint, while the emotional variety ranges from contemplation to a dramatic climax. In a certain sense therefore the presentation of the rondo theme itself includes variation.

The first episode (Con moto) is a playful, animated chain of musical images. Its double-faceted melody is heard three times; the first half of the melody, soon subjected to grand climaxes, sounds like a bear dance, and its gracefully fleeting response resembles the dance of light-moving peasant girls. Naturally the original folk-music material did not contain this promise of duality, which is the product of creative imagination.

The rondo melody first returns in the minor. The idyllic picture portrayed in the episode comes to a sudden end, the melody, now in the bass, expressing repressed *drama*, an effect further intensified by the woodwind passages that shoot downward like distant flashes of lightning. Vibrato string tremolos add to the tension, until there arrives a powerful outburst, like an exclamation.

The second episode (Moderato) seems to have the function of an extremely dense and concentrated slow movement. It is a pastoral scene, whose singular, improvisatory and richly embellished melody is heard done, first on the oboe, then the flute and the piccolo, later being reduced to a memory by the solo violin, finally being taken over by the solo double-bass. The until now fairly dense orchestration assumes a latticed fabric, resembling chamber music, and the rustling sounds of the accompaniment material conjure up nature surrounding the shepherd playing his pipe.

The second return of the rondo melody takes place in a new harmonic guise, and the most exposed, third melodic phrase is enriched also with a new element. Kodály underlines this new building stone by sharp shifts of dynamics as if wishing to draw attention to it by contrasting material. Yielding to a moment of particular inertia, the concluding section of the principal melody, a rotating motif with constantly growing kinetic energy, rolls along with increasing speed, and, as if breaking through an imaginary finishing line, leads into the most quickly whirling section of the work, the third (Vivace) episode, which perhaps functions as a scherzo. It is a fast, 2/4 dance, whose originality is enhanced by many different applications of a style of accompaniment called "esztam", in which strong and weak beats are divided between different instruments. During its further development and ornamental enrichment this dance character acquires quite demonic intensification, at the climax practically tumbling into the broad unison which prepares for the last return of the rondo theme. As a delicate mask of symmetry, the composer now restrains the material to counterbalance the growing speed of the rolling material which introduced the third episode. He puts over this curbing effect even by the "grinding" sound heard in the very strong sforzatos, in order to be able to call a halt in just four bars to the onward rush of the music.

The composer bids a soft farewell to the recurring, principal melody; none of its appearances so far has been so homogeneous in its dynamics nor so close to chamber music in its texture. And although it appears unequivocally in a bright D major, it is so replete with submission, resignation and melancholic elements that it has the effect of being only a remote echo of the earlier material *verbunkos* intonation. In the penultimate bar of the rondo melody the sound is split up dispersed along the prism of the mysterious harmonics from the three violins tinged by woodwind solos. The tremendous round-dance of the coda, which rounds off the composition, starts out in the immense distance. The dancers of this tableau are at first joined only by a few, but their number constantly increases. The music, woven from elements of instrumental folk music, bagpipe effects and ornaments, constitutes, even with its sudden standstills and repressed moments, a single large-scale climax. Particularly fine and noble are the embellishments that circumscribe the melodic outlines, the creatures of a fertile interplay between the composer's invention and the folklorist's imagination.

In its proportionate structure and varied melodic world, the characteristic nuances of orchestration, and its harmonic abundance, the *Dances of Marosszék* justifiably belongs among Zoltán Kodály's most popular works.

The Spinning Room

one-act Singspiel

COMPOSITION:	1924–1932 (?1965).
FIRST PERFORMANCE:	Budapest, April 24, 1932, Hungarian Royal Opera House; conducted by: Sergio Failoni; produced by: László Márkus; sets and costumes: Gusztáv Oláh; choirmaster: Vilmos Roubal; choreography: Jan Cieplinsky.
CAST:	Housewife: Mária Basilides; Lover: Imre Palló; Neighbour: Mária Budanovits; A Youth: Endre Rösler; A Girl: Anna Báthy; A Mummer disguised as a Flea: Oszkár Maleczky; Mute characters: Two Gendarmes, An Old Woman, A Little Girl
PERFORMERS:	soprano, 2 contraltos, tenor, 2 baritones, mixed choir, ballet.
INSTRUMENTATION:	piccolo, 2 flutes, 2 oboes (the second doubling cor anglais), 2 clarinets, 2 bassoons, 4 horns, 2 trumpets, 3 trombones, timpani, percussion (bass-drum, cymbals, triangle, side drum, tambourine), strings.
DURATION:	*c*. 80 minutes.
PUBLISHER:	Universal Edition (vocal piano score).

On April 1, 1922 Kodály first suggested to his Viennese publishers that they publish his folksong arrangements. In a letter of May 8 the same year he wrote that he was now engaged in the realization of his plan, and would select folksongs different from the ones Bartók had arranged. On July 16, 1923 he consulted the publisher as to whether his 30 to 40 arrangements should be issued in one volume or several, while on July 24, 1924 he suggested the publication in various volumes of 50 folksongs for concert performance, with ten songs per volume. Edward J. Dent, professor of music at Cambridge University, and from 1922 chairman of the ISCM, in a letter written in German of December 3, 1924 wrote to Kodály: *Many thanks for having sent me the extremely interesting Hungarian folksongs.* In a letter in French, undated, but which, judging by the contents, must have been written in 1924, Michel D. Calvocoressi reproached Kodály that Cecil Gray—instead of him—had ... *received the offer from Rózsavölgyi* (Budapest music-publishers) *to make the English translation of your 50 folksongs.* Eventually, however, the first volumes of *Hungarian Folk Music* were translated by Calvocoressi. Kodály's 57 folksong arrangements with piano accompaniment were published between 1925 and 1932. The first two volumes appeared issued jointly in 1925 by Rózsavölgyi Budapest, Universal Edition Vienna, and Oxford University Press. This was the first occasion when an English publisher cooperated in the publication of music by Kodály. Hubert Foss, head of the Music Department of Oxford University Press, discussed the publication of his works with Kodály in Budapest on May 11, 1925. The meeting took place at the suggestion of Calvocoressi, who also persuaded His Master's Voice to record 27 of the folksong arrangements of *Hungarian Folk Music*. The recording was made in 1928 in Budapest with Hungarian vocalists and Béla Bartók providing the piano accompaniment.

Hungarian Folk Music, a cycle of folksong arrangements intended for concert performance, has two links with the stage work *The Spinning Room*. On the hand Kodály experimented in the *Hungarian Folk Music* pieces with instrumental accompaniments to go with the folksong, providing portraits of landscape, people, situations and psychological sketches, later employed in *The Spinning Room*. On the other hand, 12 of the 23 folksong arrangements in the stage work come from *Hungarian Folk Music*.

It was in fact not Kodály who first had the idea of using these folksong arrangements on the stage. In the autumn of 1924 a new variety theatre was opened in Budapest. The conductor, Mihály Nádor was a former student of Kodály, and he had the idea of inserting short scenes from Kodály's folksong arrangements among the various items. The first such 15-minute scene, accompanied by a chamber ensemble, was staged on August 31, 1924, and was kept in production until October 5. The scene bore the title "Spinning Room", and the songs in it later were all included in the final stage work, which however had a completely different plot. The variety theatre planned further folksong scenes with Kodály's music, but these never came about.

When the first two volumes of *Hungarian Folk Music* appeared with an English translation, Thomas Armstrong (signing himself T. A.) had fine things to say about them in *The Musical Times* (August 1926): *A most interesting set of Hungarian folksongs from Transylvania, arranged by Zoltán Kodály, is published at Budapest by Rózsavölgyi és Társa, and in London by the Oxford University Press. The interpreter of folksong is always faced with the problem of implications; often in simple melodies there is a high concentration of feelings, and the singer or arranger must either work very simply, in the hope of letting the overtones sound clearly, or he may attempt to extract the inner meanings and re-express them in his own language. The latter is Kodály's way, and it is done with tremendous energy, command, sense of the dramatic, and many moments of beauty. In every number there are striking touches of imaginative setting, like the little accompaniment figure on No. 6. which so aptly illustrates the knocking by the children on the gravestone. 'Weeping Willow', No. 9 in vol. 2, is a particularly beautiful example in the quieter style, and the same volume contains the bitter but highly effective 'The Heartless Wife'. The danger of the method is that by saying too much of what is implied, one may repel (Rosing used to do it in his terribly dramatic way of singing 'Lord Randal'): at any rate, the arranger may overload, and one does feel in the bigger numbers of Kodály's examples that things have got beyond legitimate latitude. The settings become rhapsodies, based on folksongs, but grown into a quite different sort of a thing: and one remembers how very much more effectively, though quietly, some of Bartók's simple arrangements set off tunes which are quite well able to speak for themselves. This is a personal feeling, however, and there is no doubt about the skill and effectiveness of the setting in the present two volumes, which ought to receive careful attention.* ("Weeping Willow" and "The Heartless Wife", the two pieces the reviewer made a special point of, were included in *The Spinning Room*.)

To my knowledge it was the Budapest evening paper *Az Est* which, on September 3, 1931, first reviewed the stage work. It was in the form of an interview by Miklós Radnai, director of the Opera House, about the coming season: *This year there really will be a Kodály première in the Opera House. The Opera will stage the short-act piece entitled* In the Spinning Room, *produced already, but in a completely rearranged form. The composition of the musical pieces is also different, as both the material and the orchestration have been greatly expanded ... Songs, ballads and original Hungarian dances are to be presented in the play, all in their original intactness.* Kodály first mentioned the new work to his Vienna publisher, without naming it, in a letter of January 17, 1932: *After repeated invitations from the Opera House, I have nonetheless been obliged to have the work—you know already which one—now staged. I will presumably complete the piano score by the end of this month ... By mid-February I would reach a stage in the score when I could begin the orchestral parts.*

One can feel from the letter that the Opera House, which by 1931 already knew, at least in broad outline, what the new, complete *Spinning Room* would be like, was now pressing the composer. The Viennese music review *Musikblätter des Anbruch* still put the date of the première in March, but the first performance actually took place a month later. We know from the composer Pál Kadosa that the work of orchestration was done by him together with his fellow composer János Viski, both former Kodály pupils. This, however, probably meant quite mechanical work: realizing directions for instrumentation put down in the piano score. Kodály obviously went through their work, as the score of *The Spinning Room* shows no signs of the effects typical of the young avant-garde composer Kadosa's orchestral approach.

Universal Edition seems to have placed its trust in the work's being successful. Kodály, who usually waited for the première or even several performances of the work in question before he had it published, was also confident, and in this instance started preparations for the press well before the première. According to the composer's letter of February 29, 1932: *I enclose the corrected copy of 'The Spinning Room'. I hope the engraving has not yet passed page 42...*

Kodály hoped the folksong arrangements he had transferred from *Hungarian Folk Music* to *The Spinning Room* would also become popular in their form with orchestral accompaniment in concert halls. To reserve their copyright, he thus listed them title by title for the Vienna AKM (Austrian Copyright Society), which handled his royalties. Vienna obviously did not understand this, at least such seems to be the case from Kodály's letter of December 29, 1932 to AKM: *Regarding your question of December 20, I wish to state that the songs which had once already been registered but have been rearranged for the opera, have to be registered again if only because now they exist with orchestral accompaniment as well. Please let me know what difference it shall make if they are to be performed as parts of the opera or as individual songs. Anyway, until the opera becomes more generally known, some of them will feature on programmes as individual songs.* This expectation, however, did not materialize, as no songs from *The Spinning Room* have become repertoire pieces in orchestral concerts.

The Spinning Room was first performed abroad at La Scala Milan on January 14, 1933, and followed up there by three more performances. German opera companies were also interested in the opera, but after Hitler's accession to power opportunities for staging foreign works in Germany became extremely scarce. (*The Spinning Room* was performed on February 9, 1938 in Braunschweig, and on February 2, 1941 in Weimar, but these never came to more than two or three performances.) On March 1, 1937 the opera was given a concert performance by the Prague German Theatre, and in 1938 the Budapest Opera House Company took it to the Maggio Musicale in Florence. In 1939 it was staged by the San Carlo Opera in Naples, and on April 29 of the same year it was also performed and partly recorded by the students of Cleveland University (either in a concert performance or on the stage). The first and only British stage performance: Buxton Festival, July 24–August 8, 1982.

The BBC broadcast the opera on two occasions during the 1930s. On February 26, 1937 it transmitted a performance by the Budapest Opera House, and on May 26, 1933 the opera was conducted by Zoltán Kodály at a public studio concert, the seventh in the seventh season of the BBC series Concerts of Contemporary Music. As far as can be ascertained this was the only occasion when *The Spinning Room* was conducted by the composer. Unfortunately no recording was made of the production, though such a recording available today would be a unique and most valuable document of an authentic performance of Kodály's works.

The London production was performed by the BBC Chorus (Section B), chorus master Cyril Dalmaine, the BBC Orchestra (Section D) led by Laurence Turner, with Enid Cruickshank, Harold Williams, Parry Jones, Ina Souez and Roy Henderson as vocalists, in the English translation by Michel D. Calvocoressi. (More recent editions of the piano score contain the translation of Elizabeth M. Lockwood, who from the late 1920s onwards translated texts of Kodály's works. Quotations of folksong lyrics are from her translation.)

Kodály held altogether six rehearsals (between May 23 and 26), one with orchestra, one, the final rehearsal, with full ensemble, the remaining four devoted to choir and soloists.

The London performance was reviewed on May 27, 1933 in the *Daily Telegraph*, in an article signed H. B.: *The music is appropriately constructed of folksongs, alternating a passionate intensity, at times boisterous and humorous, and a heartbreaking melancholy. Nobody understands these songs better than Kodály, who has made himself almost one with them, unless it be Bartók, who has at late become far more radical. Kodály's music must be, in spite of its originality, as near the popular heart as that of anybody now living. The composer conducted, and secured a good performance.*

This time Kodály summarized his artistic intentions not before the Budapest première but after it: *What fault-finders cavil at is that some of the songs are already known from the concert hall and that there they are more in their proper place. I realized precisely in the concert hall that if torn out of their soil, these songs become practically unintelligible. They must be presented in an organic unity with the way of life from which they have grown out. This has been the aim of my attempts and if my life had no other result but bring, through my person, the Hungarian city closer to the Hungarian village, even if by a single step, my life was not in vain ...* The Spinning Room *is not an attempt at opera, since I could only embark on a work which today could in fact be carried through. According to certain objections the recitative is missing from it, and the songs are merely linked by mimed speech. But these objections leave out of consideration that I could not employ recitatives without a break in the style.* In 1963, during a conversation with Denijs Dille, Kodály enlarged upon the subject: *They reproached the little work with not being a drama, and having no plot, but this was not my aim; I wanted to present scenes taken from the life of the people.*

The plot of *The Spinning Room*, as Kodály outlined it, is as follows: The Lover of the Housewife is pursued by the gendarmes and he must flee. The Housewife is left alone in her home, the spinning room, which is soon filled with all those who come to try and cheer her up with play, song and dance. The gendarmes catch the Lover, but it turns out that the real culprit is the rich lad (the Big-nosed Flea). Both are dragged away, and the scene is left empty. The song of the chorus sounds from the distance; by the time they arrive at the spinning room, the Lover, having been released, also returns. General dancing ensues.

This skeleton plot develops out of a succession of folksongs. As Kodály mentioned, he employed no recitatives to link the songs. Unlike in *Háry János*, he here even eschews prose speech. So the plot becomes an extremely loose thread for the folksongs, each finer than the other, to be strung onto. The musical effect, however, is stronger than the dramatic stage effect.

In 1932, the work included 23 folksongs, 22 of them in the old style of Hungarian folk music (pentatonic, with descending melodic lines). For the 1965 Budapest revival Kodály added another folksong to the work. Twelve songs and ballads were transferred from the *Hungarian Folk Music* set, some "merely" being orchestrated and others in varying degrees arranged. The seven pantomime orchestral interludes of varying length are related to folk music only in spirit, and not melodically.

The organization of the material shows clearly the hand of the composer. The greater part of the musical material of the

Exposition returns before the Finale, dividing the overall structure into three scherzo-like and three intermezzo-like parts. The folk ballad "Fair Ilona" at the centre, functioning as a kind of "plot within a plot" is shaped like a rondo, broken into four solo parts set off by three episodes. The character-parts of the work fall by and large symmetrically around this axis.

However, the musical form is not absolutely that of an opera, with the result that the "stage work" is more effective in the concert hall, where the imagination can obediently and freely follow the series of folksongs, which Kodály has dressed so delicately in an orchestral cloak of tones and harmonies, further enhancing their beauty. The musical form can there sparkle in its full beauty, as the many fine details—and not only details—are not concealed by drab stage routine.

Everything heard in *The Spinning Room* is made credible and authentic by a kind of musical magic, like in a huge folksong symphony scored for solo voices, choir and orchestra. The orchestral ritornelles, that serve as links or partitions, though they do not make up for the dramatically missing song-speech, still express states of mind, and changing moods, while leading from song to song. Another kind of orchestral excerpt recalls the world of "speaking instruments" in piano pieces and chamber works. Among these sections are the opening music and the great interlude before the finale, which with its tempo pendulum constantly swinging out from the basic Andante appassionato e rubato, and its virtually speaking melodies, could easily find a place as a slow movement in Kodály's chamber music of the period between 1910 and 1920. After the love duet the instruments become ebulliently parlando in tone in the ascending violin solo, whose recitative rhythm is surrounded by the undulating musical material which Kodály had made use of ever since his early *Nine Piano Pieces*. The material is so freely woven that Kodály suggests, presumably for the first time in Hungarian music, an aleatory procedure in the rotation at the end, when he puts the accompaniment phrase beneath a melodic semitone marked by a fermata in repeated marks within the bar, writing above it "ad libitum".

The Spinning Room employs a different technique of folksong arrangement from that in *Háry János*, and one different from that in the cycle *Hungarian Folk Music*. In *Háry János* Kodály places the folksongs in succession, while the *trouvaille* employed in *The Spinning Room* is that (from experience gained by Kodály the choral composer) a folksong can also give rise to counterpoint, and counterpoint may also blossom from the simultaneity of several folk melodies too.

The arrangements are interlaced with instrumental folk music, for the most part specially composed, more rarely in a form closed to the original. According to Kodály, *The* i n s t r u m e n- t a l *part of folk music is hardly more than the transposition of vocal melodies to instruments, whether they are performed by musicians from the people or by gypsies*. Not infrequently therefore the folklorist-composer himself composed the instrumental configurations and instrumental variants of melodies.

The folksong structure, organized around the multilayered central ballad "Fair Ilona", in both character and emotion, form a firm fabric. A tone of profound tragedy strikes us in the introductory melodies "Elmegyek, elmegyek" (Far Away I'm Going), "A citrusfa levelestől ágastól" (We Must Part My Dearest) and in the block of songs which function as a recapitulation on the orchestra "Az hol én elmegyek" (I Rove, I Look Around), "A citrusfa". The Housewife's sense of solitude is suggested by the "Weeping Willow" in the first part, and "Tőlem a nap" (Shades of Eve Are Slowly Falling) before the finale. This emotional circle is expanded by "Te túl rózsám, te túl" (O My Love...) (Housewife with female choir), inserted after "Hess, légy, ne szállj rám" (Shoo, Shoo, Buzzing Fly). Its sensitive chamber-music texture differs from the more dense instrumentation of the work, and expresses such a personal vein of emotion that, although it echoes the communal element in Bach's chorale arrangement, we might surmise in it an autobiographical element. Did Kodály perhaps intend the song as a requiem for his first wife, Emma?

The little joy to be found in the individual lot of the people Kodály saved for the beautiful love duet "A csitári hegyek alatt" (From Far Distant Snow-capped Mountains), and for the finale's apotheosis, which makes credible the incredible, since in 1932 there was no actual solution for the life of a peasant who fell into the hands of the gendarmerie. Neither can we forget during the great, overall dance climax that "Fejérvárott zergetik a láncot" (In Fejérvár They Rattle the Chain).

Another layer, the community one, is not only for joking, but for irony too. A fine, bantering irony permeates the women's chorus "Nekem olyan emberecske kéne" (O I Want a Young and Handsome Husband), the weaving chorus, jeering at the lazy girl (the accompaniment figuration portraying the whirr of the spinning wheel is found in European music at least since Haydn's oratorio *The Seasons*). Kodály colours and lends individuality to the familiar musical gesture by reinterpreting the metre: the basic 6/8 lilt can also turn into 3/4, the two combined, or can be pressed into 2/4. Even more ironical is the male chorus beginning "Jók a lányok, nem rosszak" (Ev'ry Girl is Good and Charming), whose strident horn signals also signify, according to European convention, cuckolding. The manner of its treatment, with harmonies leading regularly to interrupted cadences, even seems to be a caricature of the style of a German *Liedertafel* (male choir).

The corresponding layer in the second part consists of "Most jöttem Erdélyből" (I Have But Just Arrived), "Egy nagyorrú bolha" (Long Nose Comes Acalling) and the folksong "El kéne indulni, meg kék házasodni" (Wise It Were and Timely Even to Go Marry). Orchestration and harmony both serve to express irony here.

The "Fair Ilona" section is balanced by two folk ballads: the playful "Kitrákotty mese" (Kitrákotty Tale), abounding in tone-painting (again a parallel is Haydn's *Seasons*) in Part I, and the great dramatic tableau of "A rossz feleség" (The Heartless Wife) in Part II. As for the question why Kodály did not choose any of the greatest ballads in the *Hungarian Folk Music* set—"Három árva" (Three Orphans), Mónár Anna", "Kádár Kata" or "Barcsai"—even though as his own librettist and dramaturg he could have made room for such tremendous dramatic material, the answer is that in all probability they would have torn apart the dreadly fragile stage form.

Kodály may have opted for "minor" ballads so as not to have anything outshine the ballad of "Fair Ilona". We know from the research of Lajos Vargyas what a wide-branching family-tree this ballad theme has, reaching from Scotland in the West to the Ukraine in the East and Greece in the South. A matchless piece of ingenuity on the part of Kodály the scholarly composer is that he visualizes the scenes of the ballad through elements taken from folk music. This is how we are shown the "magic mill" "A malomnak nincsen köve" (Though There Are Not Any Millstones), the "magic tower" in "Lányok ülnek a toronyba" (Maidens on the Tower Are Twinning), and it is also how for a moment the "death" of László Bertelaki, which forms part of the game, becomes real through the lament melody. After Bartók's *Laments* for the piano and other pieces from his composed dirge music, the listener now becomes acquainted with the rites of folk music lament in their original form. (The spectral shadows, sharp rhythms and diminished fifth chords of the instrumental setting also follow strictly Bartókian models.) The ballad melody is interwoven with these "inserts" like a rondo theme. Kodály's familiar harmonic methods drive the unchanged folk melody constantly on, exhibiting ever new facets of it, now in a martial *verbunkos* frame, now with a glowing accompanied recitative, and now again virtually accentuated into exclamation marks. Nothing here is in question marks, nothing is ironical, the play, because it is what it is, remains serious to the death. Kodály builds a rainbow bridge for the resurrection of the protagonist wishing to see his lover "Kelj fel fiam, kelj fel" (Rise Up, Dear Son, Rise Up), and he prepares the apotheosis of the ballad, which cannot be expressed in words or song, in the orchestra, fortissimo, largaments.. "Fair Ilona" is a piece of history, a piece of the life of the rural people.

The Spinning Room is a large-scale folksong symphony created by blending together sonata, rondo, and variation form.

Galánta Dances

COMPOSITION:	completed in 1933.
FIRST PERFORMANCE:	Budapest, October 23, 1933, gala concert to mark the 80th anniversary of the founding of the Philharmonic Society Orchestra, conducted by Ernst von Dohnányi.
INSTRUMENTATION:	2 flutes (second flute doubling piccolo), 2 oboes, 2 clarinets, 2 bassoons, 4 horns, 2 trumpets, timpani, side drum, triangle, glockenspiel, strings.
DURATION:	15 minutes.
PUBLISHERS:	a) score: Universal Edition, Hawkes and Son (Boosey and Hawkes), Editio Musica Budapest,
	b) piano score (by Jenő Kenessey): Universal Edition, Editio Musica Budapest.

As a child Kodály lived in Galánta (today in Czechoslovakia) from the autumn of 1885 until the spring of 1892. There he acquired his earliest musical experiences: chamber music at home and folk-music impressions from the singing of serving maids and schoolmates. It was there also that the child was given his first real instrument, a cello. The memory of this remained fresh even until 1937, as borne out by the dedication in the first volume of *Bicinia Hungarica*: *I wrote these songs in memory of my school friends of Galánta, whose voices I still hear after the passing of fifty and more years.* And the preface to the score of the *Galánta Dances* (1934), which unfortunately has been omitted from some later editions, begins: *Galánta is a small ... market town known to travellers between Vienna and Budapest. The composer passed there seven years of his childhood.* It took, however, several decades for the orchestral work to be completed, decades spent in composition and folk-music collection as well as musicological research.

Kodály the philologist had an extremely strong sense of and interest in history throughout his adult life. This historical view was certainly not free of illusions whenever the picture of a unified, happy Hungary, undivided by social strata and untouched by the struggles of such strata, loomed from the past before his eyes. This past, which he imagined he had conjured up, was in fact a foreshadowing in his creative imagination of a picture of the future, as the reality of joy in sound. On the other hand, the activity of Kodály the scholar, exploring a multitude of facts and connections, led in all certainty objectively in the direction of the fullest possible acquaintance with the real facts of the past. It was in 1933, the year he concluded the *Galánta Dances*, that Kodály wrote in an article: *One cannot be a productive Hungarian composer unless one has incorporated and blossomed within oneself the still flourishing traditions, and then continues it after his own manner. One cannot be a productive music historian either unless the flourishing tradition runs in one's veins.* ("Néprajz és zenetörténet"—Ethnography and Musicology.)

The history of Hungarian dance music became for Kodály the researcher a living preoccupation in the 1920s. On April 26, 1925 he delivered a lecture, his first on a subject from music history, under the title "Old Hungarian Dances". He illustrated his discourse with a number of old dance tunes he himself had discovered. Certain details, for example, in *Háry János* such as the "Intermezzo" and the quotation from János Bihari in the middle section of the "Recruiting Song", were the result of his studies of the *verbunkos*.

Galánta was a noted centre of *verbunkos* music. In the preface to the *Galánta Dances* Kodály recalled his childhood memories: *There existed at that time a gypsy band which has since disappeared. Their music was the first 'orchestral sonority' which came to the ears of the child. The forebears of these gypsies were known more than a hundred years ago. In about 1800, some books of Hungarian dances were published in Vienna, one of which contained music 'after several gypsies from Galánta'. They have preserved the old Hungarian traditions. In order to continue it, the composer took his principal subjects from these ancient editions.*

It was not Kodály, but the eminent Hungarian musicologist Ervin Major, who in the spring of 1927 discovered a number of Viennese published scores that included the dance music of the Galánta gypsies. He showed the scores to Kodály in the summer of the same year, this being the earliest possible date when Kodály might have considered writing his *Galánta Dances*. The work was written for the 80th anniversary of the founding of the Budapest Philharmonic Society Orchestra, the longest-standing Hungarian symphony orchestra, and was first performed at the jubilee gala concert. Kodály's composing habits are wrapped in mystery, and one thus cannot tell when the plan of the composition first emerged.

The *Galánta Dances* commenced its international career in 1934, following the publication of the score. The conductor Heinrich Jalowetz, a pupil of Schoenberg, wrote appreciatively of the first publication of the score in Vienna: *I think this is a gift in which the orchestra may find pleasure. Kodály's invention springs so deeply from the soul of instruments that with him even the simplest musical phenomenon assumes a special sparkle. This is an exceptionally fresh and transparent orchestral texture, marked by the musical joy of sound and an absolute certainty of acoustical vision.* (*Musikblätter des Anbruch*, June 1934.)

The venue of the first performance abroad was London, where the work was performed on September 22, 1934 by the BBC orchestra conducted by Sir Henry Wood at one of the Promenade Concerts in Queen's Hall. It was soon taken up by a number of the noted conductors of the time, including Mengelberg in Holland, Ansermet in Switzerland and Eugene Ormandy, who was the first to conduct the work in the USA (with the Philadelphia Symphony Orchestra on December 11, 1936). The popularity of the piece is borne out by the nearly 30 recordings which have been made of it (under the batons of Vittorio de Sabata, Artur Rodzinsky, Ionel Perlea, Miltiades Caridis, Seiji Owawa, Antal Doráti, István Kertész, Eugene Ormandy, Sir George Solti and others). But the popularity of the *Galánta Dances* was not in harmony with its reception in professional circles.

The London performance was given a tense review by W. McN. (William McNaught Jr.) in *The Musical Times* (November,

1934): *Kodály's 'Galánta Dances' on September 22, were the kind of music that does and says very little in an expert way.* The June 1943 issue of *The Musical Times* dealt with the publication in London of a number of miniature scores of Bartók and Kodály: *Bartók is represented by the 'Divertimento for String Orchestra' and the 'Sonata for two pianos and percussion'* (3 s. 6 d. and 8 s.). *For the less forbidding Kodály there is a set of 'Galánta Dances' (6 s.).* (The prices have been given merely to show the costs of music publishing fifty years ago.) The *Music Review* carried Gerald Abraham's review of the publication (February 1943): *The Kodály work written eight years ago ... is already fairly familiar; a brilliant orchestration of a suite of Hungarian gypsy dance-tunes, it has little substance.*

After the first performance of the work in the United States, conducted by Eugene Ormandy, the Philadelphia paper *The Evening Bulletin* wrote in an unsigned article: *Kodály's 'Galánta Dances' ... contributed a measure of revelation. The distinguished Hungarian is known to orchestral audiences chiefly by the suite from his opera 'Háry János' which is fairly representative of the kind of work done by Kodály and Bartók in making a distinction between folk music and gypsy music. It was a little surprising then to find in the 'Galánta Dances' a suite which stylizes gypsy music, or at least the gypsy orchestra much as the earlier suite stylized the folksong. The new work is the less even of the two but it is also the more brilliant. It is slow getting under way, and the introductory passages include some conventional music of the type one hardly expects from Kodály, but once warmed to its subject the composition plunges into an orchestral extravaganza of stunning brilliance which outdoes even Liszt, at least in virtuosity.*

The Philadelphia critic clearly misunderstood Kodály's account of the origin of the melodies in the *Galánta Dances*. This noble, popular instrumental art music, bearing a close relationship to Hungarian folk music, has nothing to do with the shallow gypsy music which the world has come to know from the 19th century onwards, and against which Bartók and Kodály waged a justified war.

The *Galánta Dances* is entertaining, bright divertimento music. The work belongs to the extensive group of those written in great numbers in the 1920s and 1930s by Hindemith, Honegger,

Milhaud, Respighi and many others, though employing widely different means. The tone of dance music from different ages found its way in many different forms into their suites. Even so, the differences evinced by the *Galánta Dances* from these are more conspicuous than any superficial similarities.

There is not the acerbity of Hindemith or Milhaud. The handling of the material and its arrangement are also widely different from the archaicizing intentions of Respighi, who otherwise seems the closest to it. In Kodály's hands the Galánta melodies undergo profound changes, and are enriched by so great a surplus in the composition, that they eventually cast off their original garb of humble naivety.

The formal plan of the work right away includes a unique feature. Like the *Dances of Marosszék*, it is a rondo, but, quite unprecedentedly, the coda of this round dance is, regarding the number of bars, almost as long as the rondo itself, complete with introduction and containing two episodes. Another feature is that this lengthy coda consists of several musical layers, so practically forming an independent rondo within the overall large form.

The orchestration, using what at the time was considered a small orchestra, is akin to that of the *Dances of Marosszék*, but gives rise to a more latticed sound, with effects closer to chamber music. But beyond these differences in sound, the two works are linked by stronger threads than the similarity of orchestra —a related tone and historicizing approach, even though the material springs from quite different sources, the *Dances of Marosszék* using folk music, and the *Galánta Dances* consisting of pseudo-folk art music.

The slow introduction (Lento)—the only part of the work not drawn thematically from the popular *verbunkos* sources—opens the portals wide, like a majestically raised curtain, to the music of the Galánta gypsies. A heroic motif, and a rustling, mysterious melodic fragment, whirling in three superimposed parts, recalls the gesture of "The Tale Begins" from *Háry János*. The "Once upon a time" atmosphere of the tale is reinforced by the insubstantial hovering of the introductory music, with a composed rubato of constantly changing tempi. The heroic theme is eventually taken over by the solo clarinet, whose sound and colour are to dominate a large part of the rondo theme. At Bar 45, its improvisations end in a cadenza, and by way of symmetry to counterbalance the form, another clarinet cadenza is heard exactly 45 bars before the end of the work.

Kodály often drew attention to the vocal melodic roots of folk or pseudo-folk dance music. The folk-music equivalents of the characteristic rondo theme of the *Galánta Dances* have also come to light. The original pattern of the rondo theme is a taut fast moving piece in Presto tempo. The notes essentially tally with the central part of Kodály's melody, and much of the suggested harmony on the bass is also preserved. Yet the arrangement has travelled very far from its model, a completely new quality being created, because the composer takes the many possibilities of the highly developed *slow* section of the *verbunkos* dance from the *fast* rolling melody he has taken over. The rhythmic values of the melody are double of the original, the tempo indication is Andante Maestoso instead of the original Presto, and the rigid, almost scanned rhythm has become flexible, dissolved and varied. The descending bass, resembling a passacaglia, so much liked by Kodály, is more consistent in the orchestral work when compared with the model, at the same time becoming a vehicle for colourful harmony. In its composed form, the rondo theme presents the original melody in a fourfold retardation.

The rhythmic lilt of the melody creates a historical atmosphere, a rich set of variations being written practically around the metrical feet of the ceriambus (long-short-short-long), the favourite rhythm of 19th century Hungarian music. The sound of clarinet and strings is merely coloured by the full orchestra, serving perhaps to recreate the mood of "historic times", and conjure up the memory of the Galánta musicians. The complete rondo melody is heard twice, first on solo clarinet and then on the string and woodwind, the repeat of the second half of the melody leading into the first episode. When heard for the second time on the clarinet, the meditative melody assumes a glowing, heroic tone, with Kodály's characteristic performance direction appassionato. The same mood marks the return of the rondo theme too, the composer reserving the mood of meditation for the moment directly before the conclusion of the work, as a pause for retrospection, checking the intense whirl of the dance. It is thus primarily the appassionato character of the rondo theme which determines the form, although both repeats are increasingly varied.

The key of the first episode, in a moderate tempo (Allegretto moderato) brings a surprise, as it is heard in the downward pulling key of A flat minor, far removed from the main key of A. The melody is latent with several tonal interpretations, and the composer makes varied use of this element of variety. The dynamic shifts seem to outline nearby and distant images even within the melody, a contrast of languid expression and great dramatic power. With the orchestration too, Kodály creates a kind of stereophonic effect by making the melodic sections answer each other on different instruments and groups of instruments, thus increasing the "depth of field" of his simple material. To spice the metre, Kodály breaks up the regular four-quaver structure of the melody rotated in 2/4 time, by inserting "lame" steps of 1/4.

After the darkened main key, the second episode (Allegro con moto, grazioso) is in a bright D major. The orchestration is also bright (triangle, glockenspiel), and sparkle too comes from the violin and woodwind harmonies, which carry the melody. Here Kodály the composer receives an impulse from Kodály the ethnomusicologist, so that his arrangement turns the Galánta legacy into a bagpipe melody. The bagpipe character is intensified by the wind parts that surround the melody, and by fragmented figurations typical of the folk instrument, while the delicate play of accents lends a characteristic hovering quality to the whole section. Two animato sections break into this idyllic scene, the second leading into a short forceful stretto, and then to the most broadly developing version of the rondo theme. Its tremendous power is counterbalanced by its short duration, like a motto, while the tension loses its energy for a moment, preparing, as it were, for the huge closing section.

The large-scale coda is built out of six dance melodies. It is twice separated by slower sections, each resembling a trio, and a third time by the memory of a fragment of the rondo theme, as if to erect a monument to the famous instrumental virtuosity of the one-time gypsy musicians of Galánta. The strings and woodwind join the rapturous joy of the movement and swirl of the rhythmic play. The extremely high part of the first violins and the fast-moving material of the oboe face performers to the present day with a most delicate and difficult task. The quotation of a few ironic moments comments on and colours the collective joy of the dance, and a few characteristic grotesque orchestral devices, such as the effect of "bawling" horns, and the rhythmic and metrical effects of accentuation, together with the slotting of irregular, triple time into the fast passages in duple time—all lend extraordinary variety to the tense closing section. Both solos and tuttis seem to project a spectacle of virtuoso dancers, stepping out of the group and then returning to the collective celebration. When the tension of the tremendous dance tableau, offset by the grotesque elements, seems to have arrived at a climax so that the kinetic energy can be intensified no further, the rondo melody appears like a vision in the colours of the rainbow. Dissolved in improvisations, followed by a chain of clarinet trills, there arrives the very last dance (Allegro molto vivace—the fastest section of the work). The syncopated rhythm, which in different forms permeates the coda at many points, marks the ending of the dance vortex and of the composition, with an emphatic exclamation mark.

Te Deum

of Budavár

COMPOSITION:	1936 (Date of completion at the end of the printed score: July 10, 1936).
FIRST PERFORMANCE:	Budapest, September 2, 1936, Matthias (Coronation) Church in Buda Castle. Performers: Irén Ritter (soprano), Melanie Kisfaludy (contralto), István Laczó (tenor), Zsigmond Mezey (bass), Antal Várhelyi (organ), choir and orchestra of the Matthias Church, conducted by Viktor Sugár.
PERFORMERS:	soprano solo, tenor solo *(ad libitum* contralto and bass solos, may be sung by choir), mixed choir *(ad libitum)*.
INSTRUMENTS:	2 flutes, 2 oboes, 2 clarinets, 2 bassoons, 4 horns, 3 trumpets, 3 trombones, tuba, timpani, organ *(ad libitum)*, strings.
DURATION:	*c.* 22 minutes.
PUBLISHERS:	Universal Edition, Boosey and Hawkes.

Before 1945, Kodály wrote more large-scale works commissioned or inspired by noted foreign conductors and orchestras than for commissions from social and cultural bodies in Hungary. One of the few is the *Te Deum*, commissioned by Károly Szendy, the mayor of Budapest, for the 250th anniversary of the liberation of Buda Castle from Turkish rule; it was to form part of the ceremony held in the Matthias Church, officially called the Buda Castle Coronation Cathedral.

The date of the commission is not known, though the letter written by the choirmaster Viktor Sugár to Kodály in connection with the work on April 24, 1936 may serve as a clue:

Dear Professor,
Please forgive me for troubling you with these lines, to ask for an opportunity to consult briefly on the **Te Deum** *you are working on, which our choir and my humble self are looking forward to...*
Sugár refers to the fact that the mayor's letter of commission had been posted, and that Kodály must have received it meanwhile. He wrote that the work was one Kodály was "working on", but how long he had been working on it we do not exactly know. It is possible that at the time Kodály had already sketched the music, which he then used for the composition after receiving the commission. It is equally possible that the *Te Deum* was inspired by the commission. If the latter supposition is correct, then it would mean that the work was completed post-haste, as Kodály would have had less than three months at his disposal, the date marking the completion of the work in the score being July 10, 1936. Taking into account also the writing out of the parts, then there could have been little time left for rehearsals, since the work was premièred on September 2, as part of the large-scale ceremonial service.

After the première, the *Te Deum* was usually given as concert performances, even when the venue was a church, rather than as part of the divine service. The reason for this has presumably been that the work is too difficult for average or small church ensembles, and the forces required, including divided chorus and the necessary number of orchestral players, goes beyond the bounds of what is available. In the early 1950s the work was ousted temporarily from the concert hall in Hungary, and it returned to the Matthias Church, where it was kept alive in unforgettable white hot concert performances by Lajos Bárdos, from 1942 the successor to Viktor Sugár in the post of choirmaster.

The work was triumphantly successful throughout the world. The second performance after the première took place in London, on November 13, 1936, at a radio concert. The BBC choir and orchestra were conducted by Sir Adrian Boult. The venue for the first public performance abroad was also Britain, at the Three Choirs' Festival on September 9, 1937. Kodály conducted the work for the first time at this festival, where it was performed by the Festival Choir and the London Symphony Orchestra.

The most telling proof of the work's success is that it was performed again at the following year's Festival (Worcester, September 7, 1938, conducted by Ivor Atkins). It was very rare for the same work to be billed at the festival in two consecutive years. To follow the work's career in Britain, on November 29, 1938 the *Te Deum* was performed, together with the *Psalmus Hungaricus*, in Newcastle-upon-Tyne, and in the last year of the Second World War, on February 3, 1945, the work was given in Glasgow performed by the Scottish Orchestra and the Choral Union conducted by Wilfrid Senior. Characteristic of the appreciation given to the work in Britain was that the April 1941 issue of the periodical *Music and Letters* carried a lengthy analytical study by W. H. Mellers on the *Te Deum*, entitled "Kodály and the Christian Epic". As far as I know this was the first study by a non-Hungarian author devoted to a single Kodály opus, and not written on a given occasion (a concert or the publication of a score).

The *Te Deum* was fairly often performed in Hitler's Germany, from 1937 onwards, when Universal Edition, Kodály's Viennese publisher, obtained the work's publishing and distribution rights. And although after the annexation of Austria Kodály changed his publisher to Hawkes and Son in London (who incidentally obtained the copyright of the *Te Deum* in 1939 only for the British Empire and the American continent), his scores and part material at the Viennese firm fell prey to the fascists. In passing, it should be mentioned that Bartók's *Music for Strings, Percussion and Celesta* was performed nowhere more frequently during the composer's lifetime than in Germany (ten confirmable performances between 1937 and 1941), and this despite the fact the work was qualified by official Nazi music critics as "degenerate" music, and that in 1938 Bartók clashed openly with Nazi "copyright" laws.

In Switzerland the *Te Deum* was first performed in Zürich, in March 1938, with the Tonhalle Orchestra and the Zürich Teachers' Choral Society conducted by Ernst Kunst. The Hungarian Palestrina Choir, led by Viktor Vaszy, during its tour of Northern Europe in early 1938, performed the *Te Deum* in Estonia, Finland and Poland. In 1939 the same ensemble took the work to Italy, where they presented it on April 18 in Naples, and perhaps other towns as well. The venue of the first overseas performance was Chicago, where it was performed by the Swedish Choral Club and the Chicago Symphony on April 27, 1938; in New York it was conducted by Ernő Rappée on March 6, 1939; and in 1941 it was given by the Cleveland Symphony Orchestra conducted by György Széll. (Aside from these performances the work was not played by any other leading orchestra in the US, nor is there any information on as to whether Kodály conducted it during his American tour in 1946—1947.)

It would be impossible and pointless to try and list all the performances of the work in Hungary. Kodály conducted it himself on many occasions. On March 15, 1948, for example, he conducted the *Te Deum*, together with the Rákóczi March by Berlioz, at a gala concert in Budapest's National Theatre marking the anniversary of the 1848 Hungarian War of Independence. His choice seemed to suggest a relationship between the musical and dramatic promptings of the two works. The concert was of key significance, as it had been organized by the Hungarian National Committee, an organization of the political parties fighting for the country's democratic transformation, and both in its choice of programme and by having invited Kodály as the conductor, the committee openly documented that it considered the *Te Deum*, a work of sacred music, as belonging to the great line of Hungarian development, expressing an emotional range including the recapture of Buda Castle from the Turks, the independence struggles waged by Prince Rákóczi, the 1848 War of Independence, and the democratic construction of the country after 1945. The choice of programme expressed what the person of the folk-centered, democratic, patriotic Kodály signified in Hungary during the years following the country's liberation.

The *Te Deum* naturally also expresses the emotional world of religion. It was written practically as the central axis of a symmetrical chronological period covering three great works for choir and orchestra (if one accepts the date of the orchestrated *Missa brevis* as 1948): *Psalmus Hungaricus* 1923—*Te Deum* 1936—*Missa brevis* (orchestral version) 1948. Religious faith is present in the music of all three works, but in none is it the sole emotional factor.

In his splendid little volume, *Úton Kodályhoz* (The Path to Kodály), Bence Szabolcsi says: *While listening to a Mozart mass in Salzburg Cathedral in the summer 1924, I realized that though being a devout Catholic, Kodály's religiousness was essentially like that of Goethe and Erasmus: he was seeking with complete devotion and trust the humane God who dwells in human hearts. This happened at the time of the 'Psalmus', later he in all probability approached dogmatic religion more closely.* Szabolcsi's thesis is borne out by Kodály's works. Though being a devoted Catholic, he wrote a whole range of Protestant works for mixed choir, and also works for an anthology entitled *Jewish Folk Choruses*.

In the preface to this study already mentioned, W. H. Mellers compares the artistic characteristics of three Central European composers: Janáček, Bartók and Kodály. He states: *Of the three composers Kodály is undoubtedly the smallest and the simplest. In his work contemporaneity of sensibility has not often sought a violent outlet, but is implicit in a certain meditative introspection, a turning inwards which is not nostalgic in origin, so that one is not surprised to discover that this harmonic idiom, with its tranquil sevenths and ninths, has some kinship with that of Debussy. But his introspection is saved from over-subjectivity by the traditional folk-sense that gives to his melodies a distinctive ripeness and soaring plasticity of contour. His melody, a natural utterance of the human singing voice, with its rhythms and inflections moulded by the Hungarian language, has therefore much of the modal suppleness of folksongs, often with a pentatonic foundation... All his representative work is vocally and lyrically conceived, in the instrumental works particularly the piano pieces and string quartets, the folky inflections tend to degenerate into perfunctory and unconvincing rhapsody, the sevenths and ninths to become precious in a sense that is almost dilettante.*

After analysing the *Te Deum*, illustrating it with music examples, Mellers concludes: *What makes the 'Te Deum' so remarkable a composition is, I am inclined to think, its polyphonic texture which implies a clarification and in a sense a deepening of Kodály's emotional processes. In the largely homophonic 'Psalmus Hungaricus' Kodály seemed to have expressed consummately all that he had to say in his direct folk-founded technique, and it seemed to me unlikely that he could develop further along those lines. He would either have to stop composing, or to repeat himself, or to become relatively factitious, or to evolve a new manner. In view of the specialized nature of his musical upbringing the last of these alternatives seemed improbable, and many of the later choral works, not to mention the instrumental ones, did seem to betray a disturbingly synthetic quality. But in the 'Budavári Te Deum' Kodály, without sacrificing any of the spontaneity and passionate simplicity of his mode of experience, incarnates it in a polyphonic technique of surprising flexibility and power, and in so doing presents to us the essence of this experience with a lucidity and a depth that he had not, in the magnificently vital songs and the 'Psalmus Hungaricus' quite approached. The experience is not fundamentally more difficult or "profound", but its implications are more exhaustively realized. Its simplicity, more so even than the simplicity of the songs, is here its strength, and it is a serene smiling simplicity such as we shall look for in vain in almost all other contemporary music of anything approaching a comparable power. The earlier music of Vaughan Williams—to cite a local example that would appear to be broadly parallel—has none of Kodály's spontaneity because Vaughan Williams's achievement in an urbanized community inevitably betrays a degree of self-consciousness that Kodály had less need of ... Although Kodály may compose other music as good as the 'Te Deum', I doubt if he will write any better and I am pretty certain that he will have no successors. Because of, rather than in spite of, his technical fluency in the 'Budavári Te Deum' he is, in the history of European music, the last great naif.*

Mellers was justified in drawing attention to the differences in style and expression between the *Te Deum* and the *Psalmus Hungaricus*, which had become so popular in Britain too. He foresaw that Kodály's art would find no followers. Let me add though that there were all the more imitations, at least among Hungarian composers, although Kodály, who taught composers over several decades, never required his students to copy or imitate his style. His aims as an educator were to give a thorough grounding in professional knowledge.

At the turn of the 1950s and 1960s, it was in the possession of this knowledge acquired from Kodály that several of his former Hungarian students applied modern composing techniques so successfully.

Ever since the disintegration of the Baroque musical vernacular, composers have been hard put to write settings of the *Te Deum*, an ancient *vers libre* arranged in lines of varying length and built on varying rhythms. Kodály created a firm musical form for the loose chain of strophes by a chain of recapitulations, providing the pylons of a grid system freely related to sonata structure. The words "Buda Castle" (Budavári) in the title refer to a more profound context than the external occasion for the composition, and differ in meaning for instance from Handel's Utrecht or Dettingen Te Deums. This is expressed right away by the allusion to the Rákóczi March in the opening fanfare. (It is a generally known fact in Hungary what an inflammatory effect the Rákóczi March had at Berlioz's concert in Pest in 1846, and also that after the crushing of the 1848 Hungarian War of Independence, it was banned as a vehicle of rebellious, revolutionary ideas.) This deeper relationship is also expressed continually by scales in the instrumental parts derived from the Rákóczi March, and, further back in time, from the folksongs of the Hungarian freedom struggle of the turn of the 17th and 18th centuries, whose scales are also related to the march. The Rákóczi fanfare that opens the work is followed by a sizzling violin passage fashioned from the same folk-music scale that served as an unambiguous expression in the history of Hungarian music. A musical and at the same time social meaning is expressed by the trumpet which interprets the section beginning "Tu gloriosus". It may be considered a simple trumpet call, but in fact it outlines the opening of the Marseillaise, the anthem of the French revolution. Thus Kodály paints an aura of the Hungarian freedom struggles and the universal struggles for freedom around the ancient Latin text, setting the historical event of the recapture of Buda from the Turks to music, yet investing it with a broader social meaning.

This meaning is further intensified by the Hungarian peasant music, which never appears in literal quotations, but whose presence is distilled almost throughout, via the many instrumental figurations using the pentatonic scale, harmony based upon folk music practice, and particularly the fact that the Latin text is given Hungarian prosody. This too all makes the *Te Deum* a "Buda Castle" Te Deum.

Kodály tackles two contradictions (also providing their resolution) of which one alone would more than suffice as an artistic task: 1) the translation of the Latin text into Hungarian, and 2) the uniting of a modern variant of the advanced, dialectical European art-music form—a freely interpreted sonata structure—with the text of a hymn about one and a half thousand years older, in such a way that neither suffers. A synthesis of Europe and Asia, which a Hungarian analyst has described as the clash between the spirit of Byzantium and that of Cluny, is achieved along other channels too: through Kodály's polyphony rooted in tradition just as through the Renaissance overtones of more than one harmonic progression. He drew not only on the original sources of Palestrina and Lassus, but turned also to an intermediary in these mysterious harmonies, namely Franz Liszt. Handel can also be heard in the work, in the double counterpoint of "In te Domine speravi"—while the soaring Sanctus is virtually a quotation from Bach; we should compare it with the Sanctus of the *Mass in B minor*. Kodály had also studied the Te Deum in Verdi's *Quattro pezzi sacri*, and learned from it in his treatment of the text, and in the use of fanfares, though it was the transparent soprano solo at the end of the Verdi work ("In te Domine speravi") that most strongly influenced Kodály when setting the same words. The only actual quotation is the Gregorian chant for the section "Venerandum tuum verum", so as not to have completely obliterated the original purpose of the Te Deum. In contrast to the enlightened spirit of Cluny at the turn of the millennium, Kodály for a moment conjures up the dark maelstroms of Byzantium, of the Christianity of the Orient. The Oriental tone of the cry "Miserere nostri Domine" seems to refer to Mussorgsky and the roots of the music of the Russian giant.

The consistent use of the intervals of a fourth and a fifth runs through the work like a kind of monothematicism, (as nearly three decades later it was to run through the *Symphony*). This is brought out by the first entry of the chorus, the fugato of "Pleni sunt", the first appearance of the solo quartet ("Tu rex"), and particularly by the penultimate, and thus formally extremely accentuated passage ("Non confundar"), where diminished fourth and fifth harmonies are piled upon columns of perfect fourths in the bass.

The beginning of the Rákóczi March is quoted immediately at the opening of the work, its soaring, jubilant tone permeating choir and orchestra alike. A magically hovering Renaissance modal harmonic progression portrays the appearance of angels and cherubim, in a chain of images fluttering like angels' wings. The hovering triplets of the Sanctus are coloured by the infiltration of notes from the Rákóczi March. At the words "Pleni sunt coeli et terra, majestatis gloriae tuae" a tremendous fugato unfolds in D flat, far removed from the main key of A. The laudatory lines of the prophets are represented by another Renaissance chord progression from Kodály ("Tu gloriosus Apostolorum chorus"), with the melody of the Marseillaise reborn above it. A unison orchestral melody, engraved in steel and rising in unison from the depths, expresses unshakeable faith; above it the choir recalls the beginning of the work, rounding off the first major formal section.

The only Gregorian quotation in the work serves as a link, whose significance Kodály underlines by assigning it no instrumental accompaniment ("Venerendum tuum"). This section leads to the first Adagio ("Tu Rex gloriae"), accompanied by a majestic trochee rhythm. It is a performing tradition that this is sung by a vocal quartet, the score insisting only on a solo soprano, the other parts being assigned to the choir or soloists. With quickening tempo and a tremendous dynamic intensification the section leads to the return of the musical material of the Sanctus ("Tu ad dexteram Dei"); here for the first time the full vocal and instrumental ensemble sounds in unison (and treble forte). A long pause separates it from the second Adagio ("Tu ergo quaesumus"), which is an unusually exquisite moment in Kodály's choral art. The singing of the male choir has rather the effect of murmuring, chanted, rhythmicized speech, as the chords are scored narrow spaced. The male voices, rich in harmonies, practically smother the feeling of pitch.

The reappearance of the section recalling the Marseillaise, followed by the return of the confessing unison melody, prepares the real recapitulation (the "reverse" order of the return suggests a kind of a bridge structure). The trumpet appears once again, and call the Te Deum melody ("Per singulos dies"). The Renaissance chord progression that follows is enriched by a broadly soaring soprano and tenor solo, leading to the choral tableau of the Miserere. With its varied rhythmic articulation, the Miserere contains virtually no melodic element. The fugato of the first section returns, newly composed to words of hope and trust, and given animated instrumental counterpoint. In conclusion, as in the first section of the work, the fugato underlines the essential interval structure of the melody by piling up into compressed fourths. After the choir stops, Kodály, in preparation for the words "Non confundar in aeternum", creates a musical image unusual for him: he portrays "eternity" by a dodecaphonic tower of fourths rising from the depths, with a firm rhythm in half note-values (perhaps the only instance in Kodály where the whole note stock is used without repeating any of the notes). In the last moment, after rolling along all the 12 notes, the tower of fourths reveals its direction of movement, which is not along a straight line but in a circle that returns to its first interval. The perfect fourths are joined by a passage of augmented fourths and diminished fifths, chromatically descending by semitones, resulting in a very cutting sound, presumably to portray "humiliation".

Having come full circle, the *Te Deum* recalls the dramatic structure of the conclusion of the *Psalmus Hungaricus*, where, as in the *Te Deum*, the key switches from the main key of A minor to a radiant D major, and the choir changes to the emphatic expression of singing without words. Kodály, however, never repeated himself exactly, and the difference is that in the moment before the conclusion, it is the fugato theme that is transfigured. In a broadly unfolding unison (an effect appearing for the second time in the work) the music avows with great emphasis: "Non confundar in aeternum". Now only the echo of the "In aeternum" is left. The tender melody of the soprano solo seems to parallel in mood the solo in *Evening* for mixed choir (1904). Just as the melody of "When as King David..." dies away at the end of the *Psalmus Hungaricus*, so also does the fugato melody melt away here, resolving the dramatic, heroic colour of the key of A minor into a warm A major on pizzicato low strings.

The Peacock

Variations on a Hungarian Folksong

COMPOSITION:	1937–1939 (?).
FIRST PERFORMANCE:	Amsterdam, November 23, 1939, Concertgebouw Orchestra, conducted by Willem Mengelberg.
INSTRUMENTATION:	3 flutes, third doubling (piccolo), 2 oboes, second doubling (cor anglais), 2 clarinets, 2 bassoons, 4 horns, 3 trumpets, 3 trombones, timpani, triangle, cymbals, bell, harp, strings.
DURATION:	27 minutes.
PUBLISHERS:	Published by the composer, Boosey and Hawkes, Editio Musica Budapest

The melody, which is a four-row pentatonic, descending, isorhythmic song (i. e. containing the same number of syllables in each line) with a quintal shift (i. e. repeating down a fifth), is a prototype of the old style Hungarian folk music, yet was discovered by ethnomusicologists relatively late, in 1935, with the "peacock" text. Soon after its collection by Vilmos Seemayer, Bartók notated it down, and passed it on to Kodály. Variants of the "Peacock" melody, however, had been known much earlier. One was used by Bartók, who incorporated it into the finale of his *String Quartet No. 1*, completed in 1909, as a gesture representing self-revelation. The opera *Bluebeard's Castle* begins and ends with a version of the Peacock melody reduced to its very essence, and from it he also shaped one of the great climaxes of his ballet, *The Wooden Prince*. The melody thus looked back to important examples of its use in art music by the time Kodály, starting in 1937, began to make use of its possibilities in three forms (male chorus 1937, orchestral variations 1939, and No. 72 in Volume II of *Bicinia Hungarica* 1941).

In Hungary the folksong "Felszállott a páva" (The Peacock has flown) has become to represent liberty, national independence and rallying against fascism. On May 25, 1937, the Central Association of the Hungarian Workers' Choral Unions commissioned Kodály to compose a choral work for male choir in commemoration of the 30th anniversary of the Association's existence, which coincided with the 60th anniversary of the birth of Endre Ady, Hungary's greatest "progressive" poet (1877–1919). One of Ady's poems is a variation of the words of the folksong "The Peacock Has Flown" and Kodály amalgamated the words of the poem with the folksong. The Chorus had a double première: on November 13, 1937 it was performed at the Bartók-Kodály recital organized by the March Front, which symbolized the rally against fascism, and on December 12 it was heard at the jubilee concert for which it had been commissioned. The police during the inter-war years reacted sharply to the revolutionary message of the work, and censored the text, sometimes even preventing performance of the work.

The chorus, retracing Endre Ady's revolutionary poem practically to the primeval source of folk music, and the orchestral variations on the folksong, belong together conceptually and aesthetically, even showing kinship of form in so far as the male chorus is also a series of variations on the folksong, even if the treatment of the two differs greatly (the chorus has a "simpler" dramatic structure and the atmosphere of the opening returns as the conclusion, while the orchestral work is much more complex, and ends with a finale redolent of optimism and brilliance).

Like the chorus, the orchestral set of variations was written to a commission, this time for the Concertgebouw Orchestra of Amsterdam, which asked contemporary composers for works to commemorate the 50th anniversary of its founding. The commission was forwarded by Dr Rudolf Mengelberg, the nephew of the conductor, Willem Mengelberg, and the administrative and artistic manager of the orchestra. How the work came to be written can be traced in the correspondence of Kodály and Rudolf Mengelberg:

May 13, 1937: Kodály accepted the commission, promising the work for possibly the spring of the next year, but giving no details.

June 3, 1937: Mengelberg suggested March 31, 1938 as a date for the première.

January 29, 1938: ... *Looking through my sketches I still think I could complete a work in variation form about 15 minutes long by the given date.* This is the first mention by Kodály of the idea of a work with variations. When he wrote the sketches for the work, and whether he already had in mind variations on the Peacock melody are not known (though if he had, the sketches could have been written any time from 1935 onwards).

May 18, 1939: ...*Nearly three months have passed*, wrote Kodály, *since I presented the score to Prof. Mengelberg. His reply at the time was that a date would soon be set for the performance.* (Mengelberg conducted in Budapest on March 16, 1939.)

May 24, 1939: Rudolf Mengelberg wrote that the première was scheduled for October 12, 1939.

June 7, 1939: Mengelberg asked Kodály to write down the dedication of the work in ink ("Belated salutation for the 50th anniversary of the Concertgebouw Orchestra and its conductor Willem Mengelberg") so that it could be reproduced in the programme notes for the première.

June 21, 1938: Mengelberg informed Kodály that the première might take place in October.

August 9, 1939: Kodály: *Regarding the dedication, I would rather write it in Dutch, and I would be much obliged if you were so kind as to send me a proper Dutch version.* Mengelberg sent the translation, and the dedication, in Kodály's hand, was printed in Dutch in the programme notes of the première.

November 23, 1939: The conductor's telegram to Kodály on the day of the première: *At today's Concertgebouw concert I conducted the world première of your splendid variations which aroused great acclaim from both orchestra and audience. My orchestra joins me in thanking you sincerely for the complimentary dedication. In true friendship Willem Mengelberg.*

The first traces of the composition of the piece therefore appear in Kodály's letter of January 29, 1938. In the same letter he states his financial conditions: *Because of Professor Mengelberg, I would prefer just a formal fee.* The amount, 300 Dutch florins, was really a token amount, even when Kodály had the orchestral parts copied out at the orchestra's expense. From the

1920s onwards, Mengelberg had done much to popularize Kodály's works both in the Netherlands and the United States, as well as later in Hungary, and the friendly gesture on the part of the composer is fully understandable.

The first reaction to the première, two telegrams from London, came to Kodály's home. After the radio broadcast of the première in Holland, Ralph Hawkes, Kodály's new publisher in London, sent the following cable: *All of us deeply moved by your beautiful variations last night stop undoubtedly one of your finest works stop BBC wish to perform as soon as possible.* And Alfred Kalmus, a former staff member of Universal Edition, Kodály's former publishers in Vienna, who had emigrated to England, sent the following telegram: *Performance made wonderful impression heartiest congratulations awaiting reply and manuscript.* Nonetheless, the work was only broadcast by the BBC after the war (on February 27, 1946, conducted by Ernest Ansermet), and the manuscript did not reach London for quite some time.

The British public learned of Kodály's new orchestral piece soon after its première. The Hague correspondent of *The Times* wrote in an unsigned article on December 6, 1939: ... *Zoltán Kodály's 'Variations on a Hungarian Folksong' for orchestra is a work precisely suited to the Amsterdam players and to the taste of the Dutch public. Essentially modern in character, it yet has a suavity and freedom from more commonplace harmonic and orchestral problems which make it welcome to music-lovers as well as to the interpreters themselves. The construction is simple, consisting of a statement of the theme, followed by 16 variations in very varied manners, though in complete succession to the great classical examples. Its general principle is to contrast a polyphonic number with one in light dance rhythm or in a sentimental song style, in one case these latter forms being supplanted by a heavy-footed funeral march, which while entirely individual, yet reminds the listener of that of Beethoven in the* Eroica. *The finale is a brilliant movement, an apotheosis of the typical Hungarian theme, in which climax succeeds climax with thrilling effect...*

Under the pseudonym Resonator, Geoffrey Sharp referred two years later to the radio broadcast and the review in *The Times*, in the column entitled "The Musicians' Gallery. Concert Musical News and Comments" of the *Music Review* (August

1941): *...a large scale set of variations on a Hungarian folksong entitled* 'Fölszállott a páva' *(The Peacock has flown), composed as a tribute to the Concertgebouw Orchestra on the attainment of its jubilee, and first given under Mengelberg on 23rd November 1939. I was fortunate enough to hear the performance by wireless, and although the reception was imperfect, it was sufficient to convince me that this was one of Kodály's finest achievements.* A notice from the Hague correspondent of *The Times*, published a few days later, was also very favourable. *The theme, equally simple in contour and rhythm, is followed by sixteen cleverly contrasted variations embracing a wide emotional range. The work does not, perhaps, mark any new advance in Kodály's art, although it has all those indigenous qualities which have won for him a high international reputation. The orchestration, in particular, seemed very individual, and on more than one occasion the sheer beauty of sound and colour was such that it was a little difficult to keep the critical faculties focused on other important elements...*

The first Budapest performance, on the Hungarian Radio, was conducted by Kodály on December 29, 1941, and the first concert performance on February 7, 1942, was given under Mengelberg. In Berlin, the Philharmonic Orchestra played the work under the baton of Ernest Ansermet on February 2, 1942, and at the Zürich performance on February 22, 1942, the conductor of the Tonhalle Orchestra was Volkmar Andreae, a devoted champion of Kodály's music. After the Second World War, Kodály himself conducted his variations during his first visit to the United States (November 22 and 23, 1946 in Philadelphia, December 12 and 13 in Detroit, and December 19 in Chicago). By the 1970s, the work had been performed on 25 occasions by 27 eminent orchestras in the USA. Kodály also conducted performances of the work in Moscow and Leningrad in the spring of 1947, and in London on December 16, 1949, when he conducted the BBC Scottish Orchestra.

After March 1939, when Kodály presented the score to Mengelberg, the *Peacock Variations* underwent a fairly great number of changes (to collate these variants is the task of a future Kodály scholar, but it is still worthwhile mentioning them here, as they throw light on the minute care of the composer's working methods).

In comparison with the first draft, there were already changes in the photoprinted second score Kodály sent to Holland in the summer of 1939: ...*The dynamic and bowing marks are more precise*, Kodály wrote on August 9, and asked that these markings should be included in the first score too. *I still have not had the work printed, as first I should like to hear it*, Kodály wrote to Mengelberg on November 26, 1939, reproaching the conductor for not having notified him in advance about the date of the première, with the result that he had not heard the radio programme. As mentioned already, the set of variations was first heard in Budapest during a radio concert on December 29, 1941, conducted by the composer. It was presumably after this, when Kodály could hear how the work sounded, that he published the score at his own expense, although the date of copyright on the publication is 1941. The later printed versions also include alterations. A final form will have to take into consideration the score Kodály himself used for performances, as well as scores into which their owners wrote corrections at the composer's request.

When plans for a critical edition of Kodály's works come to fruition, then presumably they will involve travelling half the world to collect all the changes and improvements initiated by the composer, which survive in scores used by the performers, something not only true of the *Peacock Variations*. It is to be feared, however, that with the passage of time Kodály research will be too late, as most of the performers once in direct personal contact with the composer are far from young.

In a conversation with Lutz Besch, Kodály underlined the significance of variations. *A popular theme, the melody of a folksong, is completely unsuited for the higher forms. As long as one applies the melodies in their original shape, one must be content with forms which are not counter to them. Variation is the only form which leaves the folksong and its kernel untouched, which does not develop it any further, but rather reinforces it through all its variations—at least this was the opinion of the Masters, from Mozart to Beethoven. The length of the variation in most cases —and particularly in the case of Beethoven—exactly agrees, right up to the number of bars, with the original theme. Beethoven rarely went beyond this. Later freer variations have been written, in which the length has increased. But as long as variation remains variation, the theme cannot be further developed in compliance with the sonata principle, because the theme of a folksong would not at all be suited for this.*

In the period around 1938, variation form had for long been maturing in Kodály's music. His *Meditation* for piano on a Debussy theme (1907) employs the form, as do the finales of the *First String Quartet* (1909) and the *Capriccio* for solo cello (1915), while in a broader sense, the variation idea surfaces in very many places. But in those compositions which start out from a folksong, the melody preserves its original nature virtually as a *cantus firmus*, with the "subject" of variations being the art-music accompaniment which interprets the melody, giving greater depth to its expression, and so becoming its complete equal. From this latter requirement alone originate countless character variations, which develop from the folksong, or are set beside it.

The loose formal framework of the *Peacock Variations* consists of 16 variations with an introduction and a finale. Both the opening and the conclusion themselves in a form with variations are symmetrical, if not in the number of bars (78 bars as against 235), then in their duration, both lasting for about four and a half minutes. On paper the two statements of the original form of the "Peacock has flown" are also symmetrical. The composition consists of 710 bars, the folksong appearing first in the introduction (Bars 65–72), and then in the finale (Bars 633–640). In real time (considering the tempo changes) as well as dramatically, however, the two appearances of the folksong do not follow the principle of symmetry.

The Introduction (Moderato) brings a new dramaturgy as compared to the typical "high voltage" openings of Kodály's mature style. It is enough to recall the full intensity in the opening sections of the *Psalmus Hungaricus* or the *Te Deum*, or even the heated opening bars of the chamber works, each of which begins with a broad gesture, *in medias res*. It is true that *Summer Evening* begins in a meditative tone, and the Prelude "The Fairy Tale Begins" in the *Háry János Suite* is also of a resigned tone, but *Summer Evening* is an early work, and "The Fairy Tale Begins" is, in its original function in the opera, not an opening passage.

The introduction to the orchestral variations lets the listener experience the birth of the folksong. In the first bars the melody is heard from the low strings, virtually stripped of all ornament, and reduced to its essential notes. The pentatonic basis and dark colours of this opening inevitably recall the opening bars of Bartók's *Bluebeard's Castle*. In his earlier works, the *Psalmus Hungaricus* and the *Te Deum*, Kodály reserved this bare statement of the leading melody for the concluding effect. Here he follows a different path. The phrases are set off by a full bar's rest filled by a timpani roll, and this, as well as the bassoon-horn pedal which reinforces the first notes of the phrases, impresses on our minds the main key of D.

The folksong itself is put into 3/4, while the variations, as shown right away at the start, are marked by duple time (2/4 and 4/4), with triple time appearing in only a single variation, and at an extremely accentuated point in the finale—the apotheosis of the Peacock melody.

After the exposition of the folksong, the numb calm of the night scene resolves into an exquisite passage with a dialogue between clarinet and bassoon, in canon. (We encounter many canonic forms of construction in the course of the variation.) At this point, following the analysis of Ernő Lendvai's axis system, we still sense the main key, due to the long sustained roll of G sharp on the timpani. While the note indicating the tonality changes its meaning the melody flares up in another variation on the strings, growing constantly more fierce, and from the main key, a climactic ascent towards the dominant develops. The intonation here seems to refer to the passionate orchestral opening of the *Psalmus Hungaricus*, the composer employing the musical means familiar from the *Psalm* to ease the tension and restore, after a more animated section, the Moderato opening tempo. There now comes another harmonic surprise: the tension is eased by an interrupted cadence, and the orchestration and harmony surround with question marks the original Peacock melody, heard espressivo on solo oboe. The composer applies at once so many means to estrange the melody that its introduction reinforces the feeling of a beginning.

Thus the melody that serves as a basis for the great variation structure is presented in the introduction by variative means, and enclosed within a ternary form, the composer declaring by means of sound that the melodic and harmonic elements of the work are to derive from this single melody, or, more broadly, this melodic family.

The folksong is in a slow, relaxed tempo rubato, but the first ten variations develop their material by means of strict, fixed, mostly dance rhythms, gradually deviating meanwhile from the eight-bar structure of the folk melody. Variation 1 (Con brio) is a tense dialogue between string and answering wind, this section practically a parallel with the main theme of the *Concerto*. In Variation 2, in the same tempo, high, rolling wind chords span a frame around the composed rubato of a low melodic variation. Variation 3 unfolds passionately, with a somewhat more animated tempo, in which the answering technique presented so far thickens into a canon structure. Variations 4, 5 and 6, whose calmer (Poco calmato) plane surrounds a forceful (appassionato) dramatic outburst, belong in the chain of variations as an independent, rounded off middle section. Variation 7 moves farther away from the original melody, and by way of a new element, the lively music is separated by sharp dynamic changes. Variation 8, with its playful counterpoint, is even more graceful and jaunty, its lilt reminiscent of the *verbunkos*. After this dance-like series of images with a firm rhythm, Variation 9 lends the melody, now in a parlando rubato form, an ornate garb of wind embellishments. Prototypes of the melody can be found in Kodály's piano pieces and in the piano accompaniment to the *Hungarian Folk Music* cycle. The first large formal unit is closed by an *à la chinoise* character variation (No. 10, Molto vivo), the parts leading in strict parallels, and just as the first sound in the introduction was a D tremolo on the timpani, so too is the conclusion of this large formal unit indicated by a muffled timpani stroke on D. If we think in terms of a sonata structure (although Kodály's quoted comments exclude this as a possibility), the first ten variations could be interpreted as an exposition, or even a kind of opening movement, now to be followed by a slow movement.

The middle section of the work therefore constitutes a slow section made up of four variations. Variation 11, Andante espressivo, moves right away from the hitherto strongly emphasized key of D. Above the soft string chords—this section seems to refer back to *Summer Evening*—there hovers a nasal melody on the cor anglais, portraying a mirage-haunted, sultry landscape in a dialogue with clarinet, oboe and flute. This music turns the world of dreams, and the unreal into reality. The melody, expanding into counterpoint, flares up for a fleeting moment on the strings, and then the dialogue of the wind returns, its intensity decreasing to pianissimo. The great Adagio (Variation 12) rises out of this pianissimo; it outlines an arched domed structure, only to unfold again. The strings, with a broad rubato lilt, present a new variation of the folksong, now parlando, which is surrounded by a stretto, chromatic, threateningly dramatic accompaniment first in the horn section and then on trumpets tinged with flutes, conjuring up spectral shadows. At the climax hard glittering passages on the trombones join the process. Though differently presented, and naturally different in outline, still there here returns the effect of the complaining chorus in the *Psalmus Hungaricus*. This passage into devastation and emotional depths is followed, with dramaturgical consistency, by a funeral march (Variation 13, Tempo di Marcia funebre), a communal dirge after the individuals' lament. The ostinato rhythm of the march is impressed continuously on our ears by the bass instruments, indicating a steady tread of steps, while the ceaselessly changing shape of the crowd in procession is portrayed by the trombones, trumpets and large wind sections heard above the rhythm. (The violins and violas, as vehicles of scintillating effects, remain silent in the funeral march.) By the end of this stereoscopic musical picture, the procession disappears in the distance, and after two more firmly outlined variations, the imaginary slow movement of the work dissolves into a cadenza-like section (Variation 14, Andante poco rubato). This is the first point in the work where rubato features in the form of a performance indication written out in full. This series of improvisations with a floating-like effect is deeply rooted in Hungarian instrumental folk music, here assigned exclusively to the woodwind (the brass instruments having assumed the lead in the previous two variations). A broadly laid out flute cadenza is followed by solo woodwind runs softly interlaced like chain-stitches in embroidery, over an unobtrusive accompaniment of string tremolos embellished by harp runs. This is an infinitely tender, sensitive lyrical scene.

Out of the closing passage of the Andante there develops, as the sharpest imaginable contrast, the light, playful world of Variation 15. In an Allegro giocoso tempo, the variation displays a double facet, as if to suggest the proximity of the conclusion of the work, glancing both backwards and forwards. It seems to refer to the stylized "Chinese" tone of Variation 10 and the *verbunkos* overtones of Variation 8. While so far all the section ended alone, now the music virtually dashes into the fortissimo Maestoso last variation. This is the first moment in the work when the fortissimo applies to the whole orchestra; the vehement melody radiates a threatening, dramatic force, separated by the hard beating notes of the bass instruments, including the timpani. This volcanic outburst peters out in the same way that Kodály curbed the sweep of the rondo themes in the *Dances of Marosszék* and the *Galánta Dances*.

The sizes of the groups formed by the sixteen variations resemble a waning moon (ten-four-two); in terms of real time, the duration of the performance, the first two major units are more or less proportionate. The fact that for the third unit only two variations remain serves perhaps to allow adequate time for the many striking new effects of the Finale. The closing section (Vivace) in the first place presents a new Hungarian folk tune ("Az ürögi utca"—The Ürög Street, "Volt nekem egy kecském" —I had a goat), a controlled giusto variation of the rubato Peacock melody. But here the hand of the scholar who collects and categorizes folk music, researching the structural kinship of folksongs, is guided by the composer. For at first the new folksong is not heard in its original form, Kodály consistently turning by a few "degrees" the closing notes of the phases in various directions, laying special emphasis on these twisted phrase-endings in the orchestration. By so doing he opens up a well of humour in music, as also he does by accentuating unaccented beats, sending the music a strange, fleeting effect. The giusto folksong is not heard at all in full, only a few phrases summarizing Kodály's variative creative imagination. The characteristic effect of accents on unaccented beats leads to the apotheosis of the Peacock melody (Andante cantabile). The folksong, which appeared timorously in the introduction, almost stealthily, is now all light and brilliance, the melody tinged with gold from flute and harp. The rhythms of the accompanying woodwind parts, the effect of a headlong rush created by ties placed at accented points, is an oft-employed means of Kodály to express elevated ideas. The melody once again scatters through the refractor of improvisation (as if referring to Variation 14), and then, after the moment of fulfilment, the radiantly orchestrated, sweeping closing bars bring out the pentatonic essence of the folksong.

Concerto for Orchestra

COMPOSITION:	1939–1940.
FIRST PERFORMANCE:	Chicago, February 6 and 7, 1941, Chicago Symphony Orchestra, conducted by Frederick Stock.
INSTRUMENTATION:	3 flutes (third doubling piccolo), 2 oboes, 2 clarinets, 2 bassoons, 4 horns, 3 trumpets, 3 trombones, tuba, timpani, triangle, harp, strings.
DURATION:	19 minutes, as given in the score; 22 minutes 30 seconds in the Hungarian recording (HLX 90053/55) conducted by Kodály.
PUBLISHERS:	Boosey and Hawkes, Editio Musica Budapest.

The 50th anniversary of the founding of the Chicago Symphony Orchestra was celebrated during the 1940–41 season. Its leading conductor, the German-born Frederick Stock (1872–1942), spent an astonishingly long time, practically his whole career, with the orchestra. In 1895, the year he emigrated to the United States, he became a first-desk viola player, then between 1899 and 1903 he was assistant conductor, and from 1904 until his death, the leading musical director of what originally had been called the Thomas Orchestra, after its founding conductor, Theodore Thomas. In the early 1920s, the German Riemann Encyclopaedia described Stock as *one of the most eminent American conductors.* Yet his name, it seems, was not widely known in Europe; certainly I have not found any reference to a concert conducted by him in Europe in the 1920s and 1930s.

The orchestra desired to celebrate its anniversary in a way memorable to both members and audiences, and commissioned works to be dedicated to the ensemble by eminent composers.

The commissioned works included Darius Milhaud's *Symphony No. 1* (first performed on October 17, 1940, conducted by Fr. Stock), Igor Stravinsky's *Symphony in C major* (first performed on November 7, 1940, conducted by the composer), Nikolay Miaskovsky's *Symphony No. 21* (first performed on December 26, 1940, conducted by Fr. Stock) and William Walton's overture *Scapino* (first performed on April 13, 1941). Zoltán Kodály's *Concerto* formed part of this distinguished series.

One may ask why Kodály wrote a work for Frederick Stock and the Chicago Symphony. Financial considerations can be safely excluded, as Kodály was never guided by such considerations. The composer was probably aware of the little-known fact that Stock and his orchestra had played a very great part in popularizing his works in America. From 1928 onwards, they performed the *Háry János Suite* over seven seasons, and the *Dances of Marosszék* and the *Te Deum* on one occasion each. Thus in a certain sense Kodály expressed his gratitude in this form.

In November 1939, the Hungarian press carried reports of Frederick Stock's visit to Budapest, adding that the conductor had personally forwarded the Chicago Symphony's commission to Kodály. This, however, seems most improbable, as, according to the Chicago Symphony Orchestra's kind information given us June 25, 1982, Stock conducted his orchestra in Chicago on November 2, 3, 16, 17 and 30, 1939. Considering the rehearsal and travelling conditions of the time, he could scarcely have found time for a European tour. There is no trace in the contemporary press of Stock having conducted in Europe around that time, a possibility in any case ruled out by his engagement in Chicago. In his autobiography (*Notes sans musique*, 1949, 2nd ed. 1963) Darius Milhaud says of the summer of 1939: *I was called up by Voegeli, the manager of the Chicago Symphony Orchestra, who asked me on behalf of Frederick Stock to write a work for the 50th anniversary of the existence of the orchestra.* This must have been the route by which the commission reached Kodály too, since the 67-year-old conductor in all probability asked the orchestra's manager to contact more than just one composer. No correspondence concerning the *Concerto* has come down to us either in Kodály's legacy or in the archives of the

Chicago Symphony, so it is possible that such a correspondence did not exist between the orchestra and Kodály.

The exact date of the origin of the work is also uncertain. John S. Weissmann gives 1939 as the year of composition ("Kodály's Later Orchestral Music (1)", *Tempo*, No. 17, 1950), while according to László Eősze's recent research, Kodály embarked on the composition of this *Concerto* in the summer of 1940. Since Kodály put no date on his sketches, one cannot tell what earlier notes he based the work on. A Hungarian newspaper wrote on October 6, 1940: *Kodály is just completing the orchestration of his composition.* This must have been the last corrections to the score, which was taken to the United States by Bartók and his wife, who left Budapest on October 12, 1940. There is no document in the archives of the Chicago Symphony Orchestra concerning when and how the score reached Stock. In an article announcing the première, the Chicago daily, *The American*, only mentioned: *...Concerto for Grand Orchestra, which has but recently arrived from Budapest...* (February 2, 1941). Copies of the press material concerning the concert were sent to me on October 12, 1978, by Mrs Betsey Hitchcock, Public Relations Secretary of the Chicago Symphony, for whose kind assistance I here express my thanks.

The *Concerto* was first performed on February 6, 1941, in the Orchestra Hall of Chicago, and was repeated the following afternoon as part of a youth concert. I give the whole programme, as it sounds most unusual to today's concertgoer:

Cherubini 'Anacreon' [overture]; Debussy 'Three Nocturnes'; Strauss 'On the Shores of Sorrento' (from the symphonic poem 'Aus Italien'); [Vaughan] Williams: 'Magnificat' (for chorus, contralto and orchestra); Kodály 'Psalmus Hungaricus' (for chorus, tenor and orchestra) and 'Con.[certo] for grand orchestra'; Brahms 'Hungarian Dances'. (Chicago News, February 1, 1941). Soloists were Maurine Parzybok, contralto, Robert Topping, tenor, with the 170-member University of Chicago Choir, also celebrating the 50th anniversary of its foundation, whose choirmaster Mack Evans conducted Vaughan Williams's *Magnificat*, the other works being given under the baton of Frederick Stock.

It was the first performance in Chicago of the *Psalmus Hungaricus*, and to judge from the press reaction it did not serve to the advantage of the *Concerto* that in was performed in the same programme as Kodály's most significant work. Quoting from the local papers of February 7, 1941, in the *Journal of Commerce*, Claudia Cassidi wrote a lengthy review of the *Psalmus*, and devoted a single sentence to the new work written for the Chicago Symphony: *The Concerto is a little masterpiece of clean and logical scoring, bright in color and ingenious in development.* Edward Barry's article in the *Chicago Tribune* used superlatives for the *Psalmus Hungaricus*, but switched to less enthusiastic words when writing of the *Concerto: On first hearing the piece seems to display more of Kodály's brilliance and facility than of his gift for original and significant invention. However, this remark cannot in fairness be applied to the theme of the Largo.* In the *Chicago Times* Robert Pollack also enthused over the *Psalmus*, and added concerning the *Concerto: It turned out to be a capable piece of commission work by the eminent Hungarian who always has something to say even when he is not trying his hardest.* There was a single critic who judged the new work to be equal with the *Psalmus:* Eugene Stinson in the *Chicago News: The Kodály 'Concerto' is likewise a magnificent work, athletic in its thematic material and in the development of this material, a work of classical purity though of quite contemporary idiom. It is a superb addition to a repertoire in which the composer is known best by his amusing suite from 'Háry János'.* And an unsigned review, possibly by Herman Devries, in *The American* had more enthusiastic words for the *Concerto* than for the *Psalmus: The clou in the 'evening of first performances' was the Kodály 'Concerto for orchestra' . . . Mr. Kodály can tell much in a short space of time and though a modernist in trend, his latest inspiration is a gay and exhilarating succession of well patterned bits strung together cleverly to form a festive-like dedication, although apropos, for Dr. Stock and his men richly merit such a tribute from one of the world's celebrities in the creative symphonic field.*

The first European reaction to the work appeared in London in the August 1941 number of *The Music Review*, which carried a short report by Ernest Chapman, signing himself Resonator: *The . . . 'Concerto for orchestra' designed to exhibit the characteristics of the various instrumental groups and the abilities of the performers, the work is said to be of a vivacious and exhilarating nature*. From this it is clear that Chapman himself did not hear the work.

The far from unanimous reception the *Concerto* was given in Chicago (the passages above dealing with the *Concerto* have all been quoted in full) also influenced the later career of the work in the States. By 1970 only three of the country's 27 leading orchestras had included it in their programmes. The second overseas performance was conducted by Eugene Ormándy at a concert of the Philadelphia Symphony Orchestra in 1944. One might conjecture that the orchestra which had commissioned the work had reserved all rights for its performance over a long period of time. But if that was the case, the Chicago Symphony did not make use of this right, and did not even perform the work themselves again before 1970. And this was despite the fact that during the Second World War, Kodály's music was not boycotted in the United States, even when Horthy's Hungary considered itself at war with them (December 12, 1941). Even after this the most famous orchestras of the country continued to play the *Háry János Suite* and the *Galánta Dances*. (Even the fact that Kodály himself conducted the *Concerto* on several occasions during his first visit to the USA at the end of 1946 and the beginning of 1947, did not considerably add to the work's overseas popularity.)

The first Hungarian performance of the *Concerto* took place in Budapest, on February 6, 1943, when the Budapest City Orchestra was conducted by the composer. This was in fact the second performance of the work. The daily press expressed great enthusiasm for the music, whose first performance in Hungary coincided with the Kodály Year, commemorating the 60th birthday of the composer with events bringing hope and solace to Hungary during the years of war.

It is as though Kodály had reserved for himself the right to conduct the *Concerto*. (The score too appeared in the composer's own publication, in 1942, and was only put into circulation more than fifteen years later.) After the war, on October 5, 1946 Kodály conducted the BBC Orchestra in the first performance of the work in Britain. In 1947, during his first tour of the Soviet Union, he conducted the *Concerto* with the Moscow Radio Orchestra in the auditorium of the Tchaikovsky Conservatoire on May 26, and with the Philharmonic Orchestra in Leningrad in early June. In 1948 he conducted the work on April 7 in Stockholm, and on April 11 in Malmö, while on June 17 the Budapest Philharmonic Society Orchestra performed the work under the composer's baton in Vienna.

Apart from experience gained during his student years, Kodály made his début as a conductor in April 1927, when he conducted his *Psalmus Hungaricus* in Holland. Later he conducted his own works with growing frequency, and much later, approaching his 70th birthday, he still had the physical strength to undertake the strain even of an orchestral composer's evening. Three recordings of the composer enshrine his achievements as a conductor for posterity. They display a considerably slower tempo than he himself requested in his performing instructions, with an Italianate, cantabile shaping of the parts, particularly regarding the melodic instruments, showing his vocal demands in instrumental music.

Kodály may have undertaken to conduct the *Concerto* on so many occasions because conductors showed a fairly moderate interest in the work. Apart from a recording made in the German Democratic Republic, the piece has been recorded only by Hungarian conductors—Kodály, János Ferencsik, Eugene Ormandy, and later Antal Doráti (who conducted it on the set of records of the complete orchestral works of Kodály). To illustrate by comparison: according to a Kodály discography of 1974, the *Háry János Suite* had been released 26 different times, with conductors such as Toscanini, Mitropoulos, Rodzinski, Leinsdorf, Kempe, van Beinum, not to speak of the most prominent conductors of Hungarian origin.

It is also possible that the composer did not wish to part with the score of the *Concerto* because he did not consider the work to be finally complete. A "composer's edition" has the advantage of allowing for an undisturbed chiselling away at the work. (More than one of Kodály's works underwent significant changes, at least in nuance, between two publications.) The great many differences between the "composer's" score and the "publisher's" score show that Kodály did not rest content. To evaluate the changes will be the task of the editors of any future critical edition of Kodály's œuvre.

The *Concerto* is undoubtedly one of the rarely played Kodály works. There are several explanations for its restricted popularity. Its Hungarian peasant Baroque tone relegates it to one of the "Late Melodies", an unwritten Hungarian concerto grosso. It is a little belated in another sense too. It refers to Baroque kinetic and song-like qualities at a time when, around 1940, Neo-classicism—first introduced around the turn of the century by Busoni and Reger, and accomplished from the 1920s onwards by Stravinsky, Prokofiev and Hindemith, and later Bartók, who assimilated all its features—was already on the wane. The performance of the work also poses extremely high demands. If, instead of the performance duration marked in the score, the conductor takes the recording conducted by Kodály, which is nearly four minutes longer as the authentic, then this certainly will help loosen the taut outlines of the part-writing and soften the arch outlined by the overall form full of many meanings.

It was perhaps the occasion, the anniversary greeting to the Chicago orchestra, which gave rise to the basic tone of the *Concerto* becoming so sunny and cloudless, and lending the slow section such a personal tenor. We have seen in how many different ways the dreadful experiences of the First World War affected Kodály's chamber music. By 1940, after the outbreak of the Second World War and a time of growing fascism in Hungary, Kodály seemed deliberately to shut out the outside world while writing his *Concerto*. This becomes particularly striking if one thinks of the tragic, dramatic levels of the last works Bartók composed in Europe (the *Divertimento* and *String Quartet No. 6*). But one should not think that Kodály betrayed the ideals of his youth: during the war years he formulated in his choruses the same sentiments as Bartók in the above mentioned works.

The key of the composition is D, and the material, as if continuing the *Te Deum*, contains no folk music quotations, nor any rhythmic elements originating from folklore. But here the spirit of folk music has a stronger metastatic effect: the melodic and harmonic world of the *Concerto* is based on the pentatonic scale which, if expanded, turns in the direction of the Dorian, which features so frequently in Hungarian folk music. The quintal shift structure and linear arrangement of several leading melodies are also folk-music derived. The fundamental key of D itself promises a radiant orchestral sound (a radiance indeed noted by the Chicago critics), as in this tonality the string section can make most use of open strings.

The overall form of the *Concerto* is made up of five sections of differing lengths, following on without a break. The first large section has a strict Allegro risoluto tempo; its sinewy, flexible first subject theme recalls in its character the first of the orchestral *Peacock Variations*. This rhythmically much split up melody repeating down a fifth heads the work like a solid motto; its first half is presented by the string section in unison, the answering second half coming from the orchestra, complete with wind; this section is fuller in sound and is joined by a bass counterpoint, later assigned an independent role by functioning as a second subject theme. The melodic outline of the first subject has an open effect, as its rhythmic elements may branch off in many directions, each assuming independence, and developing in detail. The fast opening section combines the exposition-development-recapitulation scheme of sonata form with the solo-tutti principle of the Baroque concerto, and its technique of constantly developing the musical material. After the statement of the first subject, its first four notes are turned as it were into a flexible spring-board, to allow the organic development of the lively convoluting woodwind parts in a smooth motion. The first subject is also suitable, practically unaltered, as a bass melody, above which the violins develop one of the motifs of the theme. One can recognize in the whole texture Bach's instrumental treatment in the *Brandenburg Concerto No. 3*. This animated play is the alternation of solo and tutti in a concerto, and the transition leading to the second subject in sonata form. The horn section, till now used soloistically, now states the second subject shaped from the recently heard bass counterpoint; its syncopated rhythm, compared to the varying rhythmic world so far, seems even and calm. The battle alarm of trumpets answering each other refers to the Hungarian freedom struggles at the turn of the 17th and 18th centuries, while the scale on the violin that answers the trumpets (a combination of melodic minor and Aeolian mode) conjures up typical folk-music phrases of this heroic period of national rallying in Hungarian history—

without, of course, any direct folksong quotation. In Kodály's musical symbolism, the role of this historical intonation is not to suggest a nostalgia for the past, but to mobilize a national, democratic joining of forces, coming into existence at the time he wrote the work. The conclusion of the "exposition" is indicated by the first subject and the second subject mounted together, and the outlines of the sinewy melody which opened the movement, now reduced to its essence, sound forcefully in the timpani.

The "development" essentially takes the first subject and reveals ever new features from it, developing the many playful contrapuntal possibilities inherent in them. The "answering" play between the woodwind and the strings is joined by the trumpets, and then, at a climax marked marcatissimo, by the horns thematically.

Via a long sustained, diminuendo chord, diminishing also in its instrumentation, the music virtually uses a cinematographic technique, by "dissolving" without any pause into the following, Largo, slow movement. A suitable title might be aria con variazioni; it is a passacaglia form, its passionate and personal aria theme, vocal in origin and of an enthralling beauty, stated by the solo cello, being followed by 12 passacaglia type variations. This is not far removed from a Baroque conception, as Handel alone produced innumerable "aria con variazioni" in a passacaglia form. A major difference of course is that the development of the melody points towards character variations. The melody at its first appearance has a completely smooth rhythm, characteristically separated into sections internally each of which begins on an unaccented beat. It is this perhaps which lends, even within the even motion, such a sensitive, hovering effect to the melody. Although radically different in line and structure, in mood it is still a late successor to the slow tenor aria ("So in Jehovah...") from the *Psalmus Hungaricus*. At this juncture the harp is first heard in the work, this itself tending to support the analogy with the *Psalm*. The slow movement is a large-scale rubato, which is indicated not only by the great many shifts in tempo written out in full, but radiated also by every note of the music. This rubato, however, is much more sparing in its means than the similar sections in Kodály's chamber music. The variations are all heard in a richer, more animated form, becoming increasingly varied rhythmically. Economy of construction shows in the fact that, while the animated rhythm of the fast, first section that brings unity in variety is held in artistic balance by relatively simple harmonic means, here in the slow section, the rhythmic lilt, less diverse within tense variations, is expressed by an extraordinary abundance of harmony. During the course of the increasingly daring harmonic explorations of the variative development, the composer focuses on three increasingly forceful climaxes. The sound of the section which is rotated in accordance with its principal key, and a key signature of three sharps, is darkened by a whole range of flattened notes. As Lajos Bárdos, the eminent Hungarian analyst of Kodály's music, writes of this section: *The darker the background the more radiant the principal figure becomes in the foreground of the picture. Here too, there prevails a Rembrandt-like feature in Kodály's music.* The richly coloured last variations embellish the aria with the tiny ornaments of instrumental folk music, and the piccolo's rallentando melodic turn in the concluding moments resembles the conclusion of the *Peacock Variations*, dissolved and dying away in improvisation.

The musical material, bending low into pianissimo, is separated from, or rather linked together with the recapitulation of the fast opening section by a long rest. Here the triple sharp key signature of the slow movement still prevails, the elements of the first subject being heard with a reintegrating function, pianissimo, and in an abbreviated form. This leading back reaches up higher and higher both in its dynamics and in the direction of the melodic line, and then returns with an elementary power to arrive at the basic key of D. The whole first subject with a fugato structure now, as a new effect, rises from the dark depths towards light and strength in the heights. The composer inserts further concerto-grosso episodes, and the "1848 Hungarian War of Independence" scale is given a much stronger emphasis. The recapitulation as a whole too is much more contrapuntal than in the first, fast section, and so may in a certain sense be considered a development too. After the many calm strata of the slow movement, the even greater number of colours and great animation have a dramatic motive. After the return of the second subject and the trumpet call, the second of the principal theme is made even more radiant by the triangle, which here appears for the first time in the work. The joint emergence of the first subject and the second subject promises a final conclusion, which however is delayed by the return of the slow movement with further variations, enriched by completely new colours in the form of improvisations so far not yet employed. Does this perhaps mean that Kodály was recalling the slow ending of the *Sonata for Cello and Piano*? The way the composer lifts the ideas of the slow section into an apotheosis in both works does have a certain kinship. But he does not repeat his own formal *trouvaille* mechanically. In its final form the *Sonata* has a slow-fast arrangement, while the *Concerto* opens with a fast section, and the balance of form and sense of proportion thus call for a fast conclusion. Kodály keeps in store a surprise new message for the brief coda: the first subject built on a framework of a fifth and a fourth, now appears in the grating sound of diminished fifths; and whereas so far the incipit pointed downwards, here it is turned upwards, and stratified with more layers than before. After an accented rest, it is condensed into a motto that brings to an emphatic end the rich, concertante texture of parts.

Mass Versions

ORGAN MASS

COMPOSITION:	(?) 1942.
FIRST PERFORMANCE:	Budapest, 11. 30 a.m. low mass, at St Stephen's Basilica, May 7, 1944, organist: Sebestyén Pécsi.
DURATION:	*c.* 30 minutes.
PUBLISHERS:	Magyar Kórus, Budapest, Boosey and Hawkes.

MISSA BREVIS
(organ version)

COMPOSITION:	1942–1944.
FIRST PERFORMANCE:	Budapest, February 11, 1945, ground-floor cloak-room of the Opera House, Júlia Orosz, Lílian Birkás, Livia Dobay, Mária Budanovits, László Nagypál, Imre Palló, János Fodor, Oszkár Maleczky, Mihály Székely (vocalists), Gusztáv Oláh (harmonium), conductor: (?).
SCORED FOR:	soprano, mezzosoprano, contralto, tenor, bass solo, mixed choir, organ.
DURATION:	32 minutes.
PUBLISHERS:	Magyar Kórus, Budapest, Boosey and Hawkes.

MISSA BREVIS
(orchestral version)

ORCHESTRATION:	(?) 1948.
FIRST PERFORMANCE:	Worcester Cathedral, Three Choirs' Festival, September 9, 1948, conducted by: Zoltán Kodály, with the Festival Choir, London Philharmonic Orchestra, Isabel Baillie, Eva Mitchell, Mary Jarred, William Herbert, Norman Walker (vocalists).
INSTRUMENTATION:	3 flutes (third doubling piccolo), 2 oboes, 2 clarinets, 2 bassoons, 4 horns, 3 trumpets, 3 trombones, tuba, timpani, organ *(ad lib.)*, strings. Vocalists as in the organ version.
DURATION:	32 minutes.
PUBLISHERS:	Boosey and Hawkes, Editio Musica Budapest.

ORGANOEDIA AD MISSIM LECTAM
Revised version of the Organ Mass, with Sebestyén Pécsi's suggested registrations, edited by: Martin Hall.

REVISION:	1966.
DURATION:	unchanged.
PUBLISHER:	Boosey and Hawkes.

The background to the mass compositions stemmed from far back in the past: the works written by Kodály as a grammar-school student and since lost include details of a mass for mixed choir and organ dating from before 1898. The student Kodály was at home in the organ-loft of Nagyszombat Cathedral, where he studied the scores of many old works (including Beethoven's *Mass in C major* and Liszt's *Missa Solemnis, the "Gran Mass"*). We do not know whether he could and did play the organ of the cathedral during his secondary school years at Nagyszombat. In a letter of July 12, 1905 he wrote to his future wife, at the time studying composition with him, that "yesterday" he had played a short fantasia on the new organ of one of the churches at Nagyszombat, and that he would play the organ at a wedding in one of the villages he had visited during his folk-music collecting tours. A photograph from 1912 shows Kodály sitting at and playing the organ of a village church.

Anyway, his interest in the "king of instruments" was fairly modest at the time. Among his published compositions the organ first featured in the *Psalmus Hungaricus*. It is true that the three Bach chorale preludes which he transcribed for cello and piano around that time were originally organ pieces, but his first organ work, which for a long time remained the only one, was the *Prelude* that appeared in 1931. But the decade and a half that preceded the *Organ Mass* did contain choral works with organ accompaniment.

In 1930, however, Kodály came into contact with the mass as a musical form in two ways. On February 3, he conducted Beethoven's *Mass in C major* and one of J. S. Bach's cantatas (apart from an occasion during his student years at the Academy of Music, this was the only concert where Kodály conducted works by other composers). Also the same year Kodály was a jury member for a Hungarian competition for the composition of a mass. The first prize was awarded to Ernst von Dohnányi's *Missa in dedicatione ecclesiae*. It is perhaps not accidental that the motif repeated three times from Bar 39 onwards (true, only in accompanying function) in the Offertorium of the Dohnányi work is identical with the principal theme of Kodály's *Organ Mass* and *Missa brevis*.

In the autumn of 1937 Kodály was commissioned by the director of a Hungarian church choir to write a mass. After lengthy deliberation, he replied on February 6, 1938: *At the moment, so far as I can see, there is no mass and for the time being there will not be one*. His plans for the near future in other words included no mass composition.

Kodály's radio statement on June 26, 1944, throws light on the origin of the *Organ Mass*:

Reporter: What was your motivation in writing the organ mass?

Kodály: *Practical need. During a lengthy stay in the country, I was asked, for want of someone better, to accompany a low mass—on a harmonium. I was suddenly faced with the problem how to avoid the faults which I had observed in the past. Because when a low mass is celebrated without the singing of any chorus or folk hymn, the organist plays solo throughout the mass. This organ solo can be of two sorts: he either plays pieces he has selected in advance or improvises. In either case the music very rarely follows the passages of the mass to express, as far as possible, the contents of the liturgical texts. I wanted something like this, and instead of an improvisation I sketched up the various movements; out of these there developed, after a great many changes, the present form of the mass.*

These sketches in all probability were first seen by the schoolteacher and priest Alfonz Nádasy, who in his recollections of Kodály recounted a conversation with the composer, who had just returned from Galyatető to Budapest: *I asked him whether in the deep snow and bitter cold he had been able to go to the little mountain chapel. He handed me his obligatory notebook with music staves, and said: 'I became an assistant cantor, and this is what I wrote'. And the story went like this: due to the deep snow the cantor could not go up from the valley. So he phoned Professor Kodály and asked him to substitute for him at the mass. Typically of Kodály's mentality, he did not wish to improvise on the spur of the moment ('it is unworthy of the liturgy', he said while I was browsing through the notes). And so he made sketches for the passages of the mass.*

No date is given. When did all this take place? All the lists of Kodály's works date the *Organ Mass* as 1942, some of them also giving the month, April. But it is scarcely credible that on or around the composer's 60th birthday his latest, completed work would not have been performed. When the *Organ Mass* was published in Budapest in 1949, with the copyright dated 1947, the reviewer of the score noted, presumably correctly, that the work had been written in the summer of 1943 at Galyatető, Kodály's favourite holiday resort, where he had a permanent apartment at his disposal until his death. Kodály presumably continued to work on the *Organ Mass* even after its première, as it is quite out of the question that the Magyar Kórus publishers should have arbitrarily withheld the publication of the score until 1949. In fact the first edition bears the marks of the work having originated on the small harmonium of the Galyatető chapel. Instead of the three-staff notation customary for the organ, it appears notated on two staves, with the direction "pedal" featuring in a few places. (In all probability this made it necessary later to publish a revised edition of the work under the title *Organoedia*.)

In his radio statement Kodály went on to say: *I wished to closely follow the liturgy. On several occasions I measured the average duration of a low mass, so that the various musical movements, and the whole work, should tally, in time too, with the relevant places of the mass. It includes neither Gregorian nor folk-music elements ... In the various themes I have tried to convey not only the overall atmospheric character but also the rhythm of the text that cannot be heard. This involuntary endeavour led to a form in which the work, almost throughout, can be sung with text as well. With tiny and insignificant changes I could rework the purely instrumental mass for mixed choir and organ.*

During the siege of Budapest at the turn of 1944 and 1945, many eminent members of the Opera House company found refuge in the safe cellars of the Opera building, and, pursued by the fascists, Kodály and his wife also took shelter there. Fighting was still going on in part of Budapest when, on February 11, 1945, two days before the liberation of the whole capital, the organ version of the *Missa brevis* was first performed by a choir made up of the company's soloists, in one of the protected cloak-rooms of the Opera House. The supplication "Dona nobis pacem" (Give us peace) had an eerie timeliness when guns were still rumbling in Buda, on the opposite side of the Danube. Oszkár Maleczky, one of the participants in the première, recalled the notable event after 15 years: *There was a harmonium in the locksmith's workshop. Here we began the rehearsals. We were rehearsing Kodály's 'Missa brevis'. The members of the choir were all soloists ... The sound was surely not ideal—the way soloists would sing in choir.* According to our knowledge, this notable performance of the *Missa brevis* was the first world première in the musical history of the newly liberated country.

The first version of the *Missa brevis* with organ accompaniment was published by Magyar Kórus, in the late autumn of 1945. (In these difficult inflationary times it required no little

effort on the part of the publisher to have the typography and the printing made of 47 pages of music.) Kodály sent the score with a letter to George Enesco in Bucharest (March 12, 1946):
...As a token of my esteem, please accept a work of mine which has been published recently; it is a mass, which to a certain extent expresses the emotions we lived through during the war.

For quite some time this publication by Magyar Kórus provided the international distribution of the *Missa brevis* (Boosey and Hawkes first advertized the work in August 1947 among the firm's new publications), while the further career of the *Organ Mass* in manuscript form is not known.

On October 3, 1946, Kodály conducted the BBC choir with George Thalben-Ball at the organ, during the recording of the mass in London. Around the same time the work was also performed in Belfast by the Co-operative Society's Choir. *The Mass did not very strongly appeal*, W. R. Anderson wrote after having listened to the Belfast concert on the radio (*The Musical Times*, November 1946).

Kodály presented his mass himself in the United States, during his first American tour. He conducted the choir of the Covenant–First Presbyterian Church in Washington on January 26, 1947. The organist was Theodore Schaefer. Interestingly, instead of the five soloists indicated in the score, the performance was given with six soloists. An unsigned article in *The Washington Post* reviewed the work the day after the performance: *...Throughout the brief span of the mass, it gave recurring evidence of Kodály's outstanding gifts as a writer of fresh-sounding melody. Both in quiet moments as in the opening Kyrie and the Qui tollis of the Gloria, as well as in the stunning unison passage of the Creed, the melodic line was of remarkable purity, reminding the listener from time to time of the plain chant so often used in choral settings of these words.*

There were moments then, too, when one remembered that Kodály shared in a common ancestry with Franz Liszt. For in the great climactic episodes, such as the close of the Gloria, or the final peroration of the Creed, Kodály has employed harmonies which combine the broadcast romanticism with daring dissonances.

The Mass was soon heard in New York (Church of Saint Mary the Virgin, April 6, 1947) and Los Angeles (Cathedral Choir,

May 25, 1947). In London it was performed on April 21, 1948 in the Church of St Martin-in-the-Fields at a concert mounted by the Westminster Music Society, where Arnold Foster conducted the choir named after him.

The orchestral version of the Mass was first performed on September 9, 1948, at a Three Choirs' Festival in Worcester Cathedral, conducted by Kodály. *This work originally written for chorus and organ has been orchestrated and in part rewritten for the occasion, The Musical Times* reported in a preliminary article on the festival (August 1948). This means that the orchestration was made specially for this long-standing festival, which had played such a significant role in spreading Kodály's work in Britain.

The London *Times* carried an extremely warm report on the première in an unsigned article by the paper's music critic (September 10, 1948): *Kodály's* 'Missa Brevis' *made an immediate impression which will be felt beyond Worcester, for it is a work which, like* 'Psalmus Hungaricus' *at a former Three Choirs' Festival, will find favour with many choral societies and their audiences. It is an adaptation in which orchestra is added to the original organ accompaniment of a liturgical mass, and a final number* 'Ite Missa Est', *reiterates the prayer for peace of* 'Dona Nobis Pacem'. *The music is compact but effective in its every note, its idiom is original but unforced, it is graceful in its vocal and stimulating in its instrumental writing. The portions of the creed which have imaginative as well as doctrinal significance (*'Incarnatus' *for instance) once more stimulate a composer to music such as has never been heard before. In short, this mass though* 'brevis' *takes its place in the line of the great settings of that inexhaustible fount of inspiration.*

The Three Choirs' Festival once again performed the orchestral mass in September 1950, this time in Gloucester, and again with considerable acclaim.

Finally, by Kodály's old age, the mass reverted to its original form. In May and June 1966, the composer made a few corrections in the *Organ Mass*, which was then edited by Martin Hall, under the title *Organoedia ad missam lectam*. Since the original formulation included no independent pedal part, Hall transferred the pedal from the organ accompaniment of the *Missa brevis* (of course with the composer's consent) into the score of the *Organoedia*.

The last phase of the process that led from the *Organ Mass* to the *Organoedia*, is in fact a corrected, finalized version of the first phase, adapted for large organ. But each previous version interprets and explains the succeeding one. The *Missa brevis* for voice may guide as it were the performer of the *Organ Mass* as the interpretation of the compact organ chords is facilitated by the vocal score, which divides the material into parts. The orchestral version makes the division between the material of primary significance and the accompanying material even more unambiguous. And since the version for choir and organ includes no instructions for registration for the instrumentalist, the organist may best mix the colours of his instrument by studying the orchestral score. And the orchestral score may come in useful for choosing shadings even for a performance of *Organoedia*, which does include suggestions for registration.

The *Organ Mass—Organoedia* does not in fact completely tally with the vocal versions. In the vocal mass the Gloria and the Credo, with their lengthy texts, are longer by 20 and 12 bars respectively, which is obviously the reference in Kodály's statement: *With tiny and insignificant changes I could rework the purely instrumental mass for mixed choir and organ.* Certain parts of the text are fitted in by expanding the original material.

Apart from the customary repeats such as 'Dona' and 'Kyrie', Kodály said, *only one motif is repeated, the 'Qui tollis' section of the 'Agnus Dei', which tallied with the 'Qui tollis' section of the 'Gloria'.* The composer's own analysis, however, is not completely accurate. It was generally typical of Kodály that he did not reveal the structural and compositional secrets of his work. In each version, the Mass has two principal themes. One appears in the fugato of the Introitus, in the Kyrie and in the jubilant tone of the Gloria. The other theme is heard in the Credo, in the virile motif of Pleni sunt and the soft motif of the Benedictus. In the Sanctus the two melodies unite.

Kodály himself drew attention to the thematic relationship of the Agnus Dei. In the *Organoedia*, the return of the Kyrie is referred to by the instruction "Tempo di 'Kyrie'" at the proper place of the Agnus Dei. (In the scores of the vocal versions, at this point there only features the instruction "tempo", which is quite misleading, since the previous bars prescribe retardation, and the opening tempo of the Agnus is Adagio, the performer therefore being justified in thinking that the Kyrie theme has to be performed Adagio instead of the previous Andante.) "Ita missa est", which closes the mass, brings a tremendous apotheosis of the Credo melody, described above as the second principal theme.

The key to the Mass appears in the sentence in Kodály's letter to Enesco: ...*to a certain extent [it] expresses the emotions we lived through during the war*. The subtitle, *tempore belli*, also referred to this. It disappeared from later editions of the score, but can still be seen on the Magyar Kórus edition of 1945. The work indeed seems to explore the emotional territory—though not the melodiousness or formal procedures—of the mixed chorus entitled *Invocation* (1943) and the chorus *Wish for Peace—The Year 1801* (1953), naturally using the much more complex means of the mass. This is illustrated by Kodály's treatment of the text (together with the musical material for the accentuated sections of the text). In the Adagio middle section of the Gloria ("Qui tollis"), the entreaty *miserere* is emphasized by an extension of 16 bars, which, with its slow tempo, is immense; the word is lent special emphasis from the chromatically descending line of the tenor and bass solos (for Kodály a rare chromatic coloration). This expansion is not required so as to "make room for" the text, as there is enough room in the relevant bars in the *Organ Mass*; the solo tenor repeats six times the word *miserere*, each time emphasizing the meaning of the deep-seated invocation by dynamics that swell and diminish. At the opening of the Agnus Dei movement—at which point the Adagio of the Gloria returns—the familiar melody becomes enriched by a new bass like a deep sigh. With "Dona nobis pacem" the movement arrives at the climax. The sopranos repeat it three times: Give us peace, and the complete material of the Kyrie movement is recapitulated to the text of the "Dona nobis pacem", until the section, given a new conclusion and dying away pianissimo, falters in almost motionless rhythm: *pacem*. The closing "Ite missa est" features in two different guises in the score of the *Missa brevis* for organ and choir (as an alternative for the choir or, with the original organ version inscription). Perhaps it was assigned a text to extend the "Dona nobis pacem" in further musical variations. Variation is here to be taken literally, as the musical vehicle of the expression of the desire for the peace is a version of the towering chord which opens the work, while the conclusion quotes the Credo. (The first edition of the sung mass did not include the vocal version of the "Ite missa est".)

Each version of the mass consists of eight movements. It is framed by the twice used direction Maestoso, the tempo marking and even more the character indication of the Introitus and the "Ite missa est". An inner circle of symmetry is shown in the recapitulation of the Kyrie (second movement) in the Agnus Dei (7th movement), which, however, is not a mechanical symmetry, as the beginning of the Agnus comes from the Adagio middle section of the Gloria (third movement). The formal weight of the Credo, which is assigned a central role (4th movement), is indicated by its slow middle section being followed, before the recapitulation, by new musical material. A further sign of inner symmetry appears in the varied return of the Hosanna that closes the Sanctus (fifth movement) at the end of the Benedictus (sixth movement).

The eight movements, each with a title, can even so equally be considered as seven, the Introitus being followed attacca by the Kyrie, which would change this inner symmetry.

The Washington critic of the *Mass* had a sharp ear when he heard in it the influence of Liszt's harmony—suffice it to mention the ethereal Christe eleison chords in the Kyrie movement (indeed, a rich mine of Lisztian harmonic passages and modulations can be found in the score). The whole tonal order of the work consists of a series of wonderful meanderings, the way leading from the dark and hopeless D minor of the opening to the victorious D major of the conclusion (perambulating along D major in the soaring fanfares of the Gloria, and then in the Credo, whose D Mixolydian becomes revealed as G major only by the conclusion of the movement). By way of tonal symmetry, in the Adagio of the Credo the mystery of birth and crucifixion is painted by a dark E flat minor with a key signature of six flats, while the Benedictus is in F sharp major with a signature of six sharps, the sharpest key throughout the whole work.

The transparent, polyphonic texture of the work and the widely employed technique of word painting, refer to times centuries before Liszt, to Palestrina and the post-Palestrina period. The augmented *nota cambiata* turn of the Sanctus alone refers to Palestrina, and the manner of treatment of the motif emphatically emphasizes its origin. The musical imagery of the Renaissance and Baroque word-painting technique, of which Kodály's a cappella choruses provide countless examples, can also be found in the score of the mass. It is enough to mention the crackling rising passages in the resurrection scene of the Credo, or the rocking accompaniment in the Benedictus—"Blessed is he that cometh". (An early version is found in the closing section of the chorus *Evening* dating from 1904, and it recurs in many works of Kodály, including the mixed chorus *Annie Miller* of 1936; this lulling gesture in both choruses expresses the feeling of homecoming, which in the mass, tracing a course of sensitive associations, refers to the long-awaited moment of the arrival of peace.) This rocking harmony presumably found its way into Kodály's vocabulary from Bach's chorale arrangements.

The mass versions are without doubt of summarizing significance. The assimilated influences are musical by-words: Palestrina, Bach and Liszt. One of the work's reviewers claims to hear echoes of the Good-Friday music in Wagner's *Parsifal* in the "Qui tollis" section of the Credo. But the blood of great, collective melodiousness also circulates hidden in the mass, such as Gregorian chant and Hungarian folk music; and it is the spirit of these that the mass has assimilated into its style. And finally, the work is of a summing up significance as well in that it was with this *Missa brevis*—a work in fact far from "brevis"—that Kodály for the last time composed such a colossal formal design throughout in perfect harmony of technique, message, and artistic expression.

Symphony

COMPOSITION:	from the 1930s to 1961.
FIRST PERFORMANCE:	Luzern, August 16, 1961, Luzern Festival, Swiss Festival Orchestra, conducted by Ferenc Fricsay.
INSTRUMENTS:	3 flutes (third doubling piccolo), 2 oboes, 2 clarinets, 2 bassoons, 4 horns, 3 trumpets, 3 trombones, tuba, timpani, triangle, cymbals, strings.
DURATION:	30 minutes.
PUBLISHERS:	Boosey and Hawkes, Editio Musica Budapest.

In 1963 Denijs Dille recorded a conversation with Zoltán Kodály: *You ask me to tell you something about my Symphony*, Kodály said. *Everyone knows that our generation has written no symphonies. We believed the form to have become obsolete. Toscanini once mentioned to me that he was looking for a symphony, as he had already conducted all the existing symphonies. I could not recommend any unknown works except two symphonies by Volkmann. He asked me why I did not or did not wish to try my hand at a symphony. We had an argument; I said it was an obsolescent genre, and he replied that a genre cannot become obsolete if one is able to fill it with new and original content. One day, on my way home from my classes, I hit upon a symphonic idea so suddenly that I noted down the first bars on the tram ticket. Arriving home I sketched up the whole exposition of the first movement. But I could not continue with it in troubled times: the '40s and the war did not leave much calm for work. When... I received the Swiss commission, I was able to complete it. That's all. I leave it to others to judge whether the genre has become obsolete or not.*

In 1964 Kodály again recalled the origin of the *Symphony*, this time to Lutz Besch: *At the time I was teaching at the Academy of Music from three till seven. You may well imagine how four hours of teaching can be exhausting. Yet once it happened that when I left the Academy at seven—I had to take the underground on my way home—I had an idea while still on the way, and indeed it came to me so suddenly and stormily that, in my anxiety lest I forget it, I wrote down the first notes on the tram ticket. At the corner I had to get off—I usually walked the rest of the way—and as soon as I got home I sat down and wrote the whole exposition of the first movement of my symphony. I had to change nothing in it later. What is called the thematic work is a much mentioned and much cursed job not infrequently calling for some kind of patching up work, but if it is to be good, then everything must come of its own accord.* Kodály taught full-time at the Academy of Music until the 1939-40 academic year, and so his reference to "from three till seven" indicates that the idea of the first movement of the *Symphony* dates from the 1930s (Besch included the draft in his volume of interviews). The composer became acquainted with Toscanini in October 1928, and they met several times during the 1930s, so Toscanini may have encouraged Kodály to write a symphony any time after 1928. The draft, taken by Kodály as essentially the final one when composing the work, leads us to believe from its general tone that it dates from the second half of the 1930s. It is difficult to decide at this date whether Kodály really was hindered from completing the symphony by the confusion of the war years, as well, let us add, as by the many forms of public activity he undertook after 1945, or whether there was some other, possibly creative reason. It was after all during the war years that he wrote, alongside his large-scale a cappella choruses, both versions of the mass. In his book on Kodály (*Zoltán Kodály*, London, 1964) Percy M. Young writes guardedly: *After the end of the war further progress was made and by the early 1950's two movements were known to be completed.*

In the score, which appeared in print in February 1962, is written: *This symphony was commissioned by the members of the Swiss Festival Orchestra.* This unusual symphony orchestra is active for just one month a year, from mid-August until mid-

September, during the period of the Luzern Festival. It recruits its members for the occasion from various Swiss orchestras. It is also remarkable that this orchestra, which practically speaking does not exist, raised from its members the money for the commissioning of new works. At a press conference on August 16, 1961, the festival opening of that year, *Eric Guignard representing the Swiss Festival Orchestra, expressed his delight in connection with the world première of Kodály's Symphony. The work has been written as a commission from the orchestra. The musicians have set up a fund for composers, which in the future also will be used for new works.* (*Luzerner Neueste Nachrichten*, August 17, 1961.) The article goes on to say: *Zoltán Kodály's 'Symphony' should in fact have been performed in 1960, but the première had to be postponed*. Writing about the première, the critic of the *Luzerner Tagblatt* wrote: *The Swiss Festival Orchestra commissioned the Symphony two years ago from Zoltán Kodály, the elderly Hungarian composer ... In 1960 he was prevented by illness from completing the work.* (August 17, 1961.)

Kodály acknowledged the commission in a letter of December 30, 1959: ...*The commission communicated to me in your letter of December 8, is a great honour for me, and I am ready in principle (if I can still manage such a thing) to write a new work, with its world première to be held in Luzern.* At this time he as yet mentioned no particular form. Passing through Zürich in the spring of 1960, Kodály discussed the new work with Eric Guignard at the airport, at which time in all probability the *Symphony* was agreed upon.

The following year, on May 14, 1961, Kodály, on learning that the opening concert of the Luzern Festival had scheduled his *Háry János Suite*, to be conducted by Ferenc Fricsay, wrote to the organizer: ...*I have just learned ... that you have billed the Háry Suite with Fricsay for the preliminary Luzern programme. From this I am driven to conclude that you no longer count on me. The present situation is that, despite an unexpected illness and 3 months of hospital treatment, I have still reached the stage where the first and third movements of the symphony are absolutely complete, with the second still taking shape. Its duration will hardly surpass that of the H. Suite, and thus they could be exchanged forthwith. Fricsay will receive the score in time, and the part material, being prepared here, will also be ready in good time.* Kodály's telegram of June 10 announced the completion of all three movements: ... *three-movement symphony Allegro, Andante, attacca Vivo. Normal orchestra.* (The Luzern programme notes featured the final tempo marking of the slow movement, Andante moderato.)

Yehudi Menuhin, at the time in Budapest giving concerts, took a copy of the score of the first movement to Ferenc Fricsay on June 25, 1961. Fricsay acknowledged receipt of the score on July 7: *Many thanks for the first movement of the Symphony...* On July 18, Fricsay again wrote to Kodály: *I would like to tell you my first impressions of the 'Symphony', the first movement of which I have studied thoroughly: I think the movement is splendid ... Let me note that I have found a fair number of errors in the first movement...* This means Kodály had no time to correct the copied score. In the same letter Fricsay mentioned that he had received the second and third movements of the work as well.

But the work of composition was not finished when the score was despatched. The eminent scholar of Kodály's works, John S. Weissmann, writes about the composition: *It should ...be pointed out here that the final printed version departs from the first completed (autograph) version in a number of points. Certain corrections and modifications were entered after the first performance at Luzern.* ("Kodály's Symphony: A Morphological Study", *Tempo*, London, No. 60, Winter 1961-2.) A part of these corrections and modifications certainly concerned the elimination of the "errors" Fricsay had mentioned with some measure of reproach; others on the other hand may help divulge secrets from the psychology of Kodály's working methods. Knowing the *fact*—even if at present not the details—that there was subsequent polishing and improvement to a great many of his works, it seems certain that Kodály completely lacked the composer's pride that makes a fetish of each work one committed to paper, also lacking was the unshakeable faith that each note and performance direction he wrote down was final. Instead, he reacted sensitively to the experience of having his works, whether gained as a conductor or as a listener. This is also why he withheld professional publication of more than one of his works, sometimes for years, and made changes to certain details, even in scores brought out by his publishers as "scripta manent". An important difference occurs in the title, though apparently a mere formality; on the photostat autograph score seen by Weissmann it was still "Symphony in C major", while the reference to the key was omitted from the printed score, perhaps because in 1961 it might have seemed a little provocative. Stravinsky (not mentioned here for aesthetic comparisons) used the title *Symphony in C* a good twenty years earlier.

The noted musicologist Willi Reich, a critic and scholar of Schoenberg and Alban Berg, reviewed the première on August 18 in the most distinguished Swiss daily, the *Neue Zürcher Zeitung*: *What is principally splendid and outstanding in this three-movement symphony—whose musical idiom keeps consistently to the traditional tonal order—is a fortunate encounter of fresh melodiousness and strong emotional tension. The melodic world of the work is rooted partly in folk music, partly, however, in the traditions of Baroque music. This melodic world is marked by exquisite qualities which by now have almost become lost: there is something natural in Kodály's melodies, the way they gather headway and burst into blossom, and radiate human warmth, while their plasticity is not least provided by the rhythm in which it is embedded. And though the main themes, particularly at the beginning of movements, are wont to emphasize their lively strength and independence in a broadly soaring unison, in the course of the extraordinarily clearly disposed symphonic consummation they never give up their intimate relationship with expressive consonance. The transparent, pure orchestral sound, whose melodically rich achievement contains Romantic, and indeed at places Impressionistic features arranged with delicate sensitivity, serves as the essential vehicle, even at the climaxes, of both musical expression, and an always clearly arranged yet never schematic structure of the movements.*

The second performance of the *Symphony* was also conducted by Ferenc Fricsay, played by the London Philharmonic Orchestra in the Royal Festival Hall, on December 7, 1961. Eugene Ormandy wished to acquire the performing rights for the United States, but his suggestion came too late. On September 28, 1961 Kodály wrote to Ormandy: *Szell, who has just been in*

Switzerland, has already secured an option for the first American performance of the Symphony, I think for January ... I am sorry that Philadelph. will not be the first, if you had written just two weeks earlier, it would still have been possible... Thereupon, Ormandy never conducted the work. The actual first American performance was conducted by George Szell, heading the Cleveland Symphony Orchestra on January 4, 1962, who later also conducted the work in New York. Of the major overseas orchestras, the San Francisco and Seattle symphony orchestras billed the *Symphony* in the 1961–2 season, and the following season it was performed in Cincinnati, and in 1963–4, in Chicago. On July 25, 1965 it was conducted, in the presence of the composer, by Mario di Bonaventura at Dartmouth College, Hanover, in the United States. Among the sporadic performances in Europe, the one at the modern musical festival in Venice in the spring of 1962 stands out, where it was conducted by Bruno Maderna, the eminent avant-garde composer and conductor. On December 19, 1963 the work was performed, in Kodály's presence by the Moscow *State Symphony Orchestra* conducted by Konstantin Ivanov, in the auditorium of the Moscow Tchaikovsky Conservatoire.

The *Symphony* is one of Kodály's rarely played works, and has never won a steady place in the repertoire either in Hungary or abroad. The 30 years or so that have passed since the work's première are not a long time historically, yet in the accelerated rate of life of today, thirty years seem much more than the same time-span meant, for instance, in the 19th century. Thus the subsequent career of the *Symphony* and the reception it has been given seem to express a kind of judgement. Certainly the music was behind the times, however enthralling the youthful beauty of some of its moments may be. After all, around the time of the work's première, Hungarian composition—precisely partly as a result of the endeavours of many former students of Kodály—was abandoning a worn out style, searching for new international landmarks, and, as we know, not without avail. Who can know what the *Symphony* would have become if its first idea, sketched on a tram ticket, together with the draft put on paper immediately afterwards had been written as a finished work, there and then in the 1930s. It is perhaps an unwritten companion to Bartók's

Concerto, which was not however produced in due time, and after the passage of three decades could no longer be brought about.

Yet the *Symphony* belongs among Kodály's most tightly constructed overall forms. Perhaps the problematic character of the work lies precisely in the fact that in it—at least in the two fast outer movements (the slow movement being a different case)—construction at many points gains the upper hand over inspiration, the regular relationship outstripping the "irregularities" that raised Kodály's works, as unique and individual, above the cultivated school of "Kodályesque" music.

Practically all the thematic details in the two fast movements can be traced back to a single "primeval" interval: the fourth, and its inversion as a fifth, which appear either in the incipit or as the melodic climax. Thus the fast movements are related to each other variationally, while the slow, middle movement is a series of variations on a different, new theme, in which the "primeval" interval is also assigned a large role.

Leafing through the score one has the feeling of turning over the pages of a never-written autobiography, transformed into notes. The resigned tone of the first section of the second subject theme of the opening movement parallels the *Summer Evening*, as does even more so its closing theme in a distilled *verbunkos* rhythm. The second theme of the second subject group, reminiscent of Brahms, heard first on the clarinets in parallels of third and fourth intervals, and then on the first and second violins and violas, seems in both colour and character to recall an even older memory (according to one of Kodály's students, the composer considered Brahms a very significant composer). The principal horn theme of the finale is a late echo of the patriotic zeal of the early 20th century found in several of Bartók's early works, and also in his letters—and even in his Hungarian national costume. Kodály had earlier employed rather ironic versions of this theme, for instance in the music of "The Battle and Defeat of Napoleon" or the "Entrance of the Emperor and His Court" in *Háry János*. The thematic material of the closing movement in fact includes countless pseudo-folk popular music phrases and motifs, lurking practically everywhere, and which Kodály had previously used for the first and last time in his published works in the theme with variations of the closing movement of the *First String Quartet*.

Listening to the slow movement, one recognizes later chapters from this would-be autobiography. The organic structure—though not the tone and melodic line—of the theme with variations seems to refer to the melody of "When as King David..." in the *Psalmus Hungaricus*, while the elevated tone may refer to the aria "So in Jehovah"; the variations also recall memorable moments from the two dance rondos and the orchestral *Peacock Variations*. And the movement seems also to be of autobiographical inspiration in a more personal context. In Kodály's telegram of June 1961 the tempo marking was Andante, and by the première the final form was Andante moderato. It could equally well have been Andante religioso, not in the Beethovenian sense of Bartók's *Piano Concerto No. 3*, but rather as a moving farewell to Emma Sándor, the composer's first wife.

But this poetic dramaturgy does not lead inevitably to the literal heroic, dance-like finale, as realized by Kodály in so many different ways in the chamber music of his youth. This, it seems, was the experience that lost most of its ardour over the course of the passing decades, which is why the dancing merry-making, though intended to be unrestrained, sounds tired and drooping—the more so the more playful. But the soul did not weary; the variations in the single-theme finale are masterpieces of elaborate compositional technique, and only one who is closely familiar with the models will notice that at places the technique is an automatic-mechanic one.

To draw attention to the key of C major on the title page would have been superfluous, as the first 52 bars of the opening Allegro impress the tonality on the listener more sharply than any written words. This contains the genesis of the first subject, as well as the thematic material of the two fast movements. The melody rising out of the pianissimo string bass, branching off and growing richer in orchestration, is itself an elaborate variation. The timpani roll a long note C, then switch to a march rhythm, thus playing an important role in marking the sections (when a professor of composition, Kodály used to make his pupils engage in brain-teasing exercises, writing out rhythms). At the peak of the first subject a violent tonal duel ensues, and we witness the estrangement of C major before arriving at the double faceted transitional section developed from it (both elements are emphasized in the development section). The first theme of the second group, soft and of course espressivo, is stated by the flute, and prepared by a sharp contrast of hard, broken chords. The incipit of the first subject peeps constantly out of the melody of the "new" material. After the intimacy of the second, Brahmsian, theme of this group, the composer sums up the material heard after the first subject in a miniature development. Presented by the strings and taken over by the woodwind, the closing theme with its *verbunkos* lilt arrives like a distant dream image. It slowly dies away, until finally only its memory remains.

The lengthy exposition (191 bars) includes many sections of variation and elaboration, but it is followed by a surprisingly short development (88 bars, or 89 if one counts the long bar's rest that precedes the recapitulation). Dramatically the development is a contrast to the exposition: the greater the role played by the thematic material in the exposition, the more modest is its function here. The "gentle" parts of the form come to the fore, and a gradual build-up prepares for the recapitulation. Both emotionally and technically the development section fulfils less of the promises of the exposition than might have been expected. Its overall effect is as if Kodály, having carefully and consistently taken over his 1930s sketch of the exposition, had lost his bearings, or failed to rekindle the impression raised by the first idea which at the time had virtually stormed him. All the more surprising therefore are the many new varied elements in the recapitulation, and the emotional enrichment of the thematic material. Elements which at the beginning of the movement were heard simultaneously are presented in succession; at the same time there is condensation, with many details given an even more subjective colouring condensation shows in the recapitulation being nearly 40 bars shorter than the exposition. For example, the sound of the second theme of the second group resembles Brahms even more closely now, and the closing theme, entrusted to the horns instead of strings and woodwind, has an even stronger, *verbunkos* dance effect. The coda consists of a single, tremendous climax, marked off by great dynamic contrasts.

The middle section (Andante moderato), which was completed last, belongs justifiably among Kodály's finest, most personal pieces of slow music. Its purely pentatonic melody in 5/4 time, striking in its internal proportions, with an A-A-B-A structure, built moreover on G sharp, forms an enormous tonal contrast with the accented C major of the opening section. No such rounded melody linear in structure, turning back to itself, has been encountered so far in the work. The phrases are separated and commented upon by the horn; the first two are stated by the viola and cello, the second time with a richer, fuller sound (as even the same melodic section cannot signify the same thing twice). The newness of phrase B is underlined at the most emphatic point of the tiny form by being played—instead of on the strings—on the clarinet. The last phrase of the theme is played by the violins, accompanied for the first time by full harmony. The theme itself is among the very best achievements of Kodály's formal art—movingly simple, profound and pure (in this sense showing a kinship with the Andante religioso of Bartók's *Piano Concerto No. 3*).

The first variation, stated on the clarinet continued by the oboe and completed by the violin, is accompanied by the descending bass so frequently employed by Kodály, already suggested at the introduction of the theme; here, however, it descends chromatically, partly to underline the interval of a fourth that forms the nucleus of the symphony, and partly in anticipation of a more relaxed, improvisatory tone. The theme itself appears only fragmentarily. Phrase A of the melody is played by the woodwind, horns and violas in a broad unison, and then by the woodwind, violins and violas with a harmonized accompaniment. The melody, treated as a *cantus firmus*, is swathed first by violin trills and ornaments turning back on themselves, then secondly by bass instrument runs—bassoon and cello. In the central, third variation the melody is felt to be even more a *cantus firmus*; not only does it double the original in scale (5/2 after the 5/4 of the opening), laid out thus broadly sounding like a creed, but the contrapuntal texture, expanding in the woodwind from two parts to five, then returning to two parts on the lower strings, evokes memories of the great polyphonic period (the style of Frescobaldi, or that of the polyphonic masters of the Netherlands). The range of the broadly phrased melody is intensified by the sharply dotted rhythm of the counterpoint formed from it, and the contrast of writing the part with the quiet mood. Here, instead of the whole theme A-A-B-A, only *A* and *B* are heard. Phrase *B* winds down in a complex and extremely taut rhythm into Variation 4, whose ascending runs on the violin and viola include only the pentatonic essence of the melody, and lead into an expressive syncopated phrase typical of Kodály's early style. Meanwhile the theme itself appears in condensed form, its chromatic line descending in semitones—how unusual is this chromaticism for the diatonic Kodály!—giving the effect of choked sobbing. The sobs for a while break out in high flutes and violins, the gesture of one unable to check his sentiments any longer. The closing fifths variation comes to us completely unwound: the parting melody appears only in outline and far from in full, surrounded by cadenza-like wind embellishments. The descending cadenza of the clarinet is answered by the rising improvisation of the violins. The short dying away coda underlines the movement's pentatonic main key of G sharp-minor together with the interval of a fourth of the symphony as a whole. Two things make the listener aware of the movement's coming to an end: the music consists of slower rhythmic values than have been heard so far in the movement, and the tempo marking calls for a slowing down. One is about to yield to the concluding main key when Kodály, after a brief pause for breath and a pianissimo, simply moves by a semitone, in a mezzopiano dynamic, the chord that determines the slow movement's tonality. He does this with the laconic simplicity that on more than one occasion is found in Beethoven, and thus re-establishes C major, the main key of the whole work, and naturally of the finale (Vivo) that follows without a pause.

A sweeping gesture leading to the first subject merges the keys of the previous movement and the finale, the C major being still haunted by the minor pentatonic G sharp (though the accidentals are now not sharps but flats), but the first subject horn call removes all doubts. A sketch with the inscription *Symph. (Finale)*, in all probability dating from before the time Kodály noted down the slow movement (a facsimile is given by Percy M. Young in his book *Zoltán Kodály*, opposite page

161), does not include naturally the "seam" connecting the two movements, but does contain the most important thematic features of the finale. The playful, dance-like second subject and codetta suggest rather a rondo form, but in intention, the finale fills a sonata framework (the contradiction outlined above thus existing also between the material and the form). Although the thematic material shows obvious links, the overall effect still remains one of listing the melodies in succession rather than of their development, even though this successive line consists of many witty ideas, particularly rhythmically. Compared with the 213 bars of the exposition, the half as many bars (121) of the development again seem to indicate difficulties in developing the material, the same being suggested by the recapitulation with just 131 bars. The broken sweep of the far from unambiguous coda (46 bars) puts a full-stop—but no exclamation mark—to end the *Symphony*.

Songs

Four Songs for Voice and Piano

COMPOSITION: 1907–1917.
PUBLISHERS: Universal Edition, Boosey and Hawkes, Editio Musica Budapest.

16 Songs on Popular Words for Voice and Piano, op.1
("Énekszó")

COMPOSITION: 1907–1909.
PUBLISHERS: Rózsavölgyi Budapest, Editio Musica Budapest.

Two Songs for Voice and Orchestra, op.5
(also in piano score)

COMPOSITION: 1913–1916.
PUBLISHERS: Universal Edition, Boosey and Hawkes, Editio Musica Budapest.

Late Melodies, *op.6* (Seven Songs for Voice and Piano)

COMPOSITION: 1912–1916.
PUBLISHERS: Universal Edition, Boosey and Hawkes, Editio Musica Budapest.

Five Songs, *op.9* for Voice and Piano

COMPOSITION: 1915–1918.
PUBLISHERS: Universal Edition, Boosey and Hawkes, Editio Musica Budapest.

Three Songs, *op.14* for Voice and Piano
(Orchestrated version: Songs 1 and 3, 1929; Song 2, before 1947).

COMPOSITION: 1918–1923.
PUBLISHERS: Universal Edition, Boosey and Hawkes, Editio Musica Budapest.

Himfy Song for Voice and Piano

COMPOSITION: (?) 1925.
PUBLISHER: Editio Musica Budapest, 1982.

Epitaphium Joannis Hunyadi for Voice and Piano

COMPOSITION: 1965.
PUBLISHER: Editio Musica Budapest.

Like the chamber music, the songs belong among the early works of Kodály. His output shows a particular "crop rotation"; before 1923 his inborn vocal bent led him in the direction of the solo voice, during which time he wrote scarcely any choruses; then from 1923 onwards, he turned his attention to choruses and composed songs only exceptionally, on very rare occasions. Catalogues of Kodály's works, still far from complete, list six works for solo voice and piano or organ among his unpublished juvenilia, up until 1907. During his lifetime, Kodály published 38 songs all but one arranged in cycles. The unity of the six song cycles lies in their kinship of tone and atmosphere, and in some cases in the poems having been taken from the same period.

Nonetheless, they cannot strictly be considered self-contained sets of connected songs. Kodály said as much, when on March 27, 1965 he wrote to Benjamin Britten, who intended to devote the Aldeburgh Festival in June 1965, to performances of Kodály's works in sequence: *I am agreeably surprised to hear about Mr. Foldi. I suppose he will sing in Hungarian?... Since there is no cyklus (cycle) in op.6, he must not sing all, he can choose what is most suitable for him.* In the same letter Kodály mentioned that only one of *Two Songs*, op.5, would be heard at Aldeburgh. Performances of the songs, which were sporadic in the 1910s, but from the 1920s onwards grew in frequency, were marked by the programmes including for the most part only excerpts of what according to the printed scores formed cycles, and more than once in a different order from the one indicated in the score. (The dates of the premières of these songs, together with the names of the vocalists, have been omitted, as this data today cannot yet be reliably ascertained.)

The volumes of songs are not always uniform regarding register. Kodály notated the first six songs in *Late Melodies* and the last four songs in *Five Songs* in the treble clef, the remaining seventh and first songs, respectively, in the bass clef. The middle one of *Three Songs*, the first to be written, dating from 1918, was originally in C minor, and the composer transposed it subsequently into D minor, a note higher, so that it could be sung by tenor or soprano. Kodály never insisted rigidly on the register and pitch he had indicated. When Andrew Foldi was preparing to perform one of the *Two Songs* at the 1965 Aldeburgh Festival, Kodály, in his letter to Britten quoted above, wrote: *As to tessiture, he [Foldi] can freely transpose, if e.g. No 1 would be too deep.* "No. 1" meant the second song of *Two Songs*, entitled "Weeping", which requires a low bass. So Kodály's song cycles, despite their dramatic coherence, do not form strictly constructed cycles, in many cases reflecting rather publisher's considerations.

Kodály's songs are immeasurably significant in 20th century Hungarian vocal music. The natural stress and accentuation of the Hungarian language differs from that of European languages, yet poets used European metrical forms and feet. In his 50th birthday lecture Kodály said: *...here are the tragic consequences* *of the exaggerated cult of the iambus practised by our nineteenth-century poets. The iambus is an absolutely natural rhythm for the English language, less so for German, French and Italian—but it is diametrically opposed to the Hungarian language. And yet, in the nineteenth century our poets surrendered unconditionally to the iambus, with the results that innumerable masterpieces in our literature were irredeemably lost to music. János Arany* already claimed that it was impossible to write Hungarian tunes to iambuses and trochees, and that if we put them to music foreign melodies would emerge unless we used violence and ignored the iambus ... producing a very distorted rhythm... Those who nevertheless tried to compose Hungarian songs on a higher level were faced with almost insurmountable difficulties. The road was long; the form and treasured quality of the Hungarian folksong had to be discovered, and learnt; only then could one cautiously attempt to write a melody that did not conflict with the natural melodic line of the Hungarian language to a poem that was non-Hungarian in form... It was in a small village, where Berzsenyi's** name had not even been heard, that it became clear to me how Berzsenyi could be expressed in songs. (The Selected Writings of Zoltán Kodály, Corvina, 1976, pp. 212-4.)*

The problem sprang from the fact that in Hungarian speech and its resultant melody there is no stressed up-beat, whereas poets had made use of one. Kodály was well versed in this matter and in 1906 wrote his doctoral thesis under the title "The Verse Construction of the Hungarian Folksong". He studied the whole system of the correlation of notes and words in Hungarian folk music, and made use of it in his compositions, bringing about a Hungarian musical "translation" of Greek and Latin metrical forms. On a scholarly basis he elaborated an artistic Hungarian prosody in which not just the rhythm is the determining factor but the melody, harmony and dynamics—all the musical means of expression.

The song cycles are settings of folk poetry (op.1), and the

---

* János Arany (1817–1882) was a great Hungarian poet. Kodály set many of his poems, and edited Arany's folksong collection for the press.

** Dániel Berzsenyi (1795–1836) was an eminent Hungarian poet, many of whose poems were set by Kodály.

very best from among Hungarian lyrics of the 16th–20th centuries, in a certain sense offering a compendium of Hungarian literary history. Kodály set nine poems by his contemporaries and twelve by poets of earlier times (fourteen, if one includes the two songs not included in any of the cycles). His songs thus embrace the essence of the whole of Hungarian poetry, and for many decades they have served as models for Hungarian composers. Kodály wrote no songs to words by non-Hungarian poets *(Epitaphium Joannis Hunyadi* is a setting of a Latin poem by the Hungarian Renaissance poet, Janus Pannonius).

The titles of the cycles refer to the German Lied, the French mélodie, or simply say "song" ("ének"). Musically, Kodály blended the French chanson and mélodie and the German Romantic Lied with the tone of Hungarian folk music, regardless of the fact that none of his songs contain a single folk-music quotation. In the spring of 1907 the young composer, reared on German music, studied Debussy's vocal music in Paris *(Pelléas et Mélisande)*, the few scores he could afford to buy with his modest scholarship, including the French maestro's song cycle *Trois chansons de France*.

This notwithstanding, Kodály's synthesis has remained, just because of his choice of poems, of a mostly local, Hungarian significance. However artistically significant the songs, the fact that the poetry is little known beyond the borders of Hungary, and extremely difficult to translate into other languages, has not furthered their spread. Kodály was aware of this and accepted its consequences, saying on his 50th birthday: ...*music written to a Hungarian text—if it follows the natural intonation of the language—is virtually impossible to translate into a European language and furthermore the melodic line flowing from a Hungarian text will sound alien to the European. And here lies the explanation as to why artistic Hungarian songs have no audience. (The Selected Writings of Zoltán Kodály*, Corvina, 1976, p. 212.) In vain did Universal Edition publish Kodály's songs with a German translation, and the firm of Rózsavölgyi publish the op.1 cycle in 1923 with Cecil Gray's splendid English text; the songs have rarely been included on the repertoires of singers abroad, even after the great international breakthrough of the *Psalmus Hungaricus* in 1926, while performances by Hungarian singers abroad cause audiences linguistic difficulties.

In Britain, the eminent concert artist Dorothy Moulton sang songs by Kodály in London in the first half of the 1920s, as did the world famous American contralto Charles Cahier in the autumn of 1925. On June 14, 1926, Herbert Heyner performed excerpts from *Late Melodies* and from op.1 on Manchester Station radio. On May 3, 1939, Keith Falkner, who later became director of the Royal College of Music, sang all 16 songs of op.1 on the BBC. On October 5, 1926, the Hungarian Mária Basilides sang seven Kodály songs during the BBC cycle of International Concerts, in Grotrian Hall (today Wigmore Hall), London. *Though one could not understand her Magyar text, and the programme gave no help, the singing of some Kodály... songs by Madame Maria Basilides was full of interest*, Edwin Evans wrote in a review signed E.E. (*The Musical Times*, November 1926). On September 12, 1937, John McKenna presented the first and third of the *Three Songs*, with orchestral accompaniment, on the BBC. The BBC orchestra was conducted by Zoltán Kodály. This recording could be an extremely valuable document of the interpretation of Kodály's work as the only sound record of how the composer conceived the performance of his songs—if the recording has survived in the archives of the BBC. What was presumably the first performance abroad of *Two Songs* took place nearly 45 years after the work was written, on June 3, 1960, at a concert entitled "A Tribute to Kodály" in the Royal Festival Hall, London. Dietrich Fischer-Dieskau sang the cycle in Hungarian, with the London Symphony Orchestra conducted by Colin Davis.

Relatively little data has survived regarding performances of Kodály's songs in other countries. His orchestral and chamber music has been much more frequently performed.

Kodály's songs are strophic in structure, and he did not write any "through-composed" (non-repeating) songs. The form of the poem he selected for musical setting served as the basic principle and starting point for the musical shape, but the composition does more than simply follow the form and content of the poem joining word and note—it brings forth a new artistic quality. Kodály respects the poetic product, but not to the extent that he necessarily set it to music without any change. He omits some material, abridges certain sections, and transposes the stress by changing the punctuation. In other words, he composes in the original sense of the term, making the poetic text suitable to transmit his musical message.

The song also served as an experimental workshop for the young composer. He issued the first three pieces of *Four Songs* (without any opus number) dating from 1907, and in them the vocal part already follows the lilt of Hungarian folksong, while the harmony of the piano part is still conceived along Romantic lines. He experimented here with the personal tone of his dream lyrics, which became so characteristic of the music of the *First String Quartet* and the *Sonata for Cello and Piano*.

In the *16 Songs*, op.1, miniatures on gems of Hungarian folk love poetry, he experimented with harmonic, melodic and atmospheric contrasts. The melodic lilt taken from folksong and the spoken Hungarian language, follows exactly the rhythm and emotional undulation of the text. Kodály often changes the metre within the same song to convey the rhythm of the poem as closely as possible. The characteristic stylistic marks of the old layer of Hungarian folksong pervade both the vocal and piano part. When in 1923 this cycle appeared, with Cecil Gray's English text, it was given a brief, but friendly reception in *The Monthly Musical Record* (April 28, 1923): *The semi-miniature edition of these sixteen little songlets, artistically bound, size 8 inches by 5, at least supplies something which really looks pleasing in a singer's hand. The music is an elaboration of the direct folk style.*

Two Songs assumes a special significance as having been written with an orchestral setting; Kodály had written nothing for orchestra since his *Summer Evening*. In 1916, there was no likelihood at all of a performance of the work, and Kodály presumably wrote these orchestral songs under the influence of Gustav Mahler, whom he held in such high esteem, without counting on their performance in the near future. They were first performed on January 10, 1921, in Budapest. ...*these works* ... *represent important contributions to modern Hungarian music* ..., Bartók wrote in the New York paper *The Musical Courier* (March 31, 1921). Kodály here experimented with the sound of the modern full orchestra, in musical settings of the greatest gems from Hungarian lyrics. *Two Songs* conveys two different moods: the first piece, "The Approach of Winter", intensifies the elegiac tone of Dániel Berzsenyi's with a musical expression of resignation so typical of Kodály. The second song, "Weeping", amplifies in music the visions of one of the greatest figures of 20th century Hungarian poetry, Endre Ady.

At this juncture the path of Kodály the song composer branched off in two directions: in *Late Melodies* he set works by old poets, and in *Five Songs* poems by his contemporaries. Already in their titles, the seven songs warn the listener of their "lateness", no one before Kodály having managed to find an adequate musical form for these truly great lyrics. *Five Songs* includes a setting of two poems by Endre Ady, the great 20th century Hungarian poet, and three by a friend from Kodály's youth, Béla Balázs (1883–1949). Balázs wrote the librettos of two of Bartók's stage works (*Bluebeard's Castle* and *The Wooden Prince*), and Kodály's songs have an atmosphere akin to that of Bartók's opera. *Three Songs* is a musical constitution of 16th and 17th century Hungarian poetry, at the same time being an artistic sketch of the tenor solo in *Psalmus Hungaricus*, thus serving as an experiment. At the request of a Hungarian singer, Kodály orchestrated the first and third songs in 1929, while the orchestration of the middle piece presumably dates from the 1940s (it was first performed in November 1947).

In his rich selection of songs Kodály shows himself to be a master of setting subjective, passionate, confessional poetry. The many moods and differences of expression which go to make his series of chamber music works ended in 1920 so valuable were first tried out in the miniature form of song, and their result can be traced as far as the *Concerto* and the *Mass*. These songs brought something completely new to Hungarian music, as well as a new colour to European music, even if not apparently indicated by their subsequent career.

Bence Szabolcsi, the eminent Hungarian champion of Kodály, wrote with lasting validity about these songs: *Each sound in this music preserves the unwithering strength and undisturbed radiance of its first appearance: the triads and seventh chords possess in full their primary tension, and unfold imperturbably the full weight of their place and position; keys have still the effect of their first revelation; a chromatic passage still sustains all the early transport of 'youthful' chromaticism. This virtually magic quality bestows scores of very simple and yet utterly intensive means of elementary expression upon the composer. But it is primarily the determining pictorialness of the musical expression that helps Kodály to fully reveal this quality. (Musikblätter des Anbruch, Vienna, August–September 1927.)*

Choral Works

The most complete Hungarian edition of Zoltán Kodály's choral works so far (Editio Musica, Budapest, 1972, 2nd ed. 1982) contains altogether 147 works: 24 a cappella male choruses, 45 mixed choruses and 78 children's and women's choruses. If we discount the various versions, most of them written by Kodály himself, some by musicians close to him (nine choruses featuring in 27 different scores), the number of original works still remains 129. Eight choruses with instrumental accompaniment (organ or piano, two of them different versions) belong really among the a cappella choruses, and so the list of works in fact includes 137 original choral pieces. It is almost impossible to draw a line between Kodály's chorus types and his works of an educational purpose. After all, the 180 movements in the four volumes of *Bicinia Hungarica*, published between 1937 and 1942, differ neither in style nor in tone from the little two-part pieces among the children's choruses, nor do the 28 three-part exercises in sight-singing of *Tricinia* (1954) differ in tone from the women's choruses.

In many of his statements and articles Kodály asserted that to conceive vocally was practically inborn within him. This seems to be backed up by the catalogue of his works: the majority of his attempts at composition dating from his student years in Nagyszombat, partly lost and partly unpublished, were vocal solos or a combination of choir and some instrument. One of these, a "Stabat mater" for four-part male choir, was probably performed in the late 1890s. This at least seems to be indicated by the fact that a set of parts of the piece in Kodály's hand and several parts copied in a strange hand are preserved in the Nagyszombat archives.

In an interview recalling his composition studies in Budapest, Kodály referred to the stimulus he received at the Academy of

Music from his professor, the German Hans Koessler. *He (Koessler) was an excellent choral composer. Even though his own pieces were not really original, they were well set for chorus ... Koessler certainly played a great part in the fact that my liking for choral music ... has increased.*

This attraction of the young composer yielded relatively few works: altogether four a cappella choral pieces date from the decades prior to the *Psalmus Hungaricus*. The earliest, *The Evening* (1904) is a mixed chorus on a poem by the 19th century Hungarian poet Pál Gyulai. Exhibiting a surprisingly mature Kodály style, it was first performed only in 1931, the year it also appeared in print. The extremely difficult women's chorus of 1908, *Two Folksongs from Zobor*, was premièred in 1917, but it gained little popularity, although in the 1920s, it was published by Universal Edition. The women's chorus without words, *Nights in the Mountains I*, dates from 1923. *Two Choruses for Male Voices* (1913-17) to words by Hungarian poets, was published in Vienna, and first performed in Düsseldorf in the autumn of 1925. Hungarian choirs included the work in their repertoires from 1927-8 onwards, but have performed it very rarely.

Hungarian choirs therefore showed an extremely moderate interest in the works of Kodály, who at the time was still little known as a composer, while for the time being Kodály's own interest was not directed towards choirs. Between 1907 and 1923 his vocal bent showed itself in his nearly 40 songs with piano accompaniment to Hungarian poems, and the broadly cantabile melodies in his instrumental music.

Psalmus Hungaricus, the work which had a decisive effect on the composer's career, also saw the origin of Kodály's life-long relationship with choral music. Chance played its part in this too. In November 1924, the organ at the auditorium of the Budapest Academy of Music was being repaired, and could not be used for the December 1 performance of the *Psalmus Hungaricus*. Kodály decided to include a children's choir to support the women's choir and substitute for the organ, and this is how he came into contact with a Hungarian school choir, for which he soon after began writing a cappella compositions.

Kodály first went to England in November 1927, in connection with performances there of the *Psalmus*, returning in September

1928 to go to the Three Choirs' Festival in Gloucester, where he became acquainted with British choral art, which was much more highly developed than the Hungarian. In 1929, he summarized his first experiences, with a measure of idealism, in his article entitled "Children's Choirs": *Is there anything more demonstrative of social solidarity than a choir? Many people unite to do something that cannot be done by a single person alone however talented he or she may be; there the work of everyone is equally important and the mistake of a single person can spoil everything. I do not want to declare that the peerless solidarity of British society and the discipline of the British individual have been created by choirs. But there may be some connections between them and the six-hundred-year-old choral culture. In the same way as one of the reasons for the difference between British and Hungarian workman is that former sing and know Bach's B Minor Mass, too.* Also in 1929, in one of his writings, Kodály suggested that after the British model, a Hungarian Three Choirs' Festival should be established with the joint forces of three towns. The sight-reading ability of English choirs led Kodály to become acquainted with John Curwen's (1816–1880) relative solmization system called *Tonic Sol-fa*, which along with his colleagues, he soon applied to the Hungarian situation. The roots therefore of Kodály's music educational concept stem from Britain.

The choirmasters Kodály became acquainted with at the Three Choirs' Festival, Ivor Atkins, Herbert Sumsion and others, played a substantial part in the performance of Kodály's choruses in England. At the festival Kodály made the friendship of Edward Elgar and Ralph Vaughan Williams.

Kodály's first children's choruses, *The Straw Guy* and *See the Gipsy*, were first heard in Budapest, on April 2, 1925, signifying a decisive day in the composer's a cappella choral art. On May 11, Hubert Foss, head of the newly established music department of Oxford University Press, visited Budapest, and at the suggestion of Michel D. Calvocoressi, the publishers' musical adviser, discussed with Kodály the publication in England of works of his not yet contracted to other publishers. This is how many of Kodály's choral works came to be included, with English translations, in the O. U. P. catalogue.

W. R. A. (W. R. Anderson) reviewed the scores of the first Kodály choruses published in England (*The Musical Times*, June 1926): *Two Hungarian folk-songs have been arranged by Kodály for S.S.S.A. (Oxford University Press). Both are in dance-mood, with the 'snap' effect we hear, nearer home in Scots songs, and (in 'See the Gipsy') crush-notes that jump a third. The second sopranos divide for a few bars near the end of the 'Straw Guy'. The part-writing is straightforward. Lively minded singers can make these songs go with a swing.* Today we still have no exact picture of the spread of the children's choruses abroad. On November 12, 1932, Kodály was able to write to Imari Krohn, the eminent Finnish folk music researcher, concerning his children's choruses: *These are so successful abroad that 4,000 to 6,000 copies have been sold of them in Britain.*

In the 1930s, the British Radio played a major role in the popularization of Kodály's choruses. Almost twenty of them were broadcast performed by the Wireless Singers and the BBC Singers. Some of them were also recorded, conducted by Cyril Dalmaine, Trevor Harvey, Stanford Robinson and Leslie Woodgate. On January 12, 1936 Kodály conducted four of his works at a studio concert of which a recording was also made : *The Angels and the Shepherds*, the children's chorus *Whitsuntide*, the motet for mixed chorus entitled *Jesus and the Traders* and the mixed chorus *Pange Lingua*, with John Wills at the organ. This was the first occasion when Kodály conducted an a cappella chorus, and since in later years he very rarely had the opportunity of conducting a choir, it would be a most valuable document of Kodály's style for posterity, should the BBC archives have preserved these recordings.

In "Wireless Notes", his permanent column in *The Musical Times*, W. R. Anderson wrote: *Four choral pieces by Kodály showed attractively his fresh fancy. He has a kind of innocence that reminds me (in nature, not in being) of Boughton's. 'The Angels and the Shepherds' (for women voices) was prettily sung. This carol and 'Jesus and the Merchants' (sic), in which the Eastern idiom is appropriately keen, pleased me best of the four works sung on January 12. How badly we need some big choral writers... The boy singers (St. Alban the Martyr's Holborn. Congratulations to Mr. R. Goodall) were extremely good.* (February 1936.) The two mixed choruses were sung by the BBC Singers.

England in fact has been of marked significance in the spread of Kodály's choral works abroad. Otherwise, from the late 1920s onwards, Europe became acquainted with these choruses principally in the interpretation of Hungarian choirs. In the United States his choruses were in all probability first heard in January 1937, when the Budapest University Choir toured twenty cities there. But in England a great many choirs have undertaken the performance of Kodály's works. An explanation for this may be that the style and tone of the pieces were close in spirit to the English choral movement. Also we would not forget that the Hungarian texts have reached England in excellent English translation, which themselves must greatly have influenced the spread of the works, something which can hardly be said of the German translations. The children's choruses published by Oxford University Press were translated into English by Michel D. Calvocoressi and Elizabeth M. Lockwood. In the autumn of 1934 Kodály sent to Edward J. Dent the manuscript of *Jesus and the Traders*, a large-scale motet for mixed voice. The eminent professor of music at Cambridge thanked him in a letter of November 23, 1934: *I will try to make a good translation,* he wrote, and added he would look for English choirs to perform the motet. He succeeded in his efforts and many English choirs have included this very difficult piece in their programmes. The English text of the *Hymn to King Stephen*—the version for mixed choir—is the excellent work of Nancy Bush, wife of Alan Bush the composer. This was the first work of Kodály's published by his new English publisher, Boosey and Hawkes (Winthrop Rogers Edition, 1940). The noted composer Edmund Rubbra wrote of the *Hymn* in the April 1940 number of *Music and Letters*: *This work depends for its effect on a cultivated and imaginative use of modern diatonic methods rather than on originality of thought. The limiting cause may perhaps be attributed to the simple but starkly suggestive folk melody (I assume it to be that) which forms the basis of each verse of the setting. In any case, the singers will mentally bless the composer for keeping to the paths of diatonism, for it makes the work easy to perform.* For Kodály I think the greatest praise must have been that the reviewer thought, even if with reservations, the strophic melody of the chorus to be a folksong, when in fact, although it exhibits the stylistic marks of the classical proportion of folk music, it is the composer's own invention.

The 1960s marked the beginning of a new period in the career of Kodály's choral pieces, when Hungarian choirmasters spread out into the world and taught his works everywhere. From the foundation of the International Kodály Society in 1975 onwards, the national sections of the society have been popularizing Kodály's choruses from the USA to Japan.

In the overwhelming majority of his choruses, Kodály arranged poems by Hungarian poets, Hungarian folksongs, popular texts and folk hymns. Presumably as a result of the intimate relationship Kodály had developed with the English choral movement, in the last years of his life he set English poems as well. In 1959, he expressed his grief over the death of his first wife, who died in the previous year, in an arrangement for mixed voices of John Masefield's poem "I will Go Look for Death". In the same year he wrote a children's chorus for the *European Song Book* edited by the Countess of Harewood and Ronald Duncan. He set a few lines from Shakespeare's *The Merchant of Venice*, under the title *Tell Me Where is Fancy Bread!*. The same text was also set to music for the song book by Benjamin Britten, Francis Poulenc and Jury Saporin, thus giving rise to a kind of noble competition. In 1963 Kodály wrote a mixed chorus entitled *An Ode for Music* on the poems "The Passion" by William Collins and "Orpheus" by Shakespeare (also attributed to John Fletcher), with the following dedication: *Written as a greeting to the Tenth Cork International Choral Festival*. Finally I would also mention here *Laudes Organi* (1966), since, although to a Latin poem and scored with organ accompaniment, this chorus is the last completed work of Kodály, written to a commission from the Atlanta-based Association of American Organists.

When writing the huge series of his choruses, Kodály naturally did not intend to conquer the world with them. These works, alongside the choral movement which from the late 1920s onwards was developing in the wake of the compositions and organizing activity of Kodály's former students, served to establish a democratic musical culture the like of which had never before existed in Hungary. *We must lead great masses to music*, Kodály wrote in his study, "Children's Choirs" of 1929. *An instrumental culture can never become a culture of masses. ... The voices and sense of our young people are so excellent that they can perform to artistic perfection anything that fits their physical and spiritual development, however difficult the task may be.*

The Hungarian choral movement developed in the mid-19th century, but due to the country's historic and cultural position, it was modelled on Austro-German patterns, borrowing a musical repertoire of little value. A typical form of community singing was the four-part male chorus with piano accompaniment, while properly trained mixed choirs, suited to perform oratories as well, were still a rarity even by the mid-1920s. The gems of Renaissance vocal polyphony were practically unknown as were the great masterpieces of oratorio literature. The repertoire of the male choirs was shoddy musically and artistically, and the Hungarian translation of the German texts, in most cases without literary value anyway, was also unsolved. The European languages and their musical setting are marked by a iambic lilt, while Hungarian is characterized by the totally contrasting trochee, Hungarian folk poetry being accented instead of metrical.

A Hungarian musical prosody which fits the unaccented followed by accented syllable structure of the iambus, and generally every metric form, was created by Zoltán Kodály. Generalizing from his first experiences as an ethnomusicologist, he applied a scholarly approach to the question of the relationship between poem and music in his doctoral dissertation entitled "The Verse Construction of the Hungarian Folksong" (1906). And parallel with extending his work of collecting folksongs, between 1907 and 1923 he elaborated in no less than 37 songs the Hungarian musical lilt to fit the European metric forms employed by Hungarian poets. On his 50th birthday, Kodály related how he had happened upon a musical tone which matched the ancient Greek metric forms used by the Hungarian poet, Dániel Berzsenyi: *It was in a small village, where Berzsenyi's name had not even been heard, that it became clear to me how Berzsenyi could be expressed in songs*. And on the same occasion he emphasized: *... it becomes clear that, whether we like it or* *not, the idiom and imagery of our greatest poets are identical with the vocabulary of the country folk.* So we are indebted to the rare and fortunate encounter in one person of a literate arts graduate, folklorist and composer that music worthy of Hungarian poetry was brought about by Kodály.

Before 1923 Kodály realized his recognition in the representative musical genre of the song. Then, in the year of the composition of the *Psalmus Hungaricus*, he became acquainted with the Danish musicologist Knud Jeppesen's study on the style of Palestrina and Renaissance vocal polyphony, and applied the lessons of this work in his own choral output, which from 1925 onwards constantly grew.

Before Kodály's choruses, the repertoire in Hungary was typified by homophonic construction, so that the melody was sung by the top part with the rest supplying the accompaniment. Kodály, by employing the lessons of Renaissance music with artistic invention, gave an impetus to each part, and so made all the members of a choir musically interested in the performance. His 129 original a cappella choruses constitute a unique accomplishment in 20th century choral literature.

The distribution of the choruses according to the performers clearly reflects Kodály's artistic and educational intentions. Most of them, 78 pieces (together with authentic transcriptions), are scored for children's and women's choirs, that is for school use; the volume of mixed choruses includes, together with the transcriptions, 45 pieces, and the collection of male choruses comprises 24 works. (The transcriptions—for instance that of a children's chorus to mixed or male chorus—were done either by Kodály or composers closely connected with him, and so are in all cases authentic.) Kodály's attention gradually turned to all fields of choral culture: disregarding his early experiments, he wrote children's choruses from 1925 onwards, and from 1931 onwards he also composed for mixed voices, after 1934 for male choirs as well. The male choruses were spurred on by his recognition that although musical expression is much more accomplished when coming from a mixed choir, male choirs with their long-standing traditions cannot be reformed overnight, and as long as these choirs exist they must be supplied with a valuable repertoire.

The artistic aim of Kodály's choruses in no way differs from that of his instrumental works. In the choral pieces too, he fills the most highly developed European forms with Hungarian musical content; cross-fertilizing the style of Palestrina with an idiom reduced from Hungarian folk music or indeed with folk melodies themselves. Apart from its incontestable artistic value, this choral output, due to its democratic trend, is of tremendous significance in Hungarian culture as a whole. By developing choral culture, Kodály hoped to make musical culture and experience the property of the great masses of the people, the workers and peasants, who, as a consequence of their position, took no part in the concert and opera life of the 1920s and '30s.

The artistic aim and technique of the choruses scored for different voices are essentially the same, but there are great differences in the way they are realized, taking into consideration the characteristics of the age groups and other qualities of the choirs. There are considerable differences in the material used for musical setting; an important element of the composition lies in what was arranged for choir. The overwhelming majority of the children's choruses are arrangements of folksongs or folk texts. They include relatively few settings of poems. This is partly due to the fact that during the first decade and a half of the origin of the children's choruses Hungarian literature was very poor in good poems intended for children, and partly to the recognition that the emotional world of children is most faithfully expressed in the game songs they themselves have created. More than two thirds of the mixed choruses are settings of literary material, with a minor proportion consisting of arrangements of folksongs or melodies taken into communal use, for instance psalms. Most of the male choruses are settings of poems, and here folksong arrangements occur with relative rarity. At the time male choruses already included fairly valueless popular pieces considered folk-like, although in fact they had nothing to do with the real folksong, but these could not be ousted from the repertoire overnight.

Kodály wrote his first children's choruses at 43, with significant international successes behind him, and on the threshold of world fame. Nonetheless these pieces show no trace of the learned composer talking down to the naive emotional world of the child. Kodály retained the innocent playfulness of a child's mentality and the memories of a childhood spent in the village of Galánta, till the end of his life. He was justified in writing in 1937, in the preface to *Bicinia Hungarica*: *I wrote these songs in memory of my school friends of Galánta, whose voices I still hear after the passing of fifty and more years. I see you still, as you were when we were children: barefooted rascals, fighting among yourselves, throwing stones into the air, exploring the countryside for birds' eggs, but ever sturdy and fearless; and the girls—demure, and always busy at home. I remember your singing and your dancing, but where have you all gone?* He preserved in his memory all his many encounters during his folksong collecting tours with singing peasant children, passing their time with century-old games accompanied by songs.

The learned folklorist and the scholarly composer has left his mark upon these masterpieces of 20th century choral literature. One group of the children's choruses demonstrated, by uniting Christian and ancient pagan memories, how the games and songs of the village child preserved the main events of the ecclesiastical year (*New Year's Greeting*, 1929; *Epiphany*, 1933; *The Voice of Jesus*, 1927; *The Straw Guy*, bidding farewell to winter and welcoming spring, 1925; *St Gregory's Day*, 1926; *Whitsuntide*, 1929; *The Angels and the Shepherds, Advent, Christmas Dance of the Shepherds*, 1935). For Kodály—and this is true not only of his children's choruses—folk music and folk poetry signified raw material for composition, to be fashioned by the composer. A whole range of his choruses give their source as "folksong" or "after folksongs", so that he not only selected from the folklore material, but also shaped it.

Kodály applied an infinite abundance of playful forms in his choruses. Sometimes he arranged a folksong for two parts, as in the *Shepherd's Song* of 1927, so that, in the spirit of Palestrina, he constructed a counterpoint to the melody, which however is also a suitable counterpoint when inverted; sometimes he elaborated a dramatized scene through dialogue among the parts (*King Ladislas's Men*, 1927), suggesting the power of irrational magic; sometimes again he composed the mocking games of a child's imagination (e.g. *The Deaf Boatman*, 1928). *Whitsuntide* is a large-scale folksong symphony in four movements, arching from the uplifting festive sentiments of Pentecost to a folk ringdance. Kodály also makes use of the special effects of Hungarian instrumental folk music (*St Gregory's Day*, bagpipe, *The Swallow's Wooing*, 1929, shepherd's pipe, etc.). The choice of words also bespeaks an exact observation of childhood imagination. The child, when absorbed in playing often says nonsense, with no rational meaning, mostly distorting words and sentences heard from adults. Such texts feature in *God's Blacksmith*, *Gipsy Lament* (1928) and *Bunnykin* (1934). Sometimes the very title cannot be translated, as it is some playful, meaningless nonsense.

A considerable part of the children's choruses may also be sung by female voices. Similarly, the fairly limited group of female choruses can in most cases also be sung by children. An exception is the passionate love song in *Two Folksongs from Zobor* (1929), in the first piece of which (*Woe is Me*) the folksong is stated by solo vocalists, while the manifold divided chorus sings, without words, meandering melodic convolutions conceived in the spirit of Art Nouveau, still new at the beginning of the century. The cycle *Mountain Nights* without words (I, 1923, II–IV, 1955–6, V, 1962) projects magic nature pictures before the listener, expressing Kodály's attraction for undisturbed alpine landscapes. In their mood, these choruses parallel surprisingly with Piece No. 4, "The Night's Music" in Bartók's piano cycle of 1926, *Out of Doors*. *Four Italian Madrigals* (1931–2) are settings of 14th and 15th century poems, employing Classical vocal polyphony. The third piece of the cycle was meant as a "wedding present" for the daughter of Arturo Toscanini, whose wedding took place in January 1931 in Budapest. The last women's chorus (*Woe is Me*, 1957) uses the same folksong which Kodály had already arranged in 1908; now, half a century later, he recalled in it the unforgettable memory of his first folksong collecting tours. This late work brings an utterly different style, the "conservative" Kodály employing virtual clusters in his dense harmonies.

The artistic significance of Kodály's male choruses lies in that their contrapuntal structure dissolves the block-like rigidity typical of German-based pieces. The choice of texts is dominated by a desire for freedom and patriotic ideas. Of outstanding significance is the *Peacock*, which Kodály wrote in 1937 at the commission of the Society of Hungarian Workers' Choirs. The melody is the same folksong as in the orchestral *Peacock Variations*, and the text draws both on folklore and composed poetry. The chorus expresses the wish for freedom of the people suffering a millennial oppression. In 1944, one of the most tragic years in Hungarian history, Kodály expressed an emotional response to fascist terror in two male choruses—*The Son of an Enslaved Country* and *Still, by a Miracle, Our Country Stands*.

Of the mixed choruses *Mátra Pictures* is a relatively early work (1931). A vocal folksong "symphony" is as a folk ballad as its point of departure and, after an arrangement of lyrical songs, the work ends in a tempestuous dance scene. *Székely Lament* (1934) is a moving song of an exile, whose folksong Kodály also arranged for piano in the op.11 cycle of *Nine Piano Pieces*. *Annie Miller* (1936) is the dramatic arrangement of a Székely folk ballad; this masterpiece of Hungarian folk poetry shows a thematic kinship with medieval English folk ballads. The wish for freedom and patriotic sentiments permeate the mixed choruses too, from *To Ferenc Liszt* (1936) to the *Hymn of Zrínyi* (1954–5). During the years of the Second World War, Kodály expressed a bitter vision of the nation's death in his mixed choruses, and wrote choruses mobilizing antifascist rallying (*The Forgotten Song of Bálint Balassi*, 1942, *Invocation, To the Székelys*, 1943). His chorus *Wish for Peace* (1953) expresses the most universal human desire.

The motet for mixed voices *Jesus and the Traders* (1934) probably represents the climax of Kodály's choral art. In the perfect English translation by Edward J. Dent, the work has featured in the repertoire of many British choirs. The composition contains in a condensed form all the means of style and content Kodály employed in his choruses. He drew inspiration from Dürer's woodcut *Die Tempelreinigung*, which refers to the Gospel according to St John (2.13) and St Luke (19.45). Kodály only refers to St John as the source of his work (2.13), but in fact he drew motifs from all four Evangelists. Instead of the Bible translation in common use in Hungary, he used a translation dating from the 17th century, not sanctioned by later usage. But even this he merely considered as poetic raw material, and in the same way he often changed the words of poems in his settings, according to the requirements raised by the musical expression, so too he formulated the rhythmic prose of his chorus with a sovereign literary and musical sense.

The archaicizing opening (in Dent's translation: "As the feast approached / then Jesus went up and entered / into Jerusalem / and into the Temple") conjures up the atmosphere of biblical times. Kodály portrays the bustle of the traders in the temple with incredible pictorialness, employing the condensed means of Renaissance vocal polyphony. There follows a visionary fugato: "And when he made / a scourge of small cords / He drove them / all out of the Temple." Jesus speaks with a captivating lyrical expressiveness and infinite gentleness in Kodály's melody: "Is it not written. / My house shall be called / of all nations / the house of prayer, / What have ye made it? / A den of robbers!" Kodály repeats the phrase "robbers" no less than 20 times. As in the *Psalmus Hungaricus*, and so many other Kodály works, it is the Lord of the poor and the oppressed whose voice is heard here: "When the scribes and chief priests / heard Him, / then did they seek / to destroy Him, / they feared Him, / for that all the people / were very attentive / to hear Him." The last chord is heard fortissimo and then dies away pianissimo, indicating, as it were, that the real redemption and thriving of "all the people" heard here was a dream of the future in 1934.

*

In 1955, Kodály expressed the essence of his whole life-work when he recalled Béla Bartók and the work done by the two of them: *Around 1900 it was necessary for the Hungarian composer first to collect folksongs. . . . To begin with we looked only for the lost ancient melodies. But seeing the village people and the great talent and fresh life being left to perish there, we gained a new idea of a cultured Hungary born of the people. We devoted our lives to bringing this about.*

Biographical Survey

1882	November 16: Zoltán Kodály born in Kecskemét.
1890–1900	Attends secondary school at the Nagyszombat Archiepiscopal Upper Grammar School; first attempts at composition; instrumental studies.
1900	Studies composition at the National Ferenc Liszt Academy of Music, and Hungarian and German in the Faculty of Arts at Budapest University.
1903	First studies of Hungarian folk music at the Ethnographical Department of the National Museum from melodies recorded on phonograph cylinders.
1905	May: Kodály meets Béla Bartók, August: Kodály's first collecting tour of folksongs. (During his life he collected and categorized tens of thousands of folksongs.)
1906	February: Doctoral thesis entitled "The Verse Construction of Hungarian Folksong". October 22: first performance of *Summer Evening*, his final examination composition, in Budapest. December 19: Appearance of *Hungarian Folksongs*, a joint publication with Bartók. The preface, signed by the two composers, was written by Kodály, who also made the harmonization of Folksongs 11–20 in the volume.
1906–1907	Study tour to Berlin and Paris. Becomes acquainted with the music of Debussy.
1907	September: Professor of music theory at the Budapest Ferenc Liszt Academy of Music. From the autumn of 1908, teaches composition there.
1909	Composition of op.1 "Énekszó"—*16 Songs on Hungarian Popular Words* (in 1923 the work appeared with the English translation of Cecil Gray),

op. 2 *String Quartet in C minor*, and op.3 *Piano Music* (later under the title *Nine Piano Pieces*).

1910 January: Completion of op.4 *Sonata for Cello nda Piano*.

March 12: The second and third movements of op.4 premièred at the Festival Hongrois in Paris. This is the first performance of a Kodály work abroad.

March 17: Kodály's first composer's evening in Budapest (op.2, 3 and 4), with Béla Bartók at the piano.

July 16: Kodály's marriage to Emma Sándor.

October–November: Kodály's works appeared in print for the first time (op.2, 3 and the *Adagio* for violin and piano of 1905). Publisher: Rózsavölgyi and Son, Budapest.

1911 Spring: Foundation of the Society of New Hungarian Music, to propagate contemporary music, with the participation of Kodály and under Bartók's chairmanship. Lacking official support and public interest, the society is dissolved after three performances, in the spring of 1912.

1912 Begins work on op.5 *Two Songs* and op.6 *Late Melodies* (seven songs).

1913 Publication of the plan for a critical edition of Hungarian folk music, in Kodály's wording and signed by Bartók and Kodály. (The first volume of the critical edition, under the title *Corpus Musicae Popularis Hungaricae*, appeared in 1951.)

1914 Composes op.7, *Duo for Violin and Cello*.

1915 Composes op.8, *Sonata for Solo Cello*, and *Capriccio*.

1916 Kodály, together with Bartók, begins the collection of folksongs in the Hungarian army.

1917 Kodály embarks on his activities as a music critic. (He published daily music reviews up till 1919, and in the early 1920s sent reviews of musical events in Budapest to music periodicals abroad.)

1918 May 7: Kodály's second composer's evening in Budapest (op.6, 7, 8, and op.10, the *Second String Quartet*.)

1919	February 14: Kodály was appointed deputy director of the Academy of Music with effect from December 31, 1918. March 21: Proclamation of the Hungarian Republic of Councils. Kodály becomes one of the three members of the Musical Directory, the other two being Bartók and Ernst von Dohnányi. Early August: Overthrow of the Republic of Councils. September 23: Kodály divested of his post as teacher and deputy director at the Academy of Music. November 22: Disciplinary action taken against Kodály for the part he played during the Republic of Councils.
1920	March: Completion of op.12, *Serenade for Two Violins and Viola*. Première: April 8. April 16: The *Sonata for Solo Cello* performed by the Verein für mus. Privataufführungen in Vienna, run by Arnold Schoenberg. The performance was mounted by Anton Webern. July 14: Although the charges brought against Kodály have not been justified, the disciplinary committee annuls his appointment as deputy director at the Academy of Music, and he is not allowed to continue teaching there. August 26: Kodály, none of whose works have been published in Hungary since 1910, agrees with Universal Edition of Vienna to the publication of his compositions.
1921	January 10: After the première of op.5, *Two Songs*, the Budapest press launch a concentrated attack against Kodály. The accusations are repudiated in writing by Béla Bartók. April: The first work by Kodály—op.8—appears in Vienna.
1922	April 22: Kodály's first English article in the *Musical Courier* in New York, a review of Budapest's musical scene.

August 5–10: He attends the Salzburg festival of modern music. Three members of the Amar-Hindemith String Quartet perform his *Serenade*. Kodály joins the founding members of the ISCM, set up at the festival. He forms a friendship with the musicologist Edward J. Dent, chairman of the ISCM.
September: Kodály begins teaching again at the Academy of Music. His students include Antal Doráti, who later earned world fame as a conductor, the musicologist Paul Henry Lang (USA), the composers Géza Fried, living in Holland, Oedoen Pártos in Tel Aviv, Mátyás Seiber in England and Tibor Serly in New York, as well as many eminent musicians in Hungary.

1923 August: Completion of the *Psalmus Hungaricus*. November 19: world première of the *Psalmus* in Budapest.
Joint publication with Bartók of their collection of folksongs: *Hungarians of Transylvania—Folk Songs*, also with English preface and notes.

1924 Kodály writes entries on Bartók, Dohnányi and Theodor Szántó for the *Dictionary of Modern Music and Musicians*, edited by Arthur Eaglefield Hull and published in London. (The entry on Kodály written by Bartók.)
December: Together with Alfredo Casella, Vaclav Talich and Egon Wallesz, Kodály sits in the jury of the ISCM.

1925 April 2: Première of his first children's choruses—*The Straw Guy* and *See the Gipsy*—in Budapest.
May 11: Hubert Foss, head of the newly established music department of Oxford University Press, has discussions with Kodály in Budapest about the publication of his works in England.

1926 July 17–18: First performance abroad of the *Psalmus Hungaricus*—in Zürich. October 16: Première of the Singspiel *Háry János* in the Budapest Opera House.

1927 March 17: Première of the piano version of the

Dances of Marosszék in Budapest, with the Hungarian-born Louis Kentner (who settled in London in the 1930s) at the piano.

March 24: World première of the *Háry János Suite* in Barcelona.

November-December: Kodály's first visit to England (performances of the *Psalmus* in Cambridge and London).

1929	Reworking of the youthful *Summer Evening*; orchestral version of the *Dances of Marosszék*.
1930	April 3: Toscanini conducts *Summer Evening* in New York.

September: Kodály launches a series of lectures on Hungarian folk music at Budapest University.

November 30: Fritz Bush conducts the first performance of the orchestral version of the *Dances of Marosszék* in Dresden.

1931	September 26: First performance abroad of *Háry János*: City Theatre, Cologne.

Kodály's study on "Hungarian Folk Music" appears in the *Hungarian Encyclopaedia of Music*. (The English translation of an enlarged edition in book form, entitled *Folk Music of Hungary*, has so far run into three editions: 1960, 1972 and 1982.)

1932	April 24: Première of *The Spinning Room* at the Budapest Opera House. (La Scala Milan staged the opera on January 14, 1933, and it was broadcast, with Kodály conducting, by BBC London on May 26, 1933.)

November 16: Kodály's 50th birthday not celebrated officially in Hungary; concerts held by his supporters and students.

1933	October 23: Première of the *Galánta Dances* in Budapest.
1934	July 24: First performance of the motet for mixed voices, *Jesus and the Traders*.
1936	September 2: Première of *Te Deum* in Budapest. (First performance abroad: BBC London, November 13, 1936.)

1937	Summer: Attack against Bartók and Kodály in the Hungarian press. Their music condemned as destructive and Bolshevik. Hungarian progressive aids repel the attacks. The Amsterdam Concertgebouw Orchestra commissions a work from Kodály.
1938	March 11–13: Nazi occupation of Austria: Kodály parts with his Viennese publishers and henceforth his works are published by Boosey and Hawkes of London. August: Edward J. Dent visits Hungary as a guest of Kodály.
1939	November 23: In Amsterdam, Willem Mengelberg premières the *Peacock Variations* written for the Concertgebouw Orchestra.
1940	October: Completion of the *Concerto* for orchestra, commissioned for the golden jubilee of the Chicago Symphony Orchestra. After Bartók's emigration to the United States, Kodály asked to be transferred from the Academy of Music to the Hungarian Academy of Sciences, to continue Bartók's work on categorizing folk music.
1941	February 6–7: Première of the *Concerto* in Chicago, conducted by Frederick Stock.
1942	December 16: Kodály's 60th birthday. He retires; the Academy of Music recommends Kodály for a high award, but he is only given the lower level. Kodály celebrations held in 1943 in Hungary.
1944	May 7: Première of the *Organ Mass* in Budapest. Kodály forced by fascist persecution to go into hiding.
1945	February 11: First performance of the choral and organ version of the *Missa brevis* in the cloak-room of the Budapest Opera House, amidst war-time conditions (fighting still going on in the capital). Spring: Kodály assumes many leading cultural functions in the liberated country. May 30: Kodály elected a member of the Hungarian Academy of Sciences.

1946	July 24: Kodály elected president of the Hungarian Academy of Sciences.

September: The first specialized primary school for singing and music set up in the spirit of Kodály's music educational principles, in the village of Békéstarhos in southern Hungary. (By the last years of Kodály's life the number of similar schools grew to 130.)

September 27: Kodály sets out on a tour abroad. October 3–5: He conducts on the BBC, London: the *Concerto*, the *Missa brevis* and *Jesus and the Traders*. His first American tour from October 28 to February 5, 1947 (New York, Pittsburgh, Philadelphia, Washington, Dallas, Detroit, Chicago). He conducts his works and attends performances of them.

1947	May–June: Kodály's first visit to the Soviet Union.
1948	March 15: Kodály awarded the newly founded Kossuth Prize, a state prize in recognition of the highest intellectual and social achievement.

On the same day the Budapest Opera House staged the first performance of *Cinka Panna*, Kodály's opera written to commemorate the centenary of the Hungarian War of Independence of 1848, to the play by Béla Balázs, a friend from his youth. Due to the libretto, the work is a failure, and it sees altogether two performances. September 9: First performance of the orchestral version of *Missa brevis*, conducted by Kodály at the Three Choirs' Festival in Worcester.

1949	October: Reorganization of the Hungarian Academy of Sciences. Kodály resigns his post as president.
1950	January: The Folk Music Research Group, led by Kodály, begins work at the Academy of Sciences. January–February: Kodály conducts his works in London.

September 25: He speaks at the ceremony held on the 5th anniversary of the death of Béla Bartók. Kodály is among the few who reject the shameful attack of Hungarian Zhdanovists on Bartók.

1951	Kodály takes part in organizing the training of

Hungarian musicologists. He undertakes the teaching of future ethnomusicologists at the first ever faculty of musicology in Hungary, set up at the Academy of Music in the autumn.

November: The first volume of the critical edition of Hungarian folk music, entitled *Corpus Musicae Popularis Hungaricae*, appears in the edition of Kodály, with Bartók as the posthumous editor, under the title "Children's Songs".

1952 March 15: Kodály awarded the highest level of the Kossuth Prize.

December 16: Celebrations for the 70th birthday of Kodály in Hungary.

1955 Completion of the large-scale composition for solo baritone and mixed voices entitled *Hymn of Zrínyi*. Première: December 16.

1956 June–July: Kodály's public press debate with leaders of Hungarian education for the better instruction of singing in schools.

1957 March 15: Kodály awarded the Kossuth Prize for the third occasion.

June: Kodály elected chairman of the Music Council of the Ministry of Culture.

December 16: Celebrations for Kodály's 75th birthday.

1958 November 22: In the 49th year of their marriage, Emma, the first wife of Kodály dies.

1959 As chairman of the Hungarian Haydn Memorial Committee, Kodály attends the celebrations and the international musicological conference held to commemorate the 150th anniversary of the death of the composer.

December 18: Kodály's second marriage. His new wife, Sarolta Péczely, comes from a family Kodály has known for several decades.

1960 May 1: Oxford University confers an honorary degree on Kodály, who returns to England after a break of ten years.

November 2: Kodály's lecture at the British Embassy

	in Budapest, under the title "English Vocal Music".
1961	August 16: In Luzern, Ferenc Fricsay conducts the première of the *Symphony*, commissioned by the Luzern Festival Orchestra in 1959.
1962	July: Kodály, honorary professor at the Accademia Santa Cecilia in Rome, is presented with the institute's highest decoration, a gold medal.
	December 16: Grand festivals held on the 80th birthday of Kodály. His former students, both living in Hungary and abroad, greet him each with variations on various Kodály themes. Kodály asks the government that the number of singing lessons should not be cut in school. His request is granted.
1963	March: The American Academy of Arts and Literature elects Kodály its honorary member.
	August 5–12: Kodály is chairman of the conference of the International Folkmusic Council in Jerusalem.
	December: His second visit to the Soviet Union, where he attends the first Moscow stage performance of *Háry János*.
1964	April: In Budapest Kodály becomes acquainted with Benjamin Britten, who soon after writes a work with variations on one of Kodály's themes *(Gemini Variations)*.
	June 25–July 3: Kodály attends the Budapest conference of the International Society of Music Education as honorary chairman.
	August 17–25: Kodály chairs the Budapest conference of the International Folkmusic Council.
	October 20: The Humboldt University of Berlin confers an honorary degree on Kodály.
1965	April 30: The Rector of Vienna University presents the Herder Prize to Kodály for his activities in developing cultural relations between East and West.
	June: Kodály attends the Aldeburgh Festival, which Benjamin Britten, Imogen Holst and Peter Pears turn into a veritable Kodály Festival.
	July–August: Kodály's second visit to the United States.

Between July 19 and 31 he is the guest of Dartmouth College in Hannover. Mario di Bonaventure, the musical director of the College, puts on a series of Kodály's works.

August: As a guest of the Ford Foundation, Kodály studies the system of musical education in American universities.

1966 February 24: Kodály's last completed work, *Laudes Organi* for mixed choir and organ.

April: In Paris Kodály attends the congress of the Fédération Internationale des Jeunesses Musicales, and addresses the Congress on April 12.

July–September: Kodály visits Canada and the USA. Toronto University confers an honorary degree on Kodály.

August 2–3: Kodály chairs the music educational conference of Santa Barbara University in California.

August 18–26: As honorary chairman of the International Society for Music Education, he attends the society's seventh international conference at Interlochen.

1967 March 6: Zoltán Kodály dies in Budapest.

Printed in Hungary, 1990
Franklin Printing House, Budapest